JOURNEY AROUND MYSELF

Books by Félix Martí-Ibáñez

JOURNEY AROUND MYSELF: IMPRESSIONS AND TALES OF TRAVELS
  AROUND THE WORLD: JAPAN, HONG KONG,
  MACAO, BANGKOK, ANGKOR, LEBANON

WALTZ AND OTHER STORIES

ALL THE WONDERS WE SEEK: THIRTEEN TALES
  OF SURPRISE AND PRODIGY

THE CRYSTAL ARROW: ESSAYS ON LITERATURE,
  TRAVEL, ART, LOVE, AND THE HISTORY OF MEDICINE

CENTAUR: ESSAYS ON THE HISTORY
  OF MEDICAL IDEAS

ARIEL: ESSAYS ON THE ARTS AND THE HISTORY
  AND PHILOSOPHY OF MEDICINE

A PRELUDE TO MEDICAL HISTORY

MEN, MOLDS, AND HISTORY

THE EPIC OF MEDICINE *(Editor)*

THE PAGEANT OF MEDICINE *(Editor)*

HENRY E. SIGERIST ON THE HISTORY
  OF MEDICINE *(Editor)*

HEALTH AND TRAVEL *(Editor)*

HISTORY OF AMERICAN MEDICINE *(Editor)*

MEDICAL WRITING *(Editor)*

MEDICINE AND WRITING *(Editor)*

In Spanish

DE NOCHE BRILLA EL SOL *(Short Stories)*

LOS BUSCADORES DE SUEÑOS *(Short Stories)*

ENSAYO SOBRE LA PSICOLOGIA Y
  FISIOLOGIA MISTICAS DE LA INDIA

SURCO *(Essays)*

OBRA *(My Work in Public Health)*

HIGIENE SEXUAL *(Sexual Hygiene)*

YO, REBELDE *(A Novel)*

AVENTURA *(A Novel)*

JOURNEY

AROUND MYSELF

IMPRESSIONS AND TALES OF
TRAVELS AROUND THE WORLD:
JAPAN, HONG KONG, MACAO,
BANGKOK, ANGKOR, LEBANON

FELIX MARTI-IBAÑEZ

Clarkson N. Potter, Inc./Publisher   NEW YORK

Library of Congress Catalog Card Number: 66-17884

Manufactured in the United States of America.

Second Printing, March, 1967

*To the immortal memory of my
beloved wife, Josephine,
who was a living symbol
of inspiration and encouragement
in so many
spiritual journeys around myself*

CONTENTS

PROLOGUE IN THREE CITIES:
ISTANBUL, CAIRO, VENICE

PROLOGUE IN THREE CITIES:
ISTANBUL, CAIRO, VENICE

THERE ARE TRAVELERS AND
there are people who simply travel. The true traveler
is the gourmet of landscapes; he who simply travels
is the gourmand of distances. The true traveler travels
for the pleasure of feeling himself flung through time
and space, absorbing fresh life wherever it is to be
found; he who only travels does so just to get somewhere and "do something." In all too many cases this
"something" is merely eating, for to many people a

3

trip is a failure unless there is a meal awaiting them at their point of destination. It is as if the meal symbolizes taking individual and private possession of the place chosen for the meal.

I am very fond of travel books, including those that merely give a prosaic account of what the traveler saw in exact relation to the purpose of his trip. Marco Polo's *Il Miglione* is one such book. The romantic adventure of the wandering Venetian (this, Dante's *Divine Comedy,* and the Crusades are three of the greatest achievements of medieval man) is one of the most luminous pages in the not so dark Middle Ages. However, Marco Polo's book is not nearly so fascinating as it might have been had the young globe-trotter given a more personalized view of the places, people, and things he encountered during his remarkable voyage from the gay Rialto of Venice to the fabulous land of Cathay.

Francisco Xavier de Balmis, the first physician to go around the world on a noble Samaritan mission—to introduce the peoples of the world to vaccination, which had only recently been discovered—journeyed at the beginning of the nineteenth century from his native Spain to the Caribbean, Mexico, the Philippines, Macao, and Canton, returning to Spain from the other side of the world months later. Yet all that he wrote regarding his marvelous adventure was a mere official account of his professional activities.

Thus, it often happens that travelers tell nothing of the marvelous world they traverse except that which has immediate pertinence to the object of their trip, perhaps because they are imposing an unconscious taboo of silence on their innermost impressions. This is a pity, for to my mind the best part of any travel book is precisely that: seeing the intimate personality of the traveler projected onto the screen of the countries visited.

How wonderful it would have been if G. K. Chesterton, who, to borrow a phrase by García Lorca, had a "child's ancient soul lined with legends," had traveled around the world and written an account of his journey. The greatest prestidigitator in all literature, Chesterton liked to "sit still and let the marvels and adventures settle on me like flies"! I am sure that he would never have related anything pertaining to economy or politics, or any data concerning the art treasures he saw. Instead, he probably would have told us that the eyes of the waitress who served him in Calcutta were as dark and sweet as the tea she poured for him, that the marauding water buffaloes of Cambodia were more ancient in spirit than the Khmer ruins of Angkor Wat, that in Kyoto he saw little Japanese girls picking up each piece of *sushi* with their chopsticks with the same love and care with which a Swiss watchmaker picks up minute springs with his pincers or a well-trained canary picks up his birdseed. But, alas! Chesterton journeyed around the world only in the enchanted vessel of his imagination. On the other hand, there are too many books of travel that seem timorous about divulging to the reader that which is the most interesting in a travel book: the traveler's inner spiritual experience.

The best part of a traveler is that which he gives to the world on his journeys: the journey around himself, the words and thoughts with which, as though they were garments of silk and gold, he transforms even the drabbest things and creatures he encounters in his path.

In most of the inns of La Mancha in Don Quixote's Spain, the only food available to a passing traveler was that which he himself carried in his saddlebags. Thus, if his bags were empty, the traveler went to bed without dinner, as often happened to many a short-sighted hidalgo. The same thing happens today to a traveler: if his heart and mind are ill provided, he runs the risk of going to bed with a hungry soul.

Today there abounds a peculiar type of tourist who, out of snobbishness, day and night wears dark glasses —symbolically and literally—which make him see the world as a monochromatic landscape. The relationship between these tourists' unicolored view and the polychromatic reality of the world is the same as that between, say, the gorgeous multicolored landscape in Nikko and a photograph of it in black and white on a magazine cover. But there are travelers who still look at the world with eyes filled with curiosity and wonder, for whom the wondrous landscapes of this world are huge vignettes illustrating the fairy tales inscribed

6

on their souls. These are the travelers that I find fascinating.

That is why, no matter how interesting the "official" account of a trip may be, I prefer a traveler's personal notebook, that schoolboy copybook in which the traveler endowed with a luminous spirit jots down not only what he sees but also what he feels, not only the unvarnished reality of strange countries and new people but also the magical unreality that these new things conjure up in his soul and that he in turn projects onto them. This is the same as giving new names to things and people even though their actual names are already well known, new names that have the same sense of awe and wonder and the same poetic freshness as those Adam called out in Paradise when for the first time he beheld a rose, a star, a lake, or a nightingale.

Not too long ago I went to Japan to deliver a lecture as the guest of honor of a distinguished medical society. This afforded me the opportunity to take a quick glance at a part of the world unfamiliar to me: the Far East. The fruit of this hurried trip, on which I was borne by the wings of whirlwind jets, was a little notebook that I filled with the impressions, images, and memories that rose in my mind like a flock of sparrows startled by the hand of a child, impressions, images, and memories stimulated by the lights and the shadows, the sounds and the silences, the places and the people, the multitudes and the solitudes of the Far East.

Aboard jet planes flying over the Arctic Circle or

7

the Arabian Desert, in the lone retreat of my hotel
room in Tokyo, while waiting for sukiyaki amid the
birdlike flutter of fans in a Kamakura garden restaurant that was like a dollhouse, aboard a Chinese ferry
plying the gray waters of the China Sea between Hong
Kong and Macao, on sampans gliding through Bangkok's sun-drenched *klongs,* on a path hacked through
the heart of a jungle of Dantesque trees leading to the
ancient ruins of Angkor, in the shade of the Biblical
cedars of Lebanon, and in the heroic castle of the
Crusaders in Byblos—in all these and other fascinating places I found myself jotting down odd words,
meaningful thoughts, or exotic images evoked by my
marvelous journey. One day, I thought to myself, when
I am back in New York and it is raining or fog shrouds
the city's gleaming towers, I shall take out this carnet
full of entries and, like chips of gold pulled out of a
chest and held up to the light, each of these words I
am now quickly scrawling with a pencil stub will
brighten the dismal day with the luminous poetry of
memory.

Months later, the, for me, precious little notebook,
which had survived a trip around the world, got lost
in the sands of the Lido Beach in Venice. *Kismet!*

But there is one priceless thing that I brought back
from my trip around the world, one that cost no money
and on which I paid no customs duty: humility, a
humility born from watching other peoples, other races,

struggling bravely and hoping humbly for the simplest things in life.

In this book I should like to reconstruct that simple little notebook in the hope that it may stimulate other travelers—whether they travel by ocean liner, on airplanes, in the brightly lit little moving houses of the international *wagons-lits,* or on the jet of their imagination as they are snugly ensconced in their fireside chairs—to gaze at the miracle of the world as if they were discovering it for the first time.

Let the reader therefore accept this book in the spirit in which it is offered: as the intimate impressions of an impressionable physician-traveler. The reader will discover no new restaurants or hotels here, no economic statistics, no study of medicine in the Orient, no critical analysis of works of art. He may even find some inaccuracies, but poetically everything is accurate. Any dates or even statistical facts that he might find have slipped in without my being aware of it, for my intention was not to compose a symphony, but only to whistle a melody.

In other words, this is only a modest notebook, a compilation of my first impressions—surface impressions to be sure, but sincere ones—with which it is my hope the reader can reconstruct in his mind the countries described, just as by gazing at the light in an Impressionist painting one can reconstruct the physical reality of the landscape concealed behind the luminous curtain evoked by the painter's brush.

9

Traveling has, I believe, three dimensions, of which I became aware in three fascinating cities that I visited on trips prior to my journey around the world. In Istanbul I perceived the dimension of space in traveling; in Cairo, the dimension of time; and in Venice, the dimension of the spirit. That is, Istanbul taught me that to travel is to live geography; Cairo, that to travel is to relive history; Venice, that to travel is to explore one's own spirit. Geography, history, spirit—these are, whether he realizes it or not, the traveler's inseparable companions.

Istanbul is like an odalisque left behind from one of its bygone seraglios, reclining on the divan formed by the age-smooth stones of its basilicas and palaces, rocked by the amber waters of the Golden Horn and the sapphire waters of the Bosporus, gazing across the latter far into the distance, past the coast of Anatolia and the enchanted cities of Smyrna and Trebizond— names that evoke myrrh and incense—and even beyond the Turkish frontiers, toward other cities with bewitching names—Damascus, Baghdad, Samarra, Palmyra, Teheran—on a geographic route that is eventually crowned with the dazzling circlet of light of the Taj Mahal and then plunges into the waters of the Indian Ocean, finally to hearken to the bugle call of Singapore resounding on the Java Sea.

Istanbul's geography explains its romantic history. Its geography, more than the walls of Theodosius, made of the city, when it was called Constantinople, an invincible fortress of the Byzantine Empire for a millennium, while its thousand gold-domed basilicas enticed the covetous eyes of the Ottomans waiting outside its walls. The city's geography was to become a mighty battering ram in the hands of the invaders, when in an incredible feat they hauled their entire fleet from the Bosporus over solid ground into the Golden Horn, which thus became a rope that throttled the last hopes of the besieged. Later, the same geography protected the barbaric Ottoman splendor in the vanquished city and the thousand and one nights of love in the perfumed shadows of the sultans' seraglios, just as before it had protected the mystical pomp of the basilicas in what had been Christ's kingdom on earth.

Istanbul, the European threshold to Asia, made me realize that instead of traveling further into the Arabian worlds, that is, North Africa, with which I was already familiar from Tangier to Cairo, or of going to the Middle East, which, like India and Pakistan, requires a trip devoted solely to it, I should visit that exotic section of the globe, Southeast Asia, and also include Japan and Hong Kong. The map reveals that girding the thorax—barrel-shaped like that of a catch-as-catch-can wrestler—of those two Asio-European giants, China and Russia, is a belt of nations, a chain of peoples in fermentation constituting Southeast Asia. These nations, bathed by the Sea of Japan and the China Sea, comprise more than ninety million people in Japan, and sixty million from Hong Kong to Malaya.

11

I loved to delve into the political and religious conformation of Southeast Asia during those long, starstudded evenings in Istanbul, at that enthralling hour when travelers exchange their wineglasses for potbellied glasses of cognac, when the golden and later scarlet sun upon the cupolas, minarets, and turrets is but a memory, when Istanbul deep in mysterious shadows reverts into Constantinople and its Western-clad inhabitants once again become the defenders of Byzantium.

In that geographic fringe of the vast Asiatic continent dwelled an astonishing variety of peoples. Although originally, I learned, they came from China and India, there are nations in that region that for two thousand years had been under Arabian influence. In quest of spices, the Arabs in their little dhows had reached as far as Malacca, Indonesia, and the Philippines. Some of these Moslem outposts are now British colonies, like Singapore; members of the British Commonwealth, like Malaya; or independent nations, like Indonesia; in addition to that crossroads of Asia, the microcosm, Hong Kong.

There are also nations that were influenced by China, like Viet Nam, a country tragically divided by its political history if not by its geography, a country in whose culture France's heartbeat is still audible. To the west of Viet Nam are nations such as Thailand, Cambodia, and Laos, on which India, through Burma, has exerted her influence (their Hinduism, Buddhism, and Sanskrit derive from India); in these nations thirty million people worship Buddha.

A little farther east and to the north, like ships perpetually anchored in the China Sea, Yellow Sea, and the Sea of Japan, stands the Christian cosmos of the Philippine Islands; the tiny Portuguese outpost of Catholicism, Macao; the Nationalist China bulwark of Taiwan; and that Chinese appendage, Korea, a funnel through which Chinese culture and religion poured into the islands of Japan. Japan closes this geographic arc of humanity with the terrible but bewitching enigma of a nation both brave and cruel, industrious and aesthetic, a samurai saber in a sheath of lotus blossoms and chrysanthemums.

This is the lesson I learned in Istanbul, the city of golden cupolas, above which the crescent moon at night is like a symbolic gift from the heavens to the city for its miraculous geographic location: the Christian mosaic of Europe behind it; the African world, on the other side of the *mare nostrum,* at its feet; the Moslem world astride the Bosporus; beyond that, the enigmatic vastness of Asia with its Hindu, Chinese, and multiracial worlds; and, almost within arm's reach, the deserts of Mesopotamia, where civilization was born, and the sun-bathed Hellenic peninsula, where, in the shade of the Parthenon—a marble lyre suspended from the blue heavens—the first philosophers, with their profound questions on nature and man, initiated the beginning of the history of Western thought.

If Istanbul prompted me to travel geographically in space and to explore the planet's wondrous vastness, Cairo incited me to travel in time, carrying with me a sense of history.

Few views in the world are as inspiring as the Nile, as seen from the terrace of one of the great hotels that line its shore, when the last rays of sun gently caress the distant pyramids and, like the necklace of a Pharaonic princess, the first lights of evening bejewel the banks of this sacred river.

While I was in Egypt I had the sensation that not only was I living history, but also that history—a flux that like the Nile itself is always changing, yet is always the same—is never over and gone. History remains with us forever, constantly enriching itself with new events, but always keeping its past alive. The *living* element in history is tradition. Historical tradition, however, is not kept alive by colossal monuments, like the megalomaniacal tombs of Cheops, Chephren, and Mycerinus, or like the Sphinx, which will never provide the answers to the unspoken questions of warriors and poets. While these monuments are mere reminders left by man in the book of history, they also appear to us like paperweights placed upon the earth by the hands of giants to prevent the landscapes from being blown away and to remind man of the different stages of history.

History lives in each one of us. History is the biography of mankind, just as the biography of one man is his history. In the history of each human being there throbs, miraculously kept alive, not only his own past but also that of all mankind.

Egypt taught me the need of always carrying *living* history with us on our travels, even as the Crusaders always carried their falcons with them; the need to view the world, its people, and its ruins with eyes filled with millennia of experience and love. No other country gives one this sensation as strongly as does Egypt.

The Akhenaton and Nefertiti gallery in the Cairo Museum, with its exquisite, delicate, fragile-looking statues, paintings, and jewels, surrounded as it is by the galleries of the other pharaohs, with their colossal, massive, funerary statues, is like the flutter of butterflies between two herds of elephants, a blinking light between two eternities of stone. With my mind still entranced by the exquisite art of Akhenaton's time and my heart still beating a little faster for the beautiful Nefertiti, I went to visit the Sakkara pyramid in the Libyan Desert. There, in the middle of August, when beneath the pounding sun even the landscape perspires and suffocates with its own sweat, gazing at the lone, proud pyramid, its ancient stones as sunburned as the faces of the wretched slaves who built it must have been, I experienced the sensation that instead of my living history, history *was living me,* that I carried it inside me, and that, as I traveled, I was restoring pieces of that history to the places I visited.

On only one other occasion in my life have I experienced the same emotion, if not stronger, that I felt upon seeing the pyramid—the oldest monument on earth today—built by my spiritual colleague, Imhotep, the Egyptian god of medicine. This second instance occurred several years ago in Guatemala, when I visited the ruins of the town of Antigua. It was a Sunday and the hour of sunset. Suddenly, behind the green immensity of the coffee plantations, a town straight out of Castile sprang up in the middle of the jungle, complete with tiny plazas, churches, houses with grilled windows, little donkeys with saddle baskets, churchgoers in black mantillas, and bells tolling the Angelus. I saw Indians kneeling in a little church, praying to Christ in their native tongue, the floor all around them littered with their offerings—pagan in style, Christian in motive—of golden cereals, brightly colored fruits, and fragrant flowers. And I would have sworn that the faces of those Indians, praying to Christ in a church whose stones had been brought over in the Christian ships of the conquistadores, were the same faces I had seen a few hours earlier in Mayan statues and bas-reliefs dating from pre-Columbian civilizations.

But returning to Egypt, that land that is all history, a history that, like a pharaoh's cloak, regally clothes the naked body of its deserts (the living flesh of the earth), I experienced as nowhere else the desire to commune with living history in my travels through the world.

Whereas in Istanbul I was filled with a sense of space

and in Egypt with a sense of time, in Venice I was filled with a sense of the spirit. Venice is the city I love most in all the world, although the most beautiful natural vista I have ever seen is the bay of Rio de Janeiro, and the most beautiful European city is Paris, and the most beautiful Oriental city is Bangkok. In Venice, an enchanting city of black swans—those graceful gondolas that have turned the dark-green canals into their dominion—the human spirit cannot but joyously surrender to its magical mists and its ever-changing iridescent lights and, floating freely, revel in the harmonious integration of its artistic tradition and its romantic history.

Not a city but a treasure trove of wonders, Venice inspires one to travel for spiritual rather than for geographical or historical reasons. Its palaces and churches, its ancient stones of lyrical beauty, its works of art evoke the tapestry of history; but its flashes of light, its diamond-like reflections, its pearly mists, its lights and shadows, its amethyst sky, its shimmering canals, the enigmatic haziness of the Adriatic Sea are the lure to a great and wonderful adventure. Venice invites one to give the spirit free rein, to let it soar to the loftiest summit of its dreams and to let it descend to the fathomless abyss of its memories, to encompass the infinite universe of its ideals and the interstellar spaces of its fantasies. Venice is the embodiment of dreams, and the best of these dreams is to be in Venice. For in Venice one's spirit learns that no journey through time

17

or space is comparable to a journey of the spirit around itself.

An intense longing to have a look at the geography of my planet and at the history of the humanity I am part of, plus the longing to journey around my spirit, inspired this simple but enthusiastic logbook of a journey around the inner world of myself.

However, since my journey around the world described in this book, I have been around the planet three more times. I have visited (and, in some places, lectured to physicians and scientists) Manila during a heat wave; Singapore, where I was almost poisoned at midnight by a bowl of *mei* in the Chinese quarter; Kuala Lumpur and the orchid farms in the jungle; Rangoon (its Golden Pagoda, the Schwedagon, is a world's wonder!) during the monsoon; and Teheran, where I had a terrifying experience during a religious holiday. Three times more have I revisited Japan, with many more days to travel and see its lovely countryside, Hong Kong during several of its worst droughts, and Bangkok during its appalling hot season. Since my first trip around the world, I have made many wonderful friends, I have explored brilliant days in many countries and probed into the mystery of their starry nights. It was most tempting to add to this book many of the new experiences I have had on those trips since that first journey, to talk about the new friends and the new places. But I have resisted that temptation (with one exception), and I will reserve the experiences of my other trips for the sequel I plan to write to this book, *More Journeys Around Myself* (Southeast Asia Revisited: Manila, Singapore, Kuala Lumpur, Rangoon, and Teheran).

I prefer to record in this book only my first impressions of my first journey, a journey around myself, sharing with my readers whatever naiveness and freshness they may have, as they are the result of my looking at the world with eyes filled with the love and wonder of an Innocent Traveler.

JAPAN

A CONFIDENCE IN A LOW VOICE:
THE SECRET OF THE GARDEN
IN KAMAKURA

ONE APRIL EVENING IN
Kamakura, a young student from Kyoto revealed to
me the secret of Japanese gardens.

It was six o'clock. Over a landscape shimmering with
a recent drizzle, one of those fine, delicate, utterly Japanese drizzles, a great golden sun lazily loitered behind
a coverlet of clouds.

I had come to Kamakura, some thirty miles from
Tokyo, to see the Daibutsu, the giant medieval Buddha.

Every year at this time, thousands of Japanese flock to Kamakura to admire the Buddha towering like a titan high over the trees.

I first explored the little streets of what had been the capital of Japan in its great Kamakura period, a cruel romantic period in which heroic art and chivalry flourished, a period famous in Japanese history for its proud, daring, sword-wielding samurai and for its courtesans, creatures more beautiful than chrysanthemums and less real than women. Afterward I was invited with a few other people to visit the home of a physician in the town. This was one of those numerous, unexpected, pleasurable courtesies to which one soon becomes accustomed in Japan.

The house had an air of quiet elegance, with its floors covered with *tatami,* mats made of fine woven straw, paper partitions decorated with birds and lotus blossoms, and smooth unpainted wooden walls. I stood fascinated before the various altars in the house: the Shinto shrine to propitiate the pagan gods, the Buddhist altar for religious contemplation, and the family altars, where the recently deceased are kept forever alive, their portraits hung in niches in front of which are placed fresh fruit and garlands of flowers, as if to revitalize the pale image of death with the fresh offerings of life.

But to me the culminating point of this delightful visit was the garden. Breaking away from the other guests, who were talking with our host, a kindly old Japanese who, every time he smiled, displayed two rows of yellow teeth, like the keys of an ancient clavichord, I walked into the garden.

I could still visualize the Daibutsu beyond the garden walls, a ninety-two-ton, forty-two-foot-high bronze Buddha, mighty in its centuries-long solitude, without a temple around it, for its temple, Kotokuin, was swept away in a tidal wave nearly four hundred years ago. More a tower than a statue, dwarfing the trees around it, the Daibutsu was built to represent Amida, the Buddhist deity, by Ono Goroemon, in 1252, in what was then the center of the Japanese government. On the other side of the walls, the Daibutsu's gigantic torso would soon be caressed by the evening breeze, and his great viridescent head with his melancholy smile would be crowned with the stars of night.

But now I was alone in a garden of singular beauty. Spacious and uncluttered, it contained only miniature trees, rocks, sand, and a small cascade of water that shimmered like crystals in a chandelier. There were no flowers, but golden bees and black butterflies hovered silently in the air like birds in a fairy tale.

The miniature trees were dwarf pines with dark-green needles and sinuous trunks posed gracefully like dancers in a lovely, silent ballet. The trees were few, mere flecks on the sea of sand, and seemingly planted by caprice, until one perceived the harmonious rhythm in their arrangement.

What set the tone of the garden were the rocks and the sand. The rocks—the muscle of Japanese gardens just as water is their blood and sand their soul—numbered a dozen, plus about as many smaller ones that served as counterpoint. Placed in a style so carefully calculated as to appear haphazard, and shaped so oddly that they looked as though they had been carved by an artistic pagan god for his own shrine, the rocks created a haunting contrast with the delicate sand.

The sand, combed, brushed, and shaped by the loving hands of some celestial gardener, formed an infinite tapestry of ripples, spirals, and zigzags, an exquisite embroidery of tiny waves folded one upon the other, and covered the ground with the silver of its grains as a veil covers the face of a chaste maiden.

For a long time I stood ecstatic, breathing in the peace of that harmonious sanctuary, while nearby the unreposing water, intoning its rhythmic chant, sounded as though the garden were reciting the evening Rosary.

Rock and sand, dwarf trees and water—I had fallen under the spell of the garden in Kamakura.

Avoiding the visitors clustered near the entrance to the house, I strolled to the opposite end of the garden, carefully stepping on those circles of stone, like huge slices of orange, embedded in the ground in perfect sequence to allow one to traverse the entire garden without ever setting foot on the miracle of its sands. It was then that the student from Kyoto approached me so quietly that I perceived her more as the guardian spirit of the garden than as a woman.

She was blessed with that divine Japanese youthful-

26

ness that remains impervious to the passage of time. She wore a white kimono patterned with large yellow roses. Her hair, anointed with camellia oil, was wound into a glossy ebony coil high on her head, like a miniature pagoda. She was tiny and moved with the quick, hopping movements of a little bird. Her bright, dark eyes, innocent of make-up, stood out of her almond-shaped face, as did the parallel lines formed by her brows and lips, the last a fine thread of coral. The only things that betrayed her modernity as a medical student in Kyoto were her bulging leather brief case and her wrist watch, which revealed her awareness of the value and tyranny of time, even though she was a Japanese woman. She had accompanied us on this visit and had helped in showing us around the house. She seemed gratified by my silent rapture at the beauty of the garden.

When I told her I had never before seen so enchanting and inspiring a garden as that one, she smiled. As she did so, millennia of wisdom suffused her face, and suddenly she looked as ancient as the Daibutsu, the great Buddha of Kamakura.

"It makes me very happy that you like our gardens so much," she said. "But if you really wish to appreciate a Japanese garden, you must look at it on your knees."

Silently I dropped to my knees, and the simple gesture of moving closer to the ground brought a startling revelation.

Seen from a standing position the garden was lovely, but seen while kneeling, its beauty acquired fresh nuances and imaginative perspectives. The large rocks were transformed into little mountains, the dwarf trees into tall pines, the little rocks into islets on the sand, and the sand itself into a silvery sea of rippling waters. Within the confined space of that garden in shorthand, all of nature was expressed, and so was all of man's inner world, with his innate desire for beauty and his vain longing for peace and contentment.

A few minutes later my knees warned me that I must rise. But I had already learned an inspiring lesson, a lesson that was to turn my journey around the world into a journey around myself. I had learned to look at lands and oceans, at exotic places and peoples of other races, on my knees, with humility, as I did that April afternoon when a Japanese girl revealed to me the secret of the garden in Kamakura.

THE JOURNEY:
FROM MANHATTAN TO TOKYO

I HAD BEEN A RESTLESS TRAVELER
for many years. I knew Europe well and had roamed
all around the Americas. I had traveled the Mediterranean from Spain to Turkey and from Greece to
Egypt, and had been around North Africa from Tangier to Morocco and Algiers. But I had never taken the
trip with the magic name: a journey around the world.

Manhattan, retreating in the distance as my taxi
speeds toward New York's airport, is like a lithographic

plate on which the engraver, in his haste to finish his task, has drawn only the most prominent lines. Manhattan, an island of oxidized silver, of old wax, of fresh stone, is a symphony of grays on the gray melancholy afternoon of my departure.

As the taxi swiftly crosses bridges and tunnels, I keep thinking that I am going around the world in twenty-eight days. "It can't be true," I say to myself. For many years I have thought of the earth as a colored globe rotating on its metal axis in the hands of schoolboys, a series of blue and green splashes—lakes, seas, and oceans—and of brown and yellow splashes—lands and countries—a minute heavenly body on the map of the skies. But suddenly, as we approach the airport, the world begins to acquire form and substance, dimension and distance. And now I am about to encircle the thick belly of that world with the rainbow belt of my fantasies.

The International Airport greets me with its usual babel of voices speaking in assorted tongues. The loudspeakers constantly bellow out embarking orders to passengers and drop names, some familiar, some exotic, of distant places and lands. It is a chaos—or is it a half-completed cosmos? At the airline counters there is an air of slightly contemptuous indifference toward travelers. Hour after hour, day after day, year after year, through the funnel of Idlewild Airport, New York pours thousands of people into the winged carpets waiting on the landing fields like flocks of flying plesiosaurs, a little mythological in appearance but with the disciplined mythology of modern aviation.

I am scheduled to take a DC-7, a plane of heavy and graceless, but reassuring, solidity.

With the final farewells, love and friendship, enveloped in a nebula of kisses and embraces, are left behind by the travelers. The door of the airplane cabin shuts with a cavernous thud, leaving me with a feeling of defenselessness inside this armored chamber, which in a few minutes will zoom across endless skies to reopen —God, the angels of the winds, and the pilot's hands, willing—in strange remote lands where I will be returned to solid ground beneath an alien sky.

The stewardesses—combinations of nurses and waitresses, with the dimensions of pinup girls—generously dispensing toothpaste-advertisement smiles, promptly begin their mission of distributing chewing gum and cigarettes, followed by cocktails and dinner. For an occasional unfortunate soul, there is a waxed paper bag. Like the flight, the stewardesses are uninteresting, even dull, but very pretty and accommodating. In each there might be sheltered either a frustrated show girl turned into a lay nun or a smiling starlet playing the part of Florence Nightingale.

The flight far above the gray flat lands, through a vast heavenly fleece of clouds, is broken by rounds of French champagne and a dreadful dinner: a salad as cold and wilted as the tomb of an old prophet, a monstrously thick, repulsively raw, unbelievably tough

31

steak, the proverbial overcooked string beans, fruit, and tea. Not even the smiles of the stewardesses can improve this meal, consumed at an altitude of thirty-five thousand feet.

I read several mystery novels, make notes, work on some articles, review my travel itinerary, revise the lecture I am to give in Japan, and play a few rounds of chess, following the moves given in a book on Paul Morphy. One of the stewardesses, a pretty blonde from Minnesota, who is as effervescent as the champagne she serves, offers to play chess with me. She loses two games and wins one—by courtesy of the passenger. She tells me that her flight run is only from New York to Seattle, Washington, and that it will be another seven years before she is assigned to the Far East. I venture the prophecy that in seven years she will be happily married and traveling on her own. Delighted, she claps her hands. I have verbalized the crystallization of her most cherished dream.

The city of Seattle, rushing to meet our plane, is like a huge, moving screen ablaze with light and color beneath a thin rain. It is not just a city seen by night: it is a kaleidoscopic fantasy out of a fairy tale. The airport is modern and very pretty, but there is no one to direct my steps. It is 8:30 P.M. here, 11:30 P.M in New York. I have already flown more than nine hours. Finally I discover a waiting room, the Imperial Lounge, Japanese in décor and so ataraxic in atmosphere that, to keep myself from falling asleep, I decide to take a stroll around the airport.

I have a hamburger in the coffee shop and a beer in one of the lounges. The whole airport is quiet, remote, melancholy. Time has stopped. The three-hour wait becomes an eternity. Finally, at 11:13 we are called. Beneath a curtain of rain that punctures the darkness with taut filaments of liquid silver, I climb aboard the plane that will take us across the ominous Arctic Circle. The craft seems weary as we take off. The Arctic Circle—ice, wind, darkness—indifferently awaits the luminous flying monster lunging with a roar, like a bull toward a bullfighter, against the belly of the northern night.

The DC-7 in which I am now flying has a fresh crew—quick, alert, smiling young men, who promptly shower us with whisky and canapés. There are now many Orientals among the passengers, some of them Japanese wearing gold-rimmed glasses. There are also several infants, every one of them bawling; substantial-looking Scandinavian businessmen; and the inevitable lone, haughty *femme fatale* in whose eyes tiny drops of vodka twinkle frostily.

The beds are made. Weary and dazed I climb into mine, and awaken soon after—in reality, seven hours later. I experience a moment of panic. My traveler's checks have disappeared. In vain I rummage through my clothes in the harrowing confinement of the berth. I finally tell a steward about it and the whole plane is soon in turmoil. Everyone jovially joins in the search, racing up and down the aisle, poking under the seats and in every other possible place, as though the plane were a hunting ground, they the hunters, and my checks the quarry. Finally I discover them in one of the pockets of my coat, where I had obviously failed to look. Embarrassed, I say that I have found them under a seat. I am sure no one believes me.

While shaving I see through the window, dark, amorphous-looking masses in the distance, the Aleutian Islands, truly "the land God gave to Cain," naked dark rocks bristling with menacing sharp points, lashed by an angry sea, drenched by a fine, icy rain. We land as if by a miracle. In an overlit, overheated shed, we are served an "Eskimo breakfast"—thick steaks, fluffy omelettes, fragrant strawberries, pastries, and coffee—while from an invisible phonograph Al Jolson bellows old Broadway melodies.

We spend an hour and a half there. When I see the size of the rock on which we have landed, I am glad that I could not see it clearly from the plane. In the distance, lofty, snow-capped mountains, topped with splashes of indigo sky, are like a huge colored post card hung over the black, frozen waters to cheer the dejected traveler. It is unbelievably beautiful, but utterly unreal. The only things real to us are the sea around us and the rock, relentlessly lashed by rain and wind.

The plane takes off. The Scandinavian businessmen return to their whisky with the frenzy of camels who

have crossed the Sahara without water and have at long
last reached a cool oasis. In turn, the babies automatically renew their howling, which has been interrupted
only by breakfast. The Oriental travelers have resumed
the hieratic position of metal idols. Clad in a dressing
gown as scarlet as the fires of hell, the *femme fatale*
only now leaps out of her berth. She walks past me
and I could swear that her body is surrounded by an
aura of mysterious sin. The stewardesses pass around
cocktails and crossword puzzles. The businessmen accept the first and turn down the second. We are passing
through great, thick, mouse-colored clouds. I read some
of Maugham's stories, more mystery books, and books
on Japan, go back to my notes, my lecture, my papers,
and fret at being so motionless and confined. We are
flying through thick, murky clouds.

Suddenly the loud-speaker informs us that we are
crossing the international date line. At that moment
I lose a day of my life. It should be Friday, but without
an instant's passing, twenty-four hours disappear and
it is Saturday. A day I have never lived is left shrouded
in the stratospheric mists.

The hours pass as slowly as the clouds in the sky.
For lack of a better diversion, one constantly eats and
drinks in this plane. More food is served, but with so
many changes of hours I no longer know what meal
it is. Is it a hearty breakfast or a light dinner? The
watch and the calendar have created chaos in the
rhythm of meals. Among the businessmen, whisky

flows as fluently as the ink from the pen of a prolific writer. Meat balls in a sharp sauce and shrimp are served. These are only the appetizers. They are soon followed by salmon in aspic, a variety of salads, a delicious saffron rice prepared in the Thai style, chicken à la Kiev with peas, and fruits, cheese, sweets, and coffee. Before dinner, we are served tray after tray of cocktails; with dinner, champagne; after dinner, liqueurs. The plane en masse feels like a limp lump of dough. Fortunately, the motors have been kept on a diet of oil and water.

By now the *femme de mystère* has almost all the men on board, with the exception of the Orientals and myself, clustered around her. She tells them that her husband has been alone in Tokyo too long, and between sips of a Martini she generously displays her teeth and legs and coyly utters further confidences. I wonder what her husband is like. Later in Tokyo, purely by coincidence, I see her several times in the shops or on the street. She is always alone, and she always wears the Biblical air of a Magdalene repentant for having repented.

The sky is now blue and silver. Fresh air pours out of the ventilators. Silently and stealthily, like a cat, Japan advances toward us. Our plane lands at Tokyo's Haneda Airport as gracefully as a bird coming to roost after a swift flight. A sleepy sun smiles at us from behind pale clouds. Japanese clad in Western dress meet the plane with outcries of greeting, and diminutive Japanese women in flowered kimonos, their arms bulging with chrysanthemums less pretty than they, welcome us. I am in Tokyo. I have really begun my journey around the world.

the plane with varying expressions of surprise and challenge announced in flowered kimonos, maple-wide belts but with a self-containment and air that they could contain the world.

"FLASHBACK" TO THE FUTURE: CATASTROPHE IN TOKYO

ALTHOUGH THIS BOOK, AS I have explained, is about my first trip around the world, I am including this account of my second landing in Tokyo as a "flashback" to the future because of its dramatic contrast with my first landing.

My second landing in Japan, one year after my first trip around the world, was very different indeed from the landing I just described, and only a miracle prevented it from being a fatal tragedy.

The journey began pleasantly enough. I traveled from New York to San Francisco in a huge jet that crossed the broad continent in a little more than five hours. These I whiled away with two novels and as many meals, meals seasoned by the stewardess's snowy smile, a "standard" smile, like a flirtation that will not blossom into love, like a drink that refreshes but does not quench the thirst.

There was a stopover in San Francisco. The airport was bathed in a sunlight that failed to warm the air, which still clawed with winter's frosty nails even though the calendar said it was now spring. A friend of mine from San Francisco, Dr. Seymour Farber, who is a world-famous physician and an educator, came to the airport to see me. He is a devoted lover of the Orient, and on my first journey around the world, he had kindly given me letters of introduction to some of his physician-friends in Japan and Hong Kong.

Aboard again—this time a jet plane of the Japan Air Lines. Burnished in solar silver, the waiting jet was as formidable and powerful looking outside as it was elegant and graceful inside. Before I boarded the plane, the publicity agent of the Japan Air Lines photographed me. Someone had told them that I was a V.I.P. He also instructed the stewardesses to see to it that I was given a special reception at the Tokyo airport. Little did I imagine what that reception would turn out to be, for both me and my fellow passengers.

The plane was decorated with the elegant simplicity

characteristic of the Japanese. The floor was thickly carpeted in a pattern representing the wavy lines of the sand in a Japanese garden, such as the Ryōanji. The walls were covered with colorful silk on which birds and flowers were depicted. To add to our comfort, we were asked to put on Japanese *happi* coats, as roomy and comfortable as they were gay and pretty. The loud-speakers diffused the subtle, melancholy tones of samisens and *kotos* playing the *sakura* music that is traditional at this time of the year when the cherry trees are about to burst into blossom.

The stewardesses, two diminutive Japanese girls, clad in exquisitely embroidered kimonos, and as lovely themselves as cherry blossoms, kept hopping up and down the aisle in their wooden clogs, distributing napkins that had been soaked in hot perfumed water, and presenting each of us with a small unpainted wooden box wrapped in silk cloth, which contained an assortment of Japanese gifts—a plastic wallet, a letter opener, a little case filled with cigarettes, a painted fan. Later they served us an "international lunch," while the jet itself devoured the miles between San Francisco and Honolulu. Beginning with caviar from Iran and smoked salmon from Scotland, the lunch then ran the whole gamut of exotic Japanese dishes, all washed down with vodka and sake and champagne. The *sakura* music floated dreamily through the air, while the plane now seemed to be hanging motionless over a carpet of sleeping white clouds. Suddenly, the music changed from *sakura* to a hula melody. We had reached Honolulu.

An hour's wait in the old gray wooden shed at Honolulu's airport passed pleasantly enough to the music of hulas as hot as the sun that showered a rain of gold over everyone and everything. Then we were summoned to reboard the plane. This time, in addition to the passengers from New York and San Francisco— businessmen, tourists, schoolteachers—our jet took on a large group of Japanese who had come to Honolulu under the auspices of a travel club in Tokyo to which they belonged. They all wore incongruous Hawaiian straw hats and garlands of red and white flowers around their necks. These *leis* were so thick, and there were so many of them, that the wearers' faces disappeared in them, giving the impression that they were mounds of flowers with feet.

Back on the plane, we again donned our *happi* and were treated to the same graceful rituals and the same subtle samisen and *koto* music. Time seemed to have stopped in a magic land without clocks or calendars. At dusk we made an unscheduled stop at Wake Island —for what reason, we were not told. Later we learned that something had gone wrong somewhere in the plane's mysterious innards. Then off again. Lulled into a pleasant lethargy by the hum of the engines, the endless parade of food and drinks, the slow ticking of time, the *sakura* music, some of the passengers, comfortably wrapped in their *happi*, finally dozed off, others, in

41

a state of aerial nirvana, musefully listened to the soft music and lazily watched the two little kimonoed stewardesses who flitted like angels through our airborne paradise.

The landing began. The plane was descending swiftly through an enveloping darkness. I felt drowsy, and to wake up I went to the washroom to sprinkle my face with water. When I tried to get out, the door was stuck and would not open. I could feel the plane coming down full tilt. For a panic-filled moment, the walls of the tiny cabin seemed to be closing in on me. After repeated yankings, the door yielded. I want back to my place and fastened my seat belt. The plane was falling too fast, like a wounded bird. In the dim distance, down below, lights blinked on and off, as if through a mist of rain.

Suddenly there was a shock. The plane had touched ground with alarming violence. Automatically I grasped my safety belt with both hands. We kept traveling on the ground at an incredible speed. A light flickered on in my subconscious. *Something is wrong. We are going to crash.* The plane kept tearing along like a mortally wounded, crazed beast. Thoughts raced through my mind: *We are going to die. How? Explosion? Fire? There is nothing we can do to save ourselves. I shall never again see those I love. My unfinished work. . . . What lies ahead?*

Suddenly the plane veered sharply. We kept going at a tremendous speed, but now the plane was bouncing up and down like a wild kangaroo. Each bounce would have catapulted me against the ceiling if it had not been for the safety belt, which was cutting into my flesh but still miraculously resisted the desperate pressure.

I had a confused vision of wax-white faces around me fixed in a look of panic. Nobody screamed. There was only the terrifying thumping of the plane on the bumpy ground. Finally, after endless agonizing minutes, during which my forehead streamed with perspiration and my heart beat faster than the speed of the plane, the craft hit something and stopped with a frightening crash.

The lights went out and darkness swallowed us. Some pipes broke and water came gurgling out in the darkness to flood our feet. And suddenly everyone burst into shouts.

I unfastened my safety belt and through the wet darkness groped my way toward the emergency exit. Suddenly I realized that I had left behind my jacket with my passport, wallet, and traveler's checks, and my brief case with my papers and books. The stupid *Homo sapiens* has been conditioned by the twentieth century to respect certain rituals—identification, money—more than his own safety, so I automatically groped my way back to my seat, recovered my possessions, and dragged them along on my second attempt to escape.

On my left, I saw flames coming from one of the engines. In their excitement the two Japanese hostesses were shouting directions in Japanese, which no one in my section of the plane understood. In the darkness I helped two old ladies to the emergency exit. The pilots gave no sign of life in their lightless cabin. The emergency evacuation slide was placed in position. Suddenly it began to dawn on us that the plane might blow up at any minute. One by one we dropped down the emergency canvas tube. I landed in a mud puddle. It was pitch black and it was hailing.

At the door of the plane faces quickly appeared and disappeared, faces so pale they had no eyes or lips. One by one, after sliding down the canvas tube, the passengers joined the group that, stupefied, waited silently nearby. We could not see that under the tremendous impact the plane had split in two. Yet, as if by a miracle, it had neither exploded nor caught on fire. Someone or something had put out the flames. A few of us, vaguely aware of the danger, uttered feeble warnings about getting away from the steel bird, which only a few hours before had stood all silver in the sun, formidable and powerful-looking, and now lay torn and dead in the mud under the pelting hail.

Spattered with mud and bombarded by hail stones, we silently set out across the dark field. The area we were crossing was under construction. There were ditches everywhere. Drainpipes, stones, and bricks littered the ground. I stumbled and fell many times. I should have broken my neck in a ditch or against a pile of stone. I did not. But this miracle was hardly important compared to the incredible miracle of not hav-

44

ing perished in the crash. The passengers, all crowded together now and forming a single human nucleus, marched dumbly under the icy hail. Halfway, one member of the crew climbed onto a mound of stones and harangued us in an English so mixed with Japanese that we never found out what he said.

The airport lights blinked in the distance, but the rescue buses seemed to be taking an eternity to reach us. Finally, we were herded into several small buses, and we headed for the airport building. In the distance, the broken silver shell of the jet, gleaming in the dark, was an overwhelming reminder of how close Death had come.

By now, except for some details that the official report filled in the next day, they told me what had happened. The plane, its hydraulic brakes out of control, had struck the ground with such force that had it not been for the skill of the pilot it would have been smashed to bits. Having survived the violent landing, the plane continued in a straight line and would have been smashed against the airport building had not the God-guided pilot veered into an open field. The plane shot at great speed across the stone-littered field until it finally struck a deep ditch, where it split in two. None of the passengers were hurt, at least as far as could be seen. It was indeed a miracle!

At the airport, shaking with cold and shock, we asked in vain for hot drinks. It was too late and everything was closed. We were told that our luggage was probably beyond salvage. Despairingly I remembered that this was barely the beginning of my journey, and that I had but one suit, one shirt, and one tie, all wet and smeared with mud. Having fulfilled all customs formalities—even under those shocking circumstances the customs inspectors carefully rummaged through our hand baggage—I reached the upper floor of the airport, preceded by the group of Japanese returning from Hawaii. They were indeed a lamentable sight. Their eyes, glassy with shock, stared out of faces that seemed more yellow than usual. Their clothes were crumpled and sodden, and with their muddied *leis* still twisted round their throats they looked as though they had wet dead chickens hanging from their necks.

As we entered the airport's main waiting room, the incongruousness of life burst upon us in a grotesque scene. Two large groups of people stood waiting. One group was clad in black, with starched white collars. Near them, on a platform hung with white streamers imprinted with red and black characters, sat a band of musicians. The leaders of the group carried the inevitable silk-wrapped boxes of presents and paper scrolls, on which were undoubtedly written words of welcome. I was told that they were waiting for a politician who had arrived on our plane. The other group was more casual and cheerful, but they too had a platform with a band and welcoming speakers and streamers and presents. They were waiting for the tourists returning home from Hawaii.

And no sooner did we appear than both bands struck up at the same time, banners waved, and the two groups pressed forward to greet and cheer the half-dazed politician and the unfortunate tourists, who were still shaking from fear.

I pushed my way through the noisy, milling crowd, while the waiting room resounded with the combined efforts of the two bands.

A seventy-yen taxi, the only one available, rocketed me through the nearly empty streets of Tokyo to the Imperial Hotel. There I found awaiting me a suite as big as a bull ring and as cold as the heart of a money-lender. But neither pleas nor threats could get me a little brandy or even a hot cup of tea to fight the cold and shock. It was past two o'clock in the morning and there was no room service! I tried a hot bath, but feeling utterly exhausted and fearing that I might fall asleep in the tub, I went to bed, piling everything I could get hold of on top of me to help warm me up.

It was a long, sleepless night, troubled by terrifying visions of what the crash could have been. The next morning, I put on my still damp, mud-spattered suit and went back to the airport. All the baggage had been rescued intact, and two officials of the airline were distributing it, after making each passenger sign a statement that he had suffered no ill effects from the accident. I protested. *"At the moment"* we were suffering no ill effects. That much I signed, after which they gave me my luggage and a glass of whisky—with the compliments of the airline!

Before leaving the airport I went out to look at the plane. It was split right in two, near the nose, which had dropped into a ditch, while the gaping hole in the body stared straight at the sky. It was good for nothing but a scrap pile. A dead bird, its electronic heart silent, its steel body smashed, its wings immobile forever, its metal head deep in mud. And, struck by the miracle of our salvation, I uttered a silent prayer.

TOKYO ONSEN

BUT ON MY FIRST VISIT I AM so entranced at being in Japan, a country I have dreamed of visiting for so long, that the usually bothersome chore of going through customs seems like a charming ritual. A smiling porter squeezes my luggage into a small rickety-looking taxi with a smiling driver. It is three o'clock in the afternoon, and the breakneck speed at which the taxi travels does not perturb me at all, because I am elatedly drinking in the sights, sounds, and smells of Tokyo.

49

We arrive at the perennially overcrowded Imperial Hotel, but my room had been miraculously secured for me by some very kind Japanese friends. The moment I finish unpacking, an overwhelming fatigue suddenly seizes every muscle in my body. The trip from New York to Tokyo had lasted forty hours.

My room is too small and is as glum and cheerless as the spirits of a maid in a Guy de Maupassant story. Through my window I can see an inner court as black, cracked, and ugly as the decayed tooth of a donkey. Squatting in one corner of the court, a Japanese boy with quick, deft fingers is making flower wreaths of paper. The melancholy sound of a noodle peddler's flute rises from below. Beyond the walls of my room, Tokyo's pulse is beating feverishly—Tokyo, with its ten million inhabitants, the most populous city in the world! Ignoring my fatigue, I quickly bathe, dress, and go out.

I am sure I walk hundreds of miles trying to find the way out to the street through the labyrinth of corridors, staircases, rooms, anterooms, hallways, reception halls, elevators, galleries, and arcades of the hotel, an experience I was to suffer not once but several times a day, every day I spent in that crowded, impersonal hotel, which to me looked as though it had had Picasso and Dali, in their most abstract periods, as planners and the Marx brothers as decorators. (On subsequent journeys to Tokyo I stayed at the Hotel New Japan, which I liked immensely.) When I finally reach the door to the street, I am warmly greeted by a brilliant indigo-blue sky that looks as though it had been painted by a gifted Japanese artist.

Out on the street, I suddenly remember that a colleague of mine from California had urged me to visit the Tokyo Onsen, the famous bathhouse, immediately upon my arrival in Tokyo. There, he assured me, all travel fatigue would be promptly chased out of my body, and I would be returned to the world beaming with renewed vitality. Filled with hope and anticipation, I hail a taxi.

The taxis of Tokyo are classified according to size, with the price increasing with the size; thus, there are seventy-yen taxis, eighty-yen taxis, one-hundred-yen taxis, and so on. There are also enormous de luxe automobiles for hire. The smaller the taxi, the greater the risk one runs among the million and a half vehicles that cram the streets of Tokyo. The Japanese, who have a great sense of humor, have christened their noisy motorcycles *kaminarizoku* (thunder breed), and their taxis *kamikazes,* after the suicide bombers used by the Japanese during World War II, whose pilots flew headlong into enemy warships, destroying themselves in order to destroy the enemy.

In a *kamikaze* on wheels I shoot forth toward Ginza (*gin* means silver, and the name "Ginza" commemorates the silver mint that stood in the same place three centuries ago), the district that in a space of a few square miles encloses a whole world of recreation: res-

51

taurants, theatres, movie houses, bars (these are end-less), cafés, night clubs, cabarets, music halls, taverns, and tea rooms. And, let us not forget the *pachinko,* or gambling machine, a Japanese version of the American pinball machine, on which, for a few cents, the player shoots tiny balls on a board and wins a prize if he strikes numbers, which light up when the balls touch them, that add up to an appropriate total. Every year young and old pour millions upon millions of yen into the machines with the innocuous-looking little balls. The number of people, especially women, who lead a precarious existence because of their passion for *pachinko* is legion, for the insatiable machines with pity for none devour the yen intended for food and rent.

The Tokyo Onsen, where my *kamikaze* finally stops after a fifteen-minute ride that has kept my heart constantly in my mouth, is an enormous ramshackle building with dingy walls lined with long, vertical Japanese signs that look more like the painted banners used as decorations at festivals. Everything a Japanese might want can be found in Tokyo Onsen, from a hall in which to practice judo to restaurants that serve *tempura* and sukiyaki, bars of all sizes flowing with sake and Japanese beer, dance halls, and, of course, the baths.

I climb several stairways and cross an interminable corridor. The place is filled with young girls who do not appear to be more than sixteen years old, although, I later find out, they are all past twenty or even thirty. Pretty, smiling, talkative, as noisy as a flock of chirping birds, they scamper about with sparrow-like little hops, forced upon them by the heavy *geta,* or wooden clogs, they wear, which are held on their feet by a narrow strap. They are dressed in white kimonos that barely reach to their knees. Their bosom poses a delightful enigma that only a gardener familiar with flowers could solve. They have fresh, clean faces, flushed from exertion, faces like frosty apples at dawn. Despite their smallness, they have a lot of sex appeal, voluptuous elfin-like creatures whose small hands hold the secret of Tokyo Onsen's success.

I am asked how long a *bassu* I want—half an hour? an hour? an hour and a half?—and I inquire—I feel so tired—if there are any longer than that. At a signal from the man in charge of the tickets, an old man as small and gray as a fresh shrimp, another man appears who is as small and pink as a cooked shrimp. He greets me in Japanese and assigns me to one of the nimble little elves, who with a luminous smile motions for me to follow her. Despite her towering *geta,* her head barely reaches my chest. I follow her down the corridor past hundreds of doors. Finally we enter a large room that adjoins another room with an individual bath.

The first room looks like a college girl's room. It is furnished with a bureau, a mirror on which are pasted pictures of Japanese film stars and one of Robert Taylor, a blue vase with fresh flowers artistically arranged, two chairs, and a wardrobe whose door is ajar, revealing another white kimono inside. Little porcelain jars and bottles filled with all sorts of cosmetic concoctions are neatly lined on the bureau. The second room contains a steam cabinet, a stool, a large sunken stone tub, and a massage table. A film of steam covers the bare walls. Everything is very clean and orderly, very Japanese.

The elf closes the door and, without wasting a moment, stands on tiptoe and quickly undoes the knot in my tie. After taking off my jacket, she reaches for my belt. I quickly turn my back and begin to remove my trousers, but she is a past master in the art of removing clothing in the face of all resistance. She then takes off my shoes and socks. Taking advantage of a knock on the door, I quickly shed my remaining cloth defenses and with one leap reach the steam cabinet. When she returns, she laughs heartily at my bashful retreat and takes off her kimono. She has nothing on underneath excepting a white bikini of scant dimensions. She is truly a Tanagra figurine, with elusive curves, all of her golden and ethereal. In faltering English she asks me how much steam I want and for how long, and as clouds of hot vapor slowly envelop me, relaxing my tense muscles, she gently wraps cold towels round my head, all the while chattering like a trained parakeet.

It is then that for the first time I come upon that peculiar custom that makes the Japanese consider it courteous to ask the sort of questions that are taboo in Western countries. I was invariably asked the same personal questions by everybody—men and women, physicians and chauffeurs, waitresses and geishas, professors and servants—all over Japan. The first question is how many children one has. The Japanese, and especially the women, take it for granted that all men are married. Therefore they never ask if you are married; instead, they immediately want to know how prolific you have been. The second question is how old you are, and the third, how much you earn. After this, nothing else can be a surprise.

In all justice it must be mentioned that in turn the same people, without waiting to be asked, voluntarily offer and elaborate on the same information about themselves. I soon discovered that the best way to answer their embarrassing questions is to counterattack with another question, whether it is related to the same subject or not. And invariably the Japanese, with an angelic smile, answers you, forgetting his own question. But on my first visit to Tokyo Onsen, I have not yet discovered this technique, and I am soon to experience the chastening results of trying to answer these questions.

Fifteen minutes later I emerge from the infernal steam contraption, my burning body haloed in thick smoke, like the devil as he appears in conventional paintings. My tormenting elf now makes me sit down on the stool, whereupon she proceeds to pour buckets of almost boiling water on my back. Then she gently pushes me toward the sunken tub and into what feels like molten lava straight from a volcano. When I emerge, a few minutes later, looking like a lobster ready to be set on the table, she bids me lie down on the massage table, after giving one good pull at the towel with which I have been attempting to cover my last bastions and replacing it with another smaller towel.

In her broken English, she asks me if I would like to eat anything, including "flied lice!" (fried rice). Craving a respite from the ordeal of fire and water, which has me panting, I tell her to order whatever she wishes.

A few minutes later a dish of fried shrimp with a hot sauce and a little porcelain bottle of warm sake are set under my nose. When I invite her to have some, she picks at the shrimp as delicately as a sparrow and then continues talking without pause about everything that comes into her head, such as movies and her Papasan. (In Japanese, the suffix "san" is a sign of respect and therefore is added to practically everything. Parents are called Papasan or Mamasan, Mount Fuji becomes Fujisan, and even a waiter is called Boysan. She calls me Martísan.) She goes on to talk about the forthcoming cherry blossom festivals and about her boy friend.

"He want to mally," she confides to me, "but I vely busy and no have time. So, if he no want to wait . . . *sayonara!*"

The word *"sayonara"* is one of the most beautiful words in the Japanese language. It means both good-by and see you soon, but it has deep nostalgic overtones and a profound emotional content; it is an expression

of farewell to people, places, and things that are loved,
a word of intense sentimental feeling.

Our conversation is somewhat surrealistic and goes
on while Ghiocco, as she is called, pounds my spine
with her energetic little fists.

"How many children you have?" she asks me.

"None," I gasp under one of her blows.

"That is vely bad," she answers, while continuing her
symphony of blows over the keyboard of my vertebra.
"You need to see a doctol!"

"But I am a doctor," I pant.

"Then you need see a bettel doctol!" she answers log-
ically.

"How do you enjoy yourself, when you finish your
work?" I ask her just to change the subject. "Do you go
to the movies?"

"No," she says earnestly. "I get one of my boy fliends
and go to a bal."

"Do you like dancing?"

"No," she answers imperturbably. "We just dlink."

"Sake, cocktails?"

"No. All that fol babies only. Whisky and beel."

"You have many boy friends, then?"

"Yes. If I have only one, any time he can say *sayonara* to me. If I have one dozen, it is me who can say
sayonara to any of them!"

She pauses, and with the pain of the pounding on
my spine, I notice in a corner of the adjoining room a
pair of street *getas* and over them her street kimono.

57

"You prefer to wear a kimono to the Western dress?"

"No. I plefel Westeln. But I have big bunyons on my feet. I no can weal high heel shoes. I need *geta*. More comfoltable. So, with *geta* I need to weal kimono."

"You are always chewing gum," I mention to her, as she has been masticating since I first saw her.

"Yes," she answers, "I have big holes in back teeth, and if I do not chew gum my mouth smells like lotten chlysanthemum."

The massage continues, until finally there is a spectacular finale. Climbing upon the table, Ghiocco begins walking on my spinal column in her bare feet. After a moment of panic, expecting every vertebra on my back to break, I experience an indescribable sensation of relief from all my fatigue. Then, without interrupting her flow of words, Ghiocco pours buckets of icy water on me, telling me meanwhile how much she likes "Lobelt Taylol" (Robert Taylor, for some reason, is very popular among the women of Japan), that she is twenty-eight years old, which surprises me, for she looks sixteen, that I should be a Papasan, and that I should go to a doctor who is "leally gud."

Then, despite my resistance, she dresses me from head to foot so quickly that all that is left for me to do is to knot my tie. Upon being given a generous tip, she chirps with joy, like a canary with a fresh piece of lettuce on a sunny day, bows to me repeatedly, and cries out that she will go with a girl friend to have a *tempura* dinner at the Ginza and to the movies. We say good-by like old friends, and I walk out of the room, my body as light as though it were made of feathers.

As I am leaving Tokyo Onsen, I notice in a corner of the entrance hall a handwritten sign in English that I copy verbatim. (I do not know whether it was someone's idea of a joke.)

Our massage girls are very nice modest maids. They give massage but no play games with anyone. We request honorable foreign visitors to give peace to them. Nothing but honest massage here. Any visitor interest in call girls must go to Ginza and ask Broadway-dressed boys for good addresses.

Bathhouses are a national institution in Japan. Besides Tokyo Onsen, the most famous, there are many others. They say that some, protected by the bathhouse sign, are dedicated to other, less sanitary, needs. The Tokyo Onsen and many others are considered a luxury by the Japanese, who go to them alone, in pairs, or with the entire family. The bathing rooms for families are larger, and custom requires that the father be the first to enter the boiling bath, where he relaxes for half an hour, while the rest of the family respectfully wait until he gives the signal. Then the oldest son follows, and later the other male children, then the wife, and finally the daughters, in order of age.

Since everyone soaps and washes himself before getting into the tub, whether at the public baths or at home, the bath is never employed for cleaning purposes in Japan; indeed, such an act would be considered barbarous. The Japanese soap and wash themselves near the bath, seated on a stool, pouring buckets of water over their heads until they are spotlessly clean. Only then do they enter the communal bath, so that although several of them—dozens in the public baths—may be sharing the same bath, the water is always clean as well as boiling hot, for the bath is to relax in and not for cleaning one's body.

The day of a Japanese—laborer, doctor, stenographer, wealthy woman, lawyer, or peasant—invariably ends with a prolonged hot *bassu,* after which the soiled clothing worn during the day is cast aside and the bather dons a kimono as soft and soothing as a caress, which helps to relax him and to induce a state of utter serenity and well-being. In hot baths the Japanese seeks his peace.

NATURE IN SHORTHAND:
THE JAPANESE GARDEN

SPREAD IN FRONT OF ME ARE green-clad hills. A stream tumbling down the hillside turns into a waterfall of crystal and foamy lace. Toads the color of emeralds doze near the water. At the foot of a hill stands a cottage with a scarlet pagoda roof. In front of the cottage, on an arched bridge spanning a pond, there is a Japanese peasant in a cart drawn by two pensive water buffaloes. In the foreground, the slender, pointed branches of a tree soar into the air like

61

silver spikes. Perched on a branch are two butterflies, their black and golden wings spread out like fans. It is a landscape of infinite grace, sweetness, and tranquillity.

I reach over with my hands. I pick up the peasant and place him on top of a hill. Then I move the two water buffaloes so that their ancient bodies are reflected in the pond near the pagoda. I am arranging, or rather disarranging, a Japanese landscape, one of those famous tray gardens that adorn every Japanese home.

Japan has two varieties of these lovely tray gardens: one, the *bonkei,* is a landscape with bridges, ponds, hills, streams, rocks, shrubs, bonsai, or dwarf trees (some of them are supposed to be up to three hundred years old), and pavilions, a reproduction in miniature of a landscape characteristic of Japan; the other, the *bonseki,* is, rather than a landscape, an abstract sketch of a landscape, modern art reducing nature to its basic elements—rocks and sand arranged on a black lacquer tray. It is an abstract study constructed on a tray even as a picture is painted on a canvas. Both types of garden are set, as are all objects in Japan, on a wooden stand, for the Japanese never put anything directly on tables.

I have seen gardens in many places of the world. I have greatly admired the Velasquezan sobriety of Madrid's rose gardens, the sophisticated splendor of Versailles' gardens, the polychrome old-world elegance of Lima's gardens; but I have never seen anything so serenely beautiful as the Japanese gardens. These gardens,

when created on nature's scale, fall into three classifica-
tions: hill gardens, flat gardens, and tea-house gardens.
In addition, as I have said, there are miniature or tray
gardens. Japanese landscapes are nature's own work of
art, but in this instance nature imitates Japanese art.

On my very first full day in Japan, I set eyes on a
Japanese landscape for the first time. It was at Hakone,
the mountain from which one can see Mount Fuji.
(Mount Fuji, the incarnation of the goddess Fujisan,
more a deity than a mountain, is supremely beautiful
with its summit of silver reflected in the blue waters
of Lake Hakone, which lies at the top of Hakone
Mountain.)

I spent that day in the country, at one of the several
gracious invitations from a Japanese friend of mine,
Takaji Oda, a very good and kind man, a truly talented
modern painter, and a brilliant business executive, who
has created a garden around his home in Tokyo that
is a wonder of artistry and imagination. In the countryside, beneath a fine, cool rain, a new kind of landscape
was revealed to me, a landscape of unique beauty—one
that contrasted with the feminine beauty of French
landscapes, with the grandiose beauty of landscapes
like Arizona's Grand Canyon, and with the spectacular
beauty of places like the bay of Rio de Janeiro. It was
a landscape of unique beauty, whose bewitching charm
lies in the infinite number of details, each more enchanting than the other, embroidered on its background. In the Japanese landscape, nature has made

full artistic use of skies, rivers, birds, and rocks, but not of flowers, which, with the occasional exception of cherry trees, lotuses, and chrysanthemums, are often absent from Japanese landscapes.

The Japanese worship their landscapes. They have mastered them and immortalized them in much the same way that man has mastered the sea by confining it within a swimming pool. Similarly, in their gardens, the Japanese reduce nature to miniature proportions, re-creating it on a small scale and at a level that requires one to look at it from one's knees.

I have seen gardens in Tokyo, Hakone, Kamakura, Yokohama, Kyoto, and Fukuoka that are sheer marvels. Each garden contained bridges, ponds, waterfalls, rocks arranged in abstract designs, shrubs, stone lanterns, pagodas, paths made of circular stepping-stones, ponds carpeted with lotus blossoms, dwarf trees, and gilded pavilions.

Nature has bestowed upon Japan a unique kind of landscape, and the Japanese lovingly reproduce it in their own gardens. One is entranced by the varicolored luminosity of the foliage, by the gentle diffused light that pours through the leaves from the sky, the charm of the bridges and streams, and especially by the magic of the rocks, boulders, and stones, so artistically placed that they alone incarnate all the beauty of the landscape. And, here and there, a lovely green haze of moss, reminiscent of the incipient beard on the chin of a country youth.

There is a garden in Kyoto—I will talk about it in greater detail later—that has carried to the ultimate that unique charm of the Japanese landscape: the rock garden of the Temple of Ryōanji. It consists exclusively of sand and rocks, without a single flower, only a few shrubs. Fifteen rocks are arranged in five clusters in such perfect balance that it would be inconceivable to think of changing them. The rocks are like mysterious islands in the solitary sea of sand. Before such a garden, with nothing to distract it, the soul expands and peace pervades the spirit, rapt in ecstasy before the miracle of art and exquisite simplicity. Simplicity, that is the secret of Japanese genius. This striving for simplicity by the Japanese has led to the elimination of everything that is perishable and ephemeral, such as flowers, and to the retention of only that which is solid and endurable: water, trees, sand, and especially rock.

(This same simplicity prompts the Japanese to build their houses with *karakami,* sliding paper walls; with *kakemonos,* hanging scrolls; and with *shoji,* painted rice-paper screens that diffuse the light, and to cover their floors with fine *tatami,* the number of *tatami* indicating the importance of a room or a house. Thus the walls and floors of the entire house can be changed periodically.)

I was especially captivated by the tray gardens, true works of art and one of the most esteemed crafts in Japan. The tray garden makes it possible to preserve a beloved landscape close to oneself, a little water and fertilizer keeping its hills, dwarf trees, and moss always green, while a little polishing keeps the streams made of glass and the lakes made with mirrors perpetually sparkling.

As a child I was fascinated by landscapes mysteriously imprisoned within sealed containers, and I used to dream of entering those miniature universes and becoming another storybook hero. All my life I have retained this fascination: Easter eggs punctured with little holes through which one sees miniature gold and silver landscapes with tiny marzipan houses and candy bridges; crystal balls enclosing snow-covered landscapes that create a snow storm when shaken; bottles that contain Mediterranean scenes with boats, lighthouses, and the blue sea; music boxes with Swiss landscapes; glass paperweights filled with enchanted forests seemingly alive with pheasants, partridges, and hunting dogs.

In Japan I made the thrilling discovery that not only tray gardens and house gardens but nature herself, for some unfathomable reason, contains the same sort of landscape, all iridescence and miniature fantasy, that I sought as a child in the unreal world of music boxes and crystal balls.

I remember one night in Tokyo when, by pure chance, I discovered a beautiful garden. As was my nightly habit, I had gone for a stroll through the Ginza, Tokyo's district of shops, restaurants, cafés, and night clubs. Whereas by day the Ginza is a boisterous aviary, punctuated by the music emanating from its great department stores, at night it is a fairylike scene of colored banners with glittering Japanese letters that look like a sorcerer's invocation, narrow streets that are an orgy of color, alleys sparkling with lights and color like a jeweler's shop window.

The traffic of human beings, automobiles, bicycles, and *jinrikishas* flows incessantly, like rice escaping from a torn bag. The women's kimonos illuminate with their rich, colorful flutter the somber Western clothes worn by the men, even as butterflies illuminate a shadowed grove of willows. Between the hours of 6 P.M. and midnight, what seems to be millions of Japanese flock to the Ginza to eat hot *tempura,* drink sake, and listen to *sakura* music. Some come to see the performance at the aristocratic *Nō* theatre, which dates from before the fourteenth century. In this drama, in which the stage is bare of almost all decoration and in which the acting is accompanied by flute and drum music, plays are presented by actors who, with the aid of a chorus and many masks, contrive to play several parts themselves. Others attend the popular sixteenth-century *Kabuki* theatre. In both these forms of drama, male actors play women's parts, just as they did in the seventeenth-century England of Shakespeare. The male impersonator of women in *Kabuki* is called an *onnagata.*

Others come to eat noodles, rice, and raw fish, to drink sake or whisky, to play *mah-jongg* or the inevitable *pachinko,* whose steel balls resound night and day in Tokyo, or they come looking for bars advertising "BEER AND GIRLS" or seeking refuge in a hall where Japanese girls, forever smiling, pluck the strings of the samisen.

Japanese men also go to the Ginza in search of quick sexual gratification. Either after work, before returning home, or after dinner, you can see them prowling about, generally alone, like alley cats in search of scraps of food or a female cat.

At eleven o'clock the Ginza, like a tired multi-eyed monster, begins to shut off its electric signs. By midnight its one hundred thousand neon eyes are closed, and almost total silence and darkness replace the fantastic medley of people, lights, and music of a few hours before.

I must have lingered too long over my sukiyaki, for when I walked out of the Japanese restaurant—after numerous good-bys and final bows from at least half a dozen kimono-clad waitresses and hostesses—which had already closed for the night and had its lights turned off, since I was the last customer, I found myself in a dark rain-washed street far from my hotel, with no one in sight.

Even under normal circumstances and in daylight, it is difficult to find any street address in Tokyo, for taxi drivers do not seem to know their own city, and expect to be directed. One soon learns to have one's destination and directions for getting there written down in Japanese. And now I was on a dark street, it was midnight, and I did not have the slightest notion of where I was.

I started walking toward some lights blinking in the distance, but I found no taxi there. Again I began walking through a dark narrow street toward another beckoning cluster of lights farther away.

I had barely taken a few steps when, as if in obedience to some signal, the lights behind me began to go out. One after another, like dying candles, I watched them disappear, creating a deepening darkness around me. I quickened my pace toward the opposite end of the street, guided by the distant blue, green, and red lights of the Japanese signs, which were reflected like fallen colored moons in the puddles on the street. Suddenly these lights also began to blink and go out.

In consternation I broke into a slight trot in the direction of the last remaining lights, which now looked like a bunch of glowing oranges, but almost immediately they too went out, leaving me completely alone in a street that had turned into a dark tunnel. Recalling with a shudder a similar situation I had experienced in 1949 in the little town of Helmstedt, Germany, while en route from Paris to Berlin, when I found myself alone in a dark lonely street, enveloped in a night that seemed proud of its impenetrable darkness, I now quickly resumed walking, turning corner after corner, clumsily feeling my way over ground muddied by the evening rain, in the hope of finding a light or a voice to guide me.

At that moment, as if the general blackout were a signal for water to replace light, it began to rain very hard, the heavy drops pelting the pavement with the violence of the steel balls in a *pachinko* machine. Within a few minutes I was drenched and, what was worse, I knew I was utterly lost. I plodded on, stumbling here and there, always clinging to the buildings with their big, silent, closed doors.

Finally, at the end of an alley, I saw a light. It was blue, a vertical Japanese sign as lovely as a garland of flowers. I walked over to it, stepped into a sandy courtyard, and found myself in front of a staircase that was faintly lit by another sign, a violet one that transformed the long strands of rain into amethyst fringes.

I knocked at the door, hoping to find a telephone. After I had knocked repeatedly, a Japanese woman in a white and red kimono opened the door, dropped to her knees as soon as she saw me, touched the ground twice with her head, and vanished in a flash amid the clatter of sandals. A few seconds later, four women in black kimonos rushed out, and they also paid me the tribute of many bows. I tried to explain what I wanted, mentioning the name of my hotel again and again and going through the motions of telephoning. Finally one of them gave me to understand that the telephone was out of order. I tried to ask her if there were any way of calling a taxi, but she merely pointed to my wet clothes and motioned to me to come in. There being nothing else I could do, I went in.

The good Samaritans, all of them middle-aged and drowsy-looking—although this did not prevent them from hopping about me as actively as squirrels—had me remove my shoes and enter a room with a flower-filled *tokonoma,* a place of honor, little bamboo tables, and an unlit fireplace, clean of all ashes. When I saw an unpainted wooden board on the wall hung with a number of keys, I realized that I was in a Japanese inn.

Preceded and followed by the Japanese women, who were now chattering rapidly and giggling like school-girls, I climbed a steep stairway in my socks and entered the room that had been assigned to me.

This was my first experience in a Japanese inn. I was given three small rooms separated by sliding wooden partitions. The main room, which had a large window covered at the moment by a screen of pink rice paper, was furnished with a small table, *tatami* on the floor, two cushions to sit on, a floor mirror, a television set and a radio—the only concessions to modern times—and a beautiful vase, set on a low table, in which three red-and-green flowers fanned out like dwarf palms. Later I discovered, behind a screen painted with blossoms and bees, a small chest, in which I placed my folded clothing, since hangers are nonexistent in Japan. The Japanese—whose world is without verticals—never hang their garments, but fold and store them horizontally.

Adjoining this room was the bathroom, with the usual deep sunken bath, so that when you are standing

71

inside it your head is at floor level, for the Japanese generally like to stand in their baths. There was also a stool to sit on and a wooden bucket used for soaping and pouring steaming water over oneself before entering the bath.

The third room was the bedroom, a perfect geometric cube, walled in by fragile screens of wood and opaque paper on which sprays of wisteria had been painted. The entire bedroom floor was covered with a mattress, thus converting the room into an island for sleeping, with the feet never touching the floor, only the mattress.

Neatly folded next to a quilt was a *yukata,* or light kimono, and a *tanzen,* the beautiful heavy cotton kimono, used by guests so that they may disrobe and be comfortable. Before retiring for the night, my Samaritans returned with more smiles and bows, a platter of bananas and oranges, a little bottle of warm sake, a steaming pot of green tea, and rice cookies. The room was softly lit, mercifully free of that odious naked bulb that hangs from the ceiling in the rooms of most provincial hotels and that somehow is perversely reflected in every mirror in the room to the detriment of one's eyes.

Cozily wrapped in the kimono, I opened the window, which in fact was a door, indeed, an entire sliding wall. And there, at my feet, only a few steps below, stood the most enchanting Japanese garden, a garden out of a watercolor painting.

It was raining hard, and the garden was like a sami-sen, a harp playing a song to itself. In the center stood a man-made pond studded with white water lilies and spanned by a miniature bridge as though by a stone bangle. Consummately arranged around the pond were dwarf willows, rocks of rare contour, tall stone lanterns, and colored lanterns that streaked the pond waters with shimmering colors, in contrast to the shadows lurking in the corners.

Beneath the rain's tremulous crystal ropes, the garden, with its little mountains, pond, waterfall, pines, and pagoda towers, was a miraculous abbreviation, a shorthand of nature. Pelted by the rain, some chrysanthemums near my window unfurled their petals like butterflies in repose.

Spellbound, I sat down on the *tatami* and spent part of the night looking at the miracle of that garden in the heart of Tokyo, dreaming, inhaling the smell of the wet earth and the foliage, watching the needles of the pine trees turn into iridescent crystal beneath the rain.

Before I finally retreated to the bedroom's padded island of dreams, my elation was absolute upon discovering in a corner of the living room, on a low red lacquer table, an exquisite tray garden, in which a few peasants in woven straw capes stood sheltered beneath the stone arches of a red pagoda perched at the foot of Mount Fuji.

It was then that I realized that the heart of Japan is

a shadowed, mysterious garden, even though between the Americanized Japanese of Tokyo and his romantic traditional past there is as much similarity as between the skin of a lion in front of a fireplace and that noble beast alive and fierce in the jungle.

In the bedroom, a small brazier, brimming with glowing charcoal, kept smoldering all night, an unexpected, fortuitous miniature of Fujiyama.

ROCKS AND SAND: A VISIT TO THE GARDEN OF RYŌANJI

O<small>NE MELANCHOLY, RAINY</small> afternoon, I went to see the Ryōanji Garden in Kyoto. I had traveled from Tokyo to Kyoto by a magnificent express train that makes the run in six hours. Early in the morning I had arrived at Tokyo's railway station and promptly got lost in that underground labyrinth with its maddening noise and confusion. A porter had grabbed my luggage and instantly disappeared, leaving me terrifyingly alone in the midst of a rushing multitude whose language I did not understand and who therefore could not direct me. After much running around, I suddenly found my luggage sitting in the middle of a platform. When the train finally arrived, the door to my compartment stood right in front of my luggage. Never have I encountered such mathematical exactitude, not even in Switzerland.

On the platform, hawkers sold lunches beautifully packed in unpainted wooden boxes wrapped in colored silk paper. All sorts of beverages were also to be had, among them cans—"Made in Japan"—of Scotch and soda, a specialty I found only in Japan. The noisy human babel milled around, a babel of confusion but with only one language—Japanese.

The train was magnificent. The car in which I sat had armchairs as large and deep as those in a bankers' club on Fifth Avenue and vases with exquisite flower arrangements, a species of decoration present everywhere, even in washrooms. (Nothing on earth is more drab and dreary than the washrooms on a train; in Japan they are redeemed by their extreme cleanliness and colorful vases of flowers.) Diminutive women dressed in white distributed, with that innocent smile that never seems to leave the Japanese lips, the inevitable and welcome napkins soaked in hot perfumed water, sandwiches, cold drinks, tea, and magazines in various languages. Beyond the windows the landscape sped by, dull and gray, except in the vicinity of the Izu Peninsula, where it is brightened by the pretty houses and hotels of Atami, clinging to the hillsides and facing the pale blue sea of the so-called Japanese Riviera. I watched my fellow travelers, all Japanese, and chatted with some of them in English. The majority were businessmen.

At lunch time, on my way to the dining car (where I was served a faultless Old Fashioned and a splendid lunch from the kitchens of the Imperial Hotel in Tokyo), I made a discovery that filled me with puzzlement. All the cars—at least a dozen—through which I passed on my way to the restaurant at the head of the train were fully occupied by utterly silent Japanese with hearing aids in their ears. For a moment I wondered if I was in the midst of a story by Edgar Allan Poe—a silent train where all the passengers are deaf and dumb.

The puzzle was solved later in my own car, when I noticed above my chair a little button like a hearing aid connected to an electric cord. It was an individual radio. Every passenger on this train was furnished with his own private radio, with which he could listen to music without disturbing his neighbors. The ear plug left everyone's hands free to open their precious lunch boxes, in which, in little squares separated by thin partitions of wood, like the blocks of paint in a child's paintbox, there was a veritable water color of inviting cold food—white rice, boiled fish, pickles, assorted greens, dried fruits—together with chopsticks sheathed in silk paper, with which most of the passengers were already picking at their rice with all the neatness of well-behaved birds.

Kyoto by day is noisy, confusing, gray. It does not have any of the modernity of Tokyo, but it does have most of its noise. Its days of splendor as the former capital of Japan are long past, but it preserves its beautiful traditions, its cultural centers, its academies and universities, its palaces and schools, all interspersed with new hotels, where the baseball games from Tokyo appear on color television screens.

At sessions of the medical congress that I was attending, I encountered many friends, some of whom I had already met and others with whom I had only corresponded. Most of them were physicians, and all of them were men who are refined, cultivated, intellectually curious, sensitive, and with exquisite manners. Their hospitality was as touching as it was amazing. A prominent Kyoto physician, Dr. Chuzo Nagaishi, invited me to a memorable *tempura* dinner in a lovely restaurant, where tiny waitresses hopped around us like happy sparrows. On another evening, some of my Japanese colleagues took me to the night club Bel-Ami (how did Guy de Maupassant's literary creation ever get to Kyoto?), and while they sat around the table drinking sake, I was lured by a kimono-clad hostess to dance the twist. There I was in the ancient capital of Japan with Kyushu colleagues, dancing the American twist with maidens from Kyoto to music played by the "Osaka Cuban Boys" in a night club with a French name!

Kyoto has more than eighteen hundred Buddhist temples and Shinto shrines, and many gardens. I visited several of the gardens in a fine rain that brought out the iridescent hues of their thousand varieties of moss. They are gardens of marvel and dream. Some of them, highly respectful of nature, add nothing to her; others have charming decorations—a bridge clasping a stream like a bracelet, a turret, like an ornamental comb, set upon a hill, a pagoda as tall as a castle. In Kyoto also are those two wonders, the gardens of the imperial villas Katsura and Shugakuin, both dating from the seventeenth century.

But what I wished above all was to see the garden of Ryöanji.

Since my arrival in Kyoto I had been feeling indisposed, perhaps from exhaustion and homesickness, both aggravated by the fact that I had put up at a hotel whose reputation is as good as its safety is bad. It was overflowing with warnings against fire written in both Japanese and English. There were signs everywhere indicating the location of emergency exits and fire escapes and signs exhorting guests not to leave anything burning in their rooms. Of course, it took no time at all for one to become obsessed with the invisible but omnipresent visions of fire. On the other hand, the rooms themselves were appalling invitations to a conflagration.

My room, the window of which looked out onto a sort of concentration camp shut in by concrete walls—actually the flat roof of a low building surrounded by the walls of higher buildings—contained such a vast collection of furniture—armchairs, rocking chairs, straight chairs, tables, wardrobes, bureaus, stools, cushions, all of them ancient and dusty—that I was forced to stack one piece on top of another in the four corners of the room before I could move around, and then I could only move sideways. The draperies (which seemed to hang everywhere) were thick and so old that I expected them to disintegrate into dust at any moment. The lamp shades were as dry as the paper of an ancient scroll. Everything seemed to be waiting for a lighted cigarette forgotten on a table, a half-extinguished match, a mere spark of any kind, for the whole place to burst into a blazing, roaring, Dantesque inferno. On my first night there, a nightmarish night, I dreamed that Kyoto had been engulfed under mountainous waves. In my dreams I was putting out what to me, both consciously and subconsciously, seemed to be an inevitable holocaust.

It was in such a state of mind that, the next afternoon, I set out in a taxi to visit the garden of Ryōanji, the "Temple of the Dragon Repose." Half an hour's drive from Kyoto brought me to the old Buddhist monastery where the garden is. I saw many monks and a few Japanese visitors crossing the flagstones on tiptoe, skirting the puddles, into which the rain was now

80

pelting down with the sound of ball shot. The temple has vast open cloisters that let in the rain. There are many statues of Buddhas, altars, and shrines, before which motionless gray-robed monks meditate in silence. Joined by the gray colonnades, wood and stone have wedded, blessed by the passage of centuries. There is a smell of damp wood and wet earth. As is often true, the commercial goes hand in hand with the religious, here in the form of small stalls where post cards, little statues, and all sorts of trinkets are sold as souvenirs of the monastery. After crossing a number of courtyards in stockinged feet—all shoes must be removed at the entrance—I reached the garden of Ryōanji, miraculously deserted at the moment. A few moments later my indisposition, my homesickness, and the thoughts of fire had all vanished.

The garden of Ryōanji is much smaller than one would expect, some twenty-three hundred square feet, rectangular in form, closed in by buildings on two sides and by walls on the other two. This Zen garden, constructed nearly five hundred years ago, epitomizes all the exquisite simplicity and elegance of the art of Japanese gardening. Hundreds of thousands of people, perhaps millions, have sat down beside its sands to pray, dream, or meditate. It is composed of fifteen rocks, gray and irregular, artistically arranged in an asymmetrical disorder, standing in groups of two, three, or five. The seeming disorder is actually the result of inspired planning. Grayish shrubs cling to the rocks.

A rippled sea of coarse white sand surrounds, integrates, and unifies the rocks. And that is all. The philosopher-gardener who designed it made it the illustration of a beautiful thought: "The universe, a grain of sand; the sea, a drop of crystal."

The rocks of Ryöanji have been compared to many different symbols, from man's sins and virtues to a lioness guarding her cubs, from fish in the sea to cabalistic figures intended to produce a psychological state of mind conducive to meditation. Its sands—which one can only look at from the edge of the garden, since walking on them is forbidden—give the impression of still, pure, serene water. Here are poetry, religion, beauty.

It was spring when I visited Ryöanji, and I tried to visualize it as it might be in the autumn and in winter. Great bronze leaves, blown in by the wind, carpeting the sands like lotuses and water lilies in a pond; snow tracing mysterious embroideries of ermine on the sea of sand, capping the rocks in shimmering white. The garden has no flowers, no water, no plants, no fruits. With the cosmic elements reduced to their utmost simplicity—rock and sand—the garden of Ryöanji offers man, like a mirror, the image of whatever desire or dream he carries in his soul.

The garden is also an oracle for the monks and for many visitors who come to seek in its sands a solution to their problems or spiritual conflicts. Sometimes they use complicated numerological systems that relate the position of the rocks and the sands at their feet with the moon and the stars overhead. Imitated throughout Japan but never equaled, Ryöanji is the answer in elemental terms of supreme beauty to the mysterious question that every human being has at some time asked himself in the solitude of his soul, for the garden of Ryöanji is just that—soul without body.

I remained seated in ecstatic admiration of the garden; this is one place that must be seen in solitude. But then an avalanche of hundreds of students arrived— young men in black uniforms that emphasized their waxlike faces—and with one last glance I walked away from the garden. At the entrance of the temple, where I had left my black shoes, I stopped in astonishment. Where there had been only a few pairs of shoes of various colors before, there were now hundreds of pairs of black shoes. I had visions of never finding my shoes and having to go back to Kyoto barefoot, like a pilgrim. (Nothing would have been more appropriate to the spiritual pilgrimage I had just experienced.) In dismay, I stared at the sea of black, dusty shoes with which the whole courtyard was carpeted, wondering if I would ever find my own. I looked, and looked, and looked. Almost an hour later I found my shoes and finally returned to the hotel, not as a pilgrim but as a plain, tired traveler.

When, a few days later, I recounted the incident of the shoes to some Japanese ladies, they made me laugh with their amusing comments. "All you had to do was to look for the only pair of polished, shiny shoes," said one girl with a smile that brought to her face all the beauty of a blossoming cherry tree. And another added: "It should have been very easy to find your shoes. They must have been the biggest in the whole monastery!"

Ryōanji is one of the most beautiful and cherished memories I have of Japan, and one of the most unforgettable of my whole trip around the world. Ryōanji, which dates from the Muromachi period, reflects Zen ascetisism, and in my opinion its most admirable feature is that it conveys the eternity of time through a limited fragment of space. To see Ryōanji is to increase the moral stature of one's soul, to enrich the treasure chest of memories with new jewels. In my castle of memories, Ryōanji is one of the most beautiful pictures that adorn its walls. It is one of the most inspiring landscapes in my spiritual geography of happiness. Simply remembering the ineffable tranquillity, the pure sweetness that breathes from its rocks and sands, makes me feel happy and serene. Ryōanji is peace and eternity. Above all, against the absurd transitory complexity of Japan's modern cities, Ryōanji, with the eternal permanence of its rocks and its sands, is a living testimony to the Japan that is immortal.

SHINTO, SHOGUNS, AND SAMURAI

IT IS VERY DIFFICULT IN A SHORT
visit to understand Japan fully. As I crossed the breadth
of Japan on my way to Fukuoka, where I was to deliver
a lecture before the National Congress of Tuberculosis,
I could see from the airplane the strange configuration
of the Japanese islands, and for a while I reflected upon
my readings on Japanese history.

With the exception of the Tokyo area, Japan lives
up to its name, *Yamato* (meaning "mountain gate-

way"). The volcanic eruptions occasionally still change its mountainous shape. Japanese mythology is filled with weddings of mountains. Japan's mountainous terrain probably accounts for the fact that the Japanese never feared invasion. In their entire history they had experienced only two invasion attempts, both in the thirteenth century by Mongolians, the second of which, according to legend, was frustrated by divine winds, or *kamikazes*. This probably bred a national complex of superiority and invincibility, which eventually led to their attack on Pearl Harbor and then culminated in the Hiroshima holocaust and proved to be their national downfall.

In order to understand Japan one would have to follow the example of Lafcadio Hearn, the Irish-American writer who originally went to Japan to write a series of travel sketches and became so enamored of the country that he adopted a Japanese name, became a Japanese citizen, and even learned, although poorly, its difficult language, a language that is derived from thousands of Chinese ideographs. These Chinese ideographs have been developed by the Japanese into two syllabaries for writing, one of which, the *katakana* syllabary, is used for words of foreign origin, and the other, the *hiragana* syllabary, for everything else. Each syllabary has forty-eight characters, in a one for one relationship. Lafcadio Hearn now reposes in the Zoshigaya cemetery, in northern Tokyo, and once a year white blossoms from the cherry trees he loved so dearly blanket his grave.

Japanese religions are as difficult to understand as Japanese script. There are Buddhist temples and Shinto shrines everywhere. One can recognize the Shinto shrines by the red *torii,* two posts made with two bars across the top that look like bird perches, and indeed this was their origin, for Shinto is an animistic religion, a pagan cult that worships the forces of nature, a cult whose numerous variations preclude both idols and a rigid ritual.

At the entrance to Shinto shrines, there are often *komusos,* or mendicant Buddhist monks, each with a basket on his chest for donations, playing a bamboo flute, and also Shinto priests in pastel-colored robes that contrast sharply with the austere black robes worn by Buddhist priests.

Shintoists worship eight million deities and believe that life is good and that the beyond is an evil place; this is exactly the opposite of Buddhists, who believe that the world is evil and that the beyond is a blissful haven from which one would not care to return. (Buddhism was imported into Japan from India via Korea in the sixth century A.D.) Japan has also been influenced by Confucianism, a code of ethical values, with modern, sophisticated rules for graceful, dignified social comportment.

Although the Japanese practice both Buddhism, which is a religion without gods, and Shintoism, which is a religion of innumerable gods, this does not seem to cause them any spiritual conflict. The Japanese are born

87

Shintoists and die Buddhists, and thus the Shintoist priests officiate for them when they are born and Buddhist priests when they die; but their marriage ritual is also Shinto. It is quite common for a Japanese to go on the same day to a Buddhist temple, either to meditate or to spin the prayer wheel, and to a Shinto shrine to make the sacrificial offering of a piece of paper covered with exhortations, which, along with thousands of others, will be hung from the trees at the entrance of the shrine.

The prevailing notion that, because Japan is so close to China, the Japanese are like the Chinese is as crass a mistake as would be the notion that Cubans and Floridians are alike because they are so close geographically. There is no more similarity between the Japanese and the Chinese than there is between Cubans and Americans.

The Japanese are a mixture of Asiatic peoples and islanders from the Pacific and Malaya. Thousands of years ago those migratory peoples overrode the aboriginal Ainus of the islands of Japan and formed a new state on the island of Honshu (Yamato). Subsequently, Chinese influence made itself felt by way of Korea. This, however, should not lead one to believe that the Japanese are mere imitators of the Chinese. They are not. They are adapters, but their adaptation has been so subtle and elegant that it has far excelled even Chinese art.

For centuries Japan remained a society of warring

tribes, with the sword and aesthetics, war and art, as ideals.

The Japanese made two great historical leaps. The first transformed them from a primitive people to a highly advanced society of Chinese origin, culturally and technologically. The second took place in the nineteenth century, when Japan shifted from a feudalistic military society to a modern scientific one.

Thus it came to pass that the proud, daring samurai took to automobiles, spoke on telephones from their lacquered, mother-of-pearl-encrusted chambers, and became pilots in Zero planes. Nevertheless, the samurai continued to be the medieval head of a clan, and his code of honor remained the same as that of the feudal lord.

Japan was ruled from 660 B.C. by an emperor who had a council of advisers and a Diet, or legislature, but the military clans continued to be the most powerful force behind the scenes. These political clans, together with the military commanders of Japan, or shoguns, and the shogun institution, ruled Japan from the twelfth century until 1868, when after a sanguinary rebellion, the country was unified. Before 1868, for fear of foreign influence, especially European, Japan closed all its ports to foreigners.

At the time of the unification, the country was under the rule of the Tokugawa shogunate. The imperial capital during this shogunate was Kyoto, and despite the fact that the emperor now resides in Tokyo, Kyoto is still the spiritual and artistic capital of Japan. From Tokyo the Tokugawa shoguns held feudal sway over one fourth of Japan, the rest of the country being the free property and hunting ground of the daimios, or feudal lords.

Japanese society during the Tokugawa period was composed of very clearly defined castes: the daimios; the samurai, or mercenary knights-errant; and soldiers, merchants, artisans, and villagers. Without an understanding of the three-way split of power among the emperor, a mere spiritual symbol, the shogun, the true ruler, and the daimios with their samurai warriors, one cannot get a true picture of Japan before its doors were opened to the West.

This was the period during which the *Bushido,* the samurai's code, flourished, and when the samurai kept the Japanese people in an ambivalent state of admiration and hatred of their swords, even as in Europe medieval knights awakened in the people both hatred and admiration of their deeds. It was the samurai or their descendants who, in World War II, manned the explosive-carrying *kamikaze* planes and destroyed the enemy by flying straight into Allied warships, thus attaining the glorious death that would enable them to join their ancestors with honor.

Some of the actions of the Japanese officers and soldiers during the last war were a psychiatric symptom of the emotional repressions forced upon them for so many centuries, for the feudal system in Japan for too long a period was extremely severe in exacting obedience.

By the onset of the Meiji era in the nineteenth century, feudalism had been undermined in Japan, and the samurai, retired with a pension by the government or thrust into the role of pensioned civil servants or officials, were compelled to hang up their invincible swords.

Many younger samurai helped to restore the emperor to his position of power. The industrialization and militarization of Japan then began on a modern scale, and with it began also the worship of the emperor as father, god, and protector of the nation. Shinto, the pagan religion that paid tribute to many deities and preached true animism, or worship of nature and its forces, extended throughout Japan and became a religious force in the service of politics, lending moral force to the emperor. According to the military clan, imperial power was essential, because they wanted to expand Japan's frontiers, since less than one sixth of her geographic area was, and still is, tillable, and she also lacked raw materials.

The process that led to Japan's great technological might before World War II began with the advent of a merchant class in the seventeenth century. By the eighteenth century, the daimios could no longer retain their warriors, the samurai, even as the European feudal lords by the end of the Middle Ages were unable to support their knights.

In Japan the daimio received as tribute from his vassals annual allotments of rice, with which he in turn paid his armed samurai. Gradually the samurai stopped receiving their payments of rice, the precious edible currency that served as barter for all their needs: housing, furniture, horses, clothes, women, and goods of all sorts.

Despite this, the shoguns forced the samurai to live in great luxury, just as in Spain (for every country has had similar cycles in history), under Philip III and Philip IV, the Spanish hidalgos were compelled by tradition to live far beyond their economic means and put up a façade of great abundance behind which the most abject poverty often reigned. At the same time, the shoguns began to raise taxes, whereupon the peasants rose in rebellion. In addition, the samurai who had lost their masters formed *ronins,* or small armed bands, that in times of disaster might fight in wolf packs.

At that point, caught between the shoguns—who withheld their payments of rice yet insisted that they live as gentlemen, causing them to borrow heavily from the merchants—and the uprisings of the peasants, the samurai likewise rebelled against the shoguns, who occasionally attempted to mollify them through *tokusei,* or forgiveness of debt. Eventually, the merchants, through their loans, gained an economic strangle hold over the samurai and the landholders. The only common denominator among them all was their hatred of foreigners, a hatred so great that the reading of European books was prohibited as late as the eighteenth century.

Japan's doors were not opened to the West by either the Russians or the English. Japan, like a ship in battle, was finally boarded by the American "barbarians," as the Japanese called them, with their clipped beards and gleaming headgear. In 1854 Commodore Matthew Perry, who the year before had demanded that Japan be opened to navigation and trade, returned with his American giants (they must have looked like towers to the small half-naked Japanese, clad in capes woven of rice straw) and triumphantly marched into Yedo, preceded by two herculean Negroes with bare torsos holding American flags, to the accompanying strains of *Yankee-Doodle.*

In full-dress uniform, Commodore Perry presented the Nipponese with weapons, perfumes, and champagne. In 1858 they signed a commercial treaty that brought to an end the isolation that for centuries had deterred the Japanese from building transoceanic vessels, since their interest had been confined to neighboring seas. Thus, the ports of Hakodate and Shimodo were opened to foreign vessels. The English and Russians soon followed the Americans.

The first consul to Japan was New York merchant Townsend Harris, who lived in a Buddhist temple and finally was received in Yedo by the shogun. In 1868 the shogun surrendered his power to the emperor. Thereafter, Western vessels plied the waters of Japan freely, including Spanish vessels carrying in their prows images of the Virgin of the Rosary, carved in Acapulco by Chinese Christians who gave the Virgin slanted eyes.

The Japanese reciprocated by sending their first ambassadorial mission to the United States in 1860, an occasion commemorated by Walt Whitman in his poem "A Broadway Pageant."

In May, 1860, the Japanese chief ambassador to the United States, Masaoki Shimmi, Lord of Buzen, and the vice-ambassador, Norimasa Muragaki, Lord of Awaji, were received by Lewis Cass, the United States Secretary of State. The Japanese diplomats were shocked because they were not offered tea. The following day they were received by President James Buchanan. For such an important occasion, the Japanese dressed in *karagigu,* wide-sleeved ceremonial robes, *eboshi,* little black skullcaps with plaited cords, embroidered silk sandals, and short gold-handled swords in silk scabbards. The Japanese ambassador presented his credentials from the Japanese state to President Buchanan in a black lacquered chest lined with silk brocade. The credential letters were encased in a vermillion silk envelope and inscribed on Japanese gold-leaf paper painted with birds and flowers. Later, at a reception given in their honor by Secretary Cass, the Japanese diplomats were amazed to see "men and bare-shoulder women hopping round the floor, arm in arm. . . . It seems very funny indeed to us, as dancing in our country is done by professional girls only and is not at all a man's pastime."

Before returning to their country, the Japanese received as a gift from a Philadelphia manufacturer an optical instrument with almost a hundred colored views of that city. The shogun was so taken with it that he refused to let it out of his sight. For it brought him magical views of an exotic city situated at the other side of the turbulent ocean, where strange people with white skin and blond hair dwelt.

DINNERS IN WATERCOLOR

O N THE TABLE IN FRONT OF
me is a coral-red shell containing a golden liquid with
a gleaming pearl at the bottom.

But no, it is not a shell; it is a red lacquered bowl
filled with chicken broth, and at the bottom, as in an
aquarium, gleams the pearly eye of a fish.

I am at the Happoen garden restaurant in Tokyo,
having lunch in a beautiful room with cool bamboo
and raffia walls.

96

(In subsequent trips to Tokyo I found even more beautiful the Chinzan-so garden restaurant. The Chinzan-so, meaning the villa of the camelias, has a park that Emperor Meije used to visit. In this park there is a beautiful pagoda, which is an exact replica of one that was there hundreds of years ago. Today, millions of fireflies are brought to Chinzan-so in the summer from other parts of Japan and set free in that fabulous park, transforming it at night into a magically luminous fairyland. The specialty of the restaurant is its succulent Mongolian—also called Genghis Khan—barbecue of pork, chicken, and vegetables.)

Behind me is the frenzied schizophrenia of Tokyo, a city bent on surrendering its traditionally serene Oriental soul in favor of feverish Western technological progress. After an hour's whirlwind ride in a *kamikaze,* a taxi whose motor seemed to be as suicide-bent as its driver, I have finally reached this oasis of peace and serenity, where there are ancient pagodas and dwarf trees more than five hundred years old.

My arrival in the midst of a pulverized rain caused a minor revolution. As I stepped out of the taxi an avalanche of Japanese attendants and waitresses rushed toward me and, prostrating themselves at my feet, they bowed repeatedly, each time lower than the time before. The attendants are young men with jet-black hair and pale complexions, clad in outfits more suited to a judo match than to a restaurant. The waitresses seem even younger, and they wear black kimonos embroidered with large roses. As they knelt on the ground, their ivory brows almost touching the mud, the rain sprinkled their lustrous black chignons with brilliants.

I entered the restaurant pavilion, which was deserted, and removed my shoes, prematurely apparently, for to the consternation of the waitresses I soon found myself splashing across wet tiles. A flurry of embroidered kimonos and little squeals of amusement followed me into the next room, my shoes having vanished along with my Western dignity. A doll-like waitress, lithe as a bamboo cane, with hands that fluttered in the air like white butterflies, motioned me to enter the private room where I was to be served lunch.

The room is large—for one man alone, enormous— a geometric cube with immaculate walls, bare of all adornment except for one *kakemono,* or scroll, and a single vase in a corner with three flaming-red flowered spears pointing toward me, the ground, and the sky. A low table, about one foot high, stands in the center of the room with cushions stacked around it. There are no windows and no light other than that filtering through the rice-paper walls. The atmosphere is one of glowing peace.

The waitress, who during the next three hours will devote herself exclusively to serving and entertaining me, motions to me to sit on the cushions and, ever smiling, leaves the room. From now until I leave, she will follow the same ritual every time she comes in or goes out: when coming in, she will softly slide the door open, kneel down and bow to the ground; then with quick little hops she will approach my table and kneel again to serve me; when leaving, she will walk backward, kneel again at the foot of the door, bow to the ground, and, still walking backward, softly close the sliding door. Each time she will scurry back and forth in her white socks as quickly as she can, as if by so doing she can have a few more minutes to devote to me.

I try to settle down on the cushions, crossing my legs, certain that within a few minutes they will ache and I shall have to stretch them out. My horizon is limited to four naked walls, a few sprigs of flowers, and the nebulous light. Yet a century-old peace is already pervading my whole being. The silence is divine.

A moment later my graceful benefactress brings me a pot of green tea, and soon afterward a little white porcelain jug of warm sake. Meanwhile, a Robinson Crusoe on this island of peace, I meditate and dream.

I have been in Tokyo only a few days and already I am dazed by the many shades of the Japanese temperament. This temperament, however, is not revealed in the daily life of Tokyo, for Tokyo, as a city, is no longer Japan. In Tokyo, the real Japan can be found only during those, for the visitor, rare moments of intimacy at meals, at the *Nō* and *Kabuki* theatres, at geisha parties, and in the heart of family life. The city, with its ten million Japanese and its lovely gardens and parks, combines the vast horizontality of London with the charm of Paris. It even has sudden outbursts of the verticality of New York, as in the downward thrust of its spotless subway and the upward thrust of its new Tokyo tower near Shiba Park, which is one thousand and ninety-two feet high, one hundred and eight feet higher than the Eiffel Tower, and which is a central transmission point for five television stations and a spacious observation platform. Viewed from this platform, Tokyo, which in 1923 was devastated by an earthquake and fire and in 1945 by the United States Air Force, now spreads out at one's feet, all reconstructed and ever growing, a strident human beehive, for Tokyo is the noisiest and the most crowded city on earth.

In automobiles, *jinrikishas* (rickshas), buses, or streetcars, one can ride on and on through the city without ever reaching the end. The things and places one can see and admire are countless. There is the Imperial Palace, with its spacious gardens and the wide ribbon of water that encircles it, where dwells the man who for the Japanese is still the symbol of the country's divine father. His spiritual prestige was once comparable only to that of the emperor of China before the advent of Sun Yat-Sen. Japan's life is focused on the patriarchal conception of the family, and the emperor is still the paternal head of the national family.

Shiba Park, near the Tokyo tower mentioned before, which is the pride of the Japanese, is built around the Zojoji Temple. Some other famous sights of Tokyo are the Buddhist temple Tsukiji-Honganji, which combines ancient Indian style in architecture with the modern;

the Meiji Shrine, which houses the relics of Emperor
Meiji, the most famous emperor in Japanese history,
and which, paradoxically, also houses a baseball field,
boxing rings, swimming pools, and race tracks; Tokyo
University, the oldest university in Japan, with its
famous *Akamon,* or red gate; Ueno Park, with its
museums of art and science; Asakusa, the Japanese
Coney Island; the Diet Building, home of the Japanese
government; the Yasukuni Shrine, dedicated to those
who have given their lives for their country; and Hibiya
Park, where azaleas bloom in May and chrysanthemums in November. And at night you can lose yourself in the whirlpool of the Ginza.

All this, however, is not the true Japan, but rather
a big city in full furor of growth, suffering from a problem that besets the rest of Japan as well. Dwelling in
the Japanese islands, comparable in size to the state of
California, is a population of more than ninety-five
million, or nearly half that of the United States. To
combat and check this disproportionate growth, a birth-
control program has been instituted.

Upon reaching its spatial limits, Tokyo, like New
York, promptly stood on tiptoe and is now trying to
reach the sky. Great soaring skyscrapers are springing
up everywhere, dwarfing the pagodas, Buddhist temples, and Shinto shrines. Steel and concrete are annihi-
lating the delicate geometry of the cherry blossoms and
chrysanthemums.

One day, after a breathtaking spin around the city,

which included visits to see the *go* players (many of whom are cooks at *sushi* street stands), the University, and the judo and jiujitsu contestants at the Kodokan Hall, I went to visit Asakusa, the shopping center, a labyrinth of streets swarming with hundreds of thousands of people shopping, strolling, bickering, stopping at street stands to eat *sashimi*—thin, exquisite strips of raw tuna fish or salmon, served with shredded radish and seaweed, which you dip in a sauce—or seeking pleasure in all its forms. In the midst of this labyrinth rises one of Tokyo's biggest stores, a cement mastodon fourteen stories high, where one can buy every article devised by Japanese ingenuity and Western technique to satisfy hunger and thirst, cold and heat, locomotion and sports, sleep and the senses. Hundreds of girls in blue uniforms bow to the throngs of customers ten thousand times daily. As you climb toward the roof terrace, you see them by the hundreds—on the automatic escalators and in the elevators, in corridors and behind the counters, ever smiling, ever accommodating, ever bowing, a living symbol of the Japanese woman's desire to serve and please men.

A good part of Tokyo can be seen from the roof-top terrace of this department store: the fragile houses, which seem to be waiting for the earthquake that will destroy them; the shops, some modern and elegant, some provincial; the street stands peddling all sorts of trinkets or food; the red and black streamers waving over the stores—a veritable human anthill seething with activity. *Pachinko* signs are a perpetual reminder of the great national passion, gluttonous gambling machines attended by smiling, accommodating girls. And everywhere there are cafés crowded with youngsters of the new generation, listening as they sip their coffee to more rock'n'roll than samisen music.

This is a world far removed from one's image of Tokyo. But on the roof terrace of one of the stores I saw a nest of swallows, which even the children dared not touch. It is things such as this that reveal the existence of another Japan.

But now, in the garden restaurant of Happoen, another swallow keeps fluttering around me. A swallow, surrounded by azalea blossoms, is embroidered on the kimono of my waitress Kimiko (the suffix "ko" in Japanese names indicates that it is feminine), one of those eternally ageless, childlike Japanese women, with hair like a black-lacquered helmet hugging her pale oval face. Her lips, a mere scarlet line, repeat the brilliant red of the wide obi wound around her imaginary waistline.

Following the Japanese ritual, Kimiko leaves me alone to enjoy my first cup of tea. Later she returns and sets on the table in front of me a miniature blue porcelain holder for the ivory chopsticks, a little black box with boiled rice, three red-and-gold-lacquered saucers with mysterious-looking greens, and a red bowl with golden chicken broth, garnished with a sprig of parsley shaped like a dwarf tree and a pearly fish eye at the bottom.

She has also brought me the customary porcelain jug of sake—rice wine as clear as water—warmed in hot water, and some excellent Japanese beer in a bottle filmed with ice.

Ritual demands that one's cup of sake never be completely empty nor completely full, and a waitress or hostess considers it her gravest fault if she forgets your cup and you have to serve yourself. I did it only once, at a Japanese party, when the hostess was very busy. I shall never forget how her lovely ceramic-like face turned a flaming red.

According to the custom, you pick up your cup—a fragile thimble-sized porcelain cup that holds barely a few drops of sake—and move it close to the jug as soon as the waitress lifts it from the table. Sake is the sacred drink of Japan. It is the inseparable accompaniment to both the humble repast and the sumptuous banquet; it is sipped at weddings, christenings, and burials. In conjunction with samisen music and geisha dances, it forms a vital part of the hours of recreation.

Kimiko serves me the sake. She is thirty-eight years old, for she had promptly told me her age and asked mine. She speaks little English, but her pantomime language is explicit. She quickly conveys to me that she is a widow by first touching her heart, then, closing her eyes, by putting her hands together next to her cheek to conjure up the idea of sleeping, and finally by pointing to heaven to indicate where her beloved one dwells.

Kimiko, after attentively watching from her knees the progress I am making with my soup and sake, rises from her kneeling position, bows to me, and goes through the usual ritual of leaving. Upon returning she repeats the ritual all over again, even though her hands are burdened with a bowl of salad, plus all the ingredients for sukiyaki, which she will prepare for me in a few minutes on my own table. The salad is a miniature garden, with scallions shaped like irises, lotus roots, ferns, dried algae, and tender bamboo shoots, all sprinkled with a soy and vinegar sauce.

I would be utterly content to subsist entirely on Japanese food. I find all their dishes delightful. Breakfast in the Japanese home—served to the father with a smiling *Ohayo,* or good day—can include such varied things as boiled rice, steamed fish, lentil or mushroom soup, radishes, dried algae, vegetables in vinegar, and boiled eggs. Some of the Japanese dishes I enjoyed most were *chawanmushi,* boiled chicken, beef and pork in a custard-like sauce; pickled gherkins and sprouts; *magi no kabayaki,* sliced eel boiled and then charcoal broiled, served on a bed of rice; *soba,* or noodle, soup, with onions and red peppers; *sushi,* a delight to the palate, boiled rice shaped into small balls filled with chopped prawns, eels, smoked or raw fish, and wrapped in paper-thin leaves made of algae dried in the sun;

sashimi, white rice seasoned with sugar, salt, vinegar, and sake; and especially *tempura* and sukiyaki.

For *tempura* one should go to the *tempura* bars, as I so often did in Tokyo and in Fukuoka. There you sit down at a low wide counter of unpainted wood, smooth and cool to the touch, shaped into a zigzag pattern to assure the diner of relative privacy, so dear to the Japanese while eating.

The inside of a *tempura* bar smells of savory fried fish and sea food. The cook, his teeth perpetually exposed in a wide grin, right before your eyes selects the finest crabs, prawns, shrimps, and chunks of assorted fish, one by one, deftly coats them in a batter of flour and sake, drops them into a cauldron of boiling fat, and after a few seconds transfers them one at a time directly to the paper-lined straw tray waiting in front of you, never allowing more than two pieces of fish on your tray, so that they will be hot. A smiling kimono-clad waitress makes sure that your sake is warm and your beer cold. Exotic vegetables, also dipped in batter and fried, are served with the fish. There is always something optimistic and gay about a *tempura* meal. It is a gastronomical spree.

I cannot imagine a more delightful lunch in the world than a good *tempura,* with morsels of sea food smoking hot in the little wicker and bamboo baskets or in golden fish-shaped straw trays from which, with the aid of wooden chopsticks to mar none of their flavor, they travel straight into your mouth.

106

But let us return to Kimiko. While she arranges the huge tray with the raw ingredients for my sukiyaki, I feast on exotic bits of *nori,* dried marine algae, *tako,* fried squid, and *sashimi.* She laughs like a little schoolgirl every time a piece of food slips off my clumsy *hashi,* or chopsticks, and plops on my plate, and cheers me each time I successfully manipulate a difficult piece, as if I were a skillful *banderillero* and the food a difficult bull.

The tray of ingredients for the sukiyaki is as colorful as a van Gogh painting. Artfully arranged on it are thin slices of delicately marbled, red and pink beef from Matsuzakaka and Kobe cattle, the best in the world, silky slices of onion, mushrooms, bamboo shoots, coiled noodles, tiny cubes of bean curd, salt pork; and a sauce made of sugar, soysauce, and sake. The beef is delicious, even when eaten raw. I learned that its ivory-tinted veins of fat are the result of the peasant's constant massaging the cattle with straw.

Once the little charcoal stove is lit, Kimiko is transformed into a priestess performing a sacred rite. While she deftly serves the beef and mixes the various ingredients, she keeps up a steady stream of talk—in Japanese with a word or two in English—laughs constantly, is alert to my slightest movement, and watches my cup to make sure that it contains just the right amount of sake. When the sauce begins to simmer in the pan, she tosses in the slices of beef. The Japanese like beef very much, but the average Japanese can afford only seven pounds of beef a year per person, to about forty-eight pounds of fish.

Despite her ceaseless activity, the marvelous Kimiko remains impeccably cool. Her face is as fresh as a white rose, and not one single hair has escaped from her lacquered coiffure. When the beef is browned, with her chopsticks she tosses several pieces into the bowl of rice, which serves both as a bed for the meat and as bread. With my chopsticks I pick up a piece of beef and, to cool it, I dip it in a saucer containing beaten raw egg. The meat is so hot that it immediately becomes coated with a set film of egg. The tender beef melts in my mouth, its delicate flavor heightened by the taste of the warm sake.

With the sukiyaki now under way, Kimiko rises from her knees, hops silently toward one of the walls, and swiftly slides it open. And suddenly all the magic of Happoen's famous garden fills every corner of the room. Startled, dazzled, I stare at the enchanted tapestry.

It is still drizzling. Happoen garden, like most Japanese restaurant gardens, is laid out so that every room in the restaurant faces the garden, and every patron can enjoy it in complete privacy. The air of peace that permeates the garden seems even greater beneath the fine rain. The beauty of the trees, shrubs, ponds, and rocks is heightened by the absence of flowers.

One of the pine trees at Happoen was planted three hundred years ago by the third of the Tokugawa shoguns, Iemitsu, on the occasion of his visit to the Daimio, or feudal lord, Okubo-Hikozaemon, owner of the garden. The pine tree, then a dwarf tree, is now a giant, although it still preserves the *bonsai*-style branches, which spread out in fanlike fashion.

There are many birds in the maples and pines, and every now and then they dash out and streak the silver of the sky with red and blue. There are lanterns that were carved in the rock eight hundred years ago. One of them was done by Midaroky, the famous stone carver and soldier-patriot. The rock lanterns, with their broad stone tops, have withstood Tokyo's earthquakes, even as the pine trees have survived the all too frequent fires. In the distance, encircled by silvery dwarf trees from the Kurile Islands, rises a pagoda with thirteen steps, built in Korea more than a thousand years ago.

The atmosphere of the garden, shrouded in a hazy light and a gentle rain, is one of utter silence, solitude, and peace. I shall always remember this lunch. For here, over a dish of sukiyaki, I had a glimpse into Japan's poetic soul.

The name sukiyaki is derived from the words *suki,* a spade, and *yaki,* meaning to roast, designating the manner in which the peasants in the middle of the fields would roast chunks of beef held in their spades. This rustic method evolved into that epicurean delight sukiyaki, with its various trays of ingredients and its beautiful lacquered, porcelain, ceramic, and unpainted wooden bowls and plates.

This meal combines everything that a human being can desire: food of subtle flavors, sake as warm as the maternal milk we fed on as infants, a waitress who is both mother and willing slave and who is as exotic as a maharani and as solicitous as a Samaritan, an infinite silence and solitude, a sense of isolation suggestive of the protection a glass case bestows upon a rare butterfly in a museum—even the waitresses are more like butterflies than like women—an enchanted garden which seems to belong to the observer, a total return to the fantasy world of childhood, when the world around was a magic carpet and one had the all-embracing maternal protection and was fed without lifting a finger.

So far as I know, no one has ever tried to discover the reason why the Japanese, who publicly are one of the most gregarious people in the world, who are unconcerned about bathing in the nude in a communal bath, men and women together, or even about performing some of the most intimate bodily functions before one another, who live under the sign of collectivity, place so much importance on solitude and privacy during their meals, in their leisure time, and in their homes. Perhaps the urge for this form of privacy indicates a desire to compensate for the lack of solitude and privacy in public life. More than ninety-five million Japanese live cramped together in an area that would still be too small for half that number of people. Perhaps that is why they try to provide all the privacy possible for their most precious moments—their meals, their moments of relaxation—equipping their homes with mobile partitions that can be shut or opened, or removed altogether to suit their moods, thus allowing each person to shut himself, if he so wishes, into a world of his own, a world, however, enclosed by translucent paper and light wood, and therefore free from claustrophobia and endowed with a fragile beauty and subtle charm.

At the same time, this privacy and the combination of food with a serenely beautiful garden, a gracious waitress, and often the melodious voice and graceful movements of a dancing geisha, makes eating transcend a mere physiological need and become a subtle spiritual experience. It would seem that, by surrounding their intimate moments with solitude and beauty, the Japanese seek to compensate for the confined space, the deafening noise, and the inevitable sordidness that their crowded islands impose upon them.

A Japanese dinner is a work of art. It is more a watercolor to be admired than food to be eaten. It appeals to the eye even more than to the sense of smell. It is felt more than it is tasted. There is no other country in the world that serves you eel in a little black lacquered box, rice in a golden bowl, golden soups in red bowls with a green sprig conjuring up a garden at the bottom of the bowl, carp in little blue porcelain chests, or *tai*—the best fish of all—its shimmering silver and coral-tinted skin garnished with a wreath of emerald-green leaves and set in what looks like a music box.

There are few spectacles in the world as lovely as a

group of Japanese girls in flowered kimonos having dinner. They look like dolls, sitting at little red- or black-lacquered tables, delicately maneuvering their chopsticks in and out of toy-sized boxes made of colorful lacquered wood, ceramic, porcelain, and even jade, containing food even more beautiful, their backdrop of haunting garden, with only a few rocks and trees, and a pool flecked with lotuses or a fountain humming in the entrancing silence.

Outside, far from all this, is Tokyo, an orgy of multicolored lights at night as I saw it from the café on the roof of the Hotel Okura, when I was the guest of two of my most admirable friends, the distinguished physician Dr. Jo Ono, and Mrs. Kimi Tamura, a truly charming lady who has done important humanitarian work with children. During the day, Tokyo is ugly and sordid and noisy; with its police directing the suicidal *kamikaze* traffic with paper lanterns; its jungle of television antennas; the big hats, woven straw mantles, and high boots on rainy days; its Buddhist temples and Shinto shrines with their gleaming roofs; its kiosks filled with crime, gossip, and sex magazines; its drugstores, where all sorts of pharmaceuticals are sold without prescriptions, from tranquilizers to aphrodisiacs; its sidewalk display counters where automatic calculating machines stand side by side with abacuses, which the Japanese prefer; its scribes squatting on the streets with their *yatate,* a little brush inside a tubular metal inkwell, with which they trace their beautiful calligraphy; its

112

infernal noise, punctuated by the shrill sound of the whistle of the *amma,* or masseurs, the majority of whom are blind; its cafés, rehearsing for the evening the favorite Broadway and rock'n'roll records of the *moga* (a contraction of the words *modan gar,* or "modern girl," as pronounced by the Japanese); its people wearing white gauze masks on their faces when they have caught a cold and wish to protect themselves against additional microbes and also to protect others; its dance halls with their Japanese taxi dancers who are intoxicated with American movies and hungry for American dollars and whose faces and kimonos are the only Japanese thing left to them; its factories, with thousands of pale girls, clad in pants and sweaters, pouring in and out; and its offices, where business correspondence is still conducted in handwriting because Japanese typewriters must have more than two thousand symbols.

Outside is the city—both beehive and nest of lice, palace and pigpen, garden and stable, treasure chest and manure dump—a city that is the symbol of a strange complicated country, where things are done in reverse from the rest of the world! For in Japan they build houses from the roof down, ending with the foundation; they write their family name and the name of their country before their given name; they read books and magazines from back to front; they saw wood by pulling the saw toward them instead of pushing it away; they sharpen pencils with an inward rather than outward motion; they read from right to left; they smile when they are sad; they strike matches outwardly instead of inwardly; they say yes when they mean no; they express denial by nodding the head up and down; they beckon to people by making, with the palm of the hand, the motion for them to go away; they wear black at weddings and white at funerals.

Having already consumed the succulent sukiyaki, my reflections are interrupted by Kimiko returning with a dish of almond cookies, a gelatin-like paste made of kidney beans, pastries in the shape of chrysanthemums, wrapped in camellia, bamboo, and cherry leaves, more tea, more smiles, and many more bows.

When I am finished, she leads me across the garden to the pavilion where the tea ceremony is held. A dozen Japanese men and women are attentively watching the movements of an old woman, mistress of the tea ceremony. She is as old as an ancient fable and as wrinkled as the bark of a cork tree. Her blue kimono, with a darker blue obi, is as wrinkled as her skin. In her hands there is age-old wisdom, and a pale smile accompanies all her movements.

The old sorceress, after making three ritual bows, mixed several varieties of tea in a boiling copper pot, stirs them with a bamboo stick, mixes some more tea in another pot, brings both pots to a boil several times, and finally mixes both pots together. After the long, gentle ritual, she passes around a wooden bowl with just a few spoonfuls of a soft, sweet, greenish liquid that is the merest suggestion of tea, mild and fragrant, with a fragrance that is the very breath of the enchanted garden.

Yes, outside, in the city, Japan is a beehive and trash can, but here Japan is a music box, a jewel case, the poetic embodiment of a race from whom we Westerners could learn the secret of how to turn life into a symphonic poem.

DOCTORS AND DOLLS: SHADOWS AND LIGHTS OF FUKUOKA

I AM ALONE ON THE HUGE STAGE. Seated before me in the great auditorium are thousands of Japanese physicians, an army of motionless shadows, with that immobility people have only in newspaper photographs of public demonstrations.

I am in Fukuoka, on the island of Kyushu, the southernmost Japanese island. The date is April 8, Buddha's birthday, the day on which more than ninety-five million Japanese pay homage to the man-god who inspired

116

the Oriental world with the ideals of his life and the achievement of his death. It is also the day on which the cherry trees burst into flower and the people flock to the parks to see the wondrous miracle of the *sakura* in bloom.

In a few moments my lecture before the Japan National Congress for Tuberculosis will begin. I have flown more than six thousand miles to attend the Congress. Dr. Arnold Rich, of Johns Hopkins University School of Medicine, and I are the guest speakers from the West. To Dr. Katsumi Kaida, President of the Congress, I owe the honor of addressing such a distinguished assemblage of Japanese physicians and also the opportunity of becoming acquainted with enigmatic, enchanting Japan. Now, while we wait for the arrival of the honorary committee that will preside at this session, I find myself alone on the stage with the venerable Professor Onodera, from Kyoto, who despite his advanced age came expressly to preside over this occasion. The audience lies in shadows before me, impressive in their polite immobility and respectful silence.

From the rear of the cavernous auditorium, dancing cones of light from the reflectors carve long luminous slices across the audience. The light sparkles on the polished jet-black hair of the men and the lily-pale faces of the women. Now and then there is the flash of a gold tooth, like a bee in flight, in a smiling mouth. The spotlights reach the stage. For a few moments two brilliant circles of light dance a waltz on the floor of the stage, pursue one another, dance together again, and finally join in happy wedlock upon my body, which for the next two hours they will never leave. I too remain motionless in the golden light, like the captain of the guards in Rembrandt's *Night Watch,* gazing unseeingly at the shadows who are waiting for me to speak.

In the minutes that follow this prelude of silence and shadows, as I await the signal to begin, I reminisce, meditate, and dream.

To reach Fukuoka I had crossed the Japanese islands by airplane, one of those small, efficient planes that fly from Tokyo to Fukuoka, making a stop at Osaka, a great business metropolis of Japan.

The plane was filled with Japanese businessmen dressed in dark Western suits and carrying brief cases as large as military staff maps. Many of them knew one another. Most of them spoke English, and from time to time a few English words would reach me, for they like to practice that language. My neighbors promptly offered me cigarettes, magazines, information on the land we were traversing. Quiet, serious, and reserved looking, but extremely courteous, the industrial future of the nation resides in the papers locked in their brief cases, which they pulled out as soon as the plane took off. The stewardesses, in green uniforms that failed to mar their linnet-like beauty, walked up and down the aisle, three for each side, offering caramels less sweet than the smiles on their faces.

We flew over the Japanese islands. Only from the air

can one fully comprehend Japan's geographic problem. Except for a few areas near Tokyo, the islands consist of endless chains of mountains and hills, bald rock and naked sierras. The Japanese have had to fecundate their country's volcanic terrain by sheer force in order to obtain the rice so vital to them, the indispensable accompaniment to the fish that abound in the seas and the rivers.

Japan's geography, as fierce and severe as a samurai, has dictated her economy. Malaysia, with its ten million people—not counting the ninety-seven million inhabitants of Indonesia—produces one third of the world's tin and ninety per cent of its natural rubber. But Japan, with no natural riches to offer the world, has had to turn her back on geography and concentrate on workmanship, on her arts and crafts, on manufacturing techniques for the production of a wide assortment of goods, ranging from toys and cameras to radios and boats. In some of these fields of manufacture, Japan has already become a leader in the world. Her innate ingenuity and skill and her incredibly cheap labor have made her a little giant in the present-day world.

Fuji!

The magic word traveled like a fireball through the entire plane. The businessmen raised their heads from their papers and, forgetting their statistics and contracts, twisted their necks to capture one more mental picture of the magic mountain. To a Japanese it does not matter how many times he has seen Mount Fuji;

each time it incites in him anew the same shudder of pleasure that the sight of his beloved incites time and again in a true lover.

Three times have I seen Fujiyama—or Fujisan, as the Japanese call it with affectionate respect—once from Kamakura, once from Hakone, and this time from the plane en route to Fukuoka. This last was the most beautiful view of all. On the distant horizon, Fuji suddenly appeared against a sky of a livid color, as if it had been flayed by the wind, like the flesh of saints in medieval depictions of scenes of martyrdom. Clouds, soft and white as the feathers on a swan, hovered on both sides. The mountain, chiseled by the hands of the gods in a misty gray and crowned with the ermine of clouds, glimmered like a silver Holy Grail.

The name, image, and shape of Fujiyama—an inactive volcano since its last eruption in 1707—dominates all of Japan. There are Fuji-shaped hats and Fuji-shaped novelties of all kinds, and infinite are the things compared to Fujiyama—a pagoda, the brow of a beautiful girl, the beak of a bird, the contours of a flower bud. Countless people travel the seventy-five miles from Tokyo to climb the mountain and see the sunrise or the sunset from its summit. The romantic young American adventurer Richard Halliburton scaled it twice, once in January, amid terrible snows, climbing thirteen miles and reaching an altitude of more than twelve thousand feet. When he reached the top he took a picture of its crater to corroborate his feat, which he later sent to the

Tokyo newspapers. When the heroic picture was published in the English newspaper in Tokyo, it appeared inverted, with everything upside down, because of a printer's error.

At Osaka, the plane to Fukuoka was half emptied and then filled again with more businessmen. Each person carried one of the three important national newspapers published in Tokyo and in Osaka: the *Asahi,* which has a circulation of more than four million, the *Mainichi,* and the *Yomiuri,* both of which follow close behind. These newspapers—all of which interviewed Dr. Rich and myself in Fukuoka—have an enormous circulation, bearing testimony of the Japanese thirst for information and culture, which is also evident in the huge book shops in Tokyo and in the astounding and ever-mounting production of books and magazines throughout the country.

On my arrival in Fukuoka, I made the acquaintance of two physicians, who became my inseparable companions during my stay, hosts nonpareil and friends to whom I feel bound in human as well as professional fraternity: Dr. Katsumi Kaida,* whose gracious family I also had the honor of meeting, and the perennially smiling Dr. Masuo Mori, the brilliant director of the Kyuden Hospital, who on my later trips to Japan would become my devoted friend and kind and gracious host and guide. I also met hundreds of other ever-smiling,

---

* This great physician and warm friend has since died.

ever-courteous, ever-eager-to-help Japanese colleagues, among them, talented, charming Dr. Tatsunori Okamura, who also became a close friend.

As I now wait to deliver my speech, I gently finger the white chrysanthemum that has been placed in my lapel to indicate that I am a guest speaker. In other countries they give one a little ribbon or a card. Here, one of the national flowers, the chrysanthemum, artistically reproduced in silk, serves as identification, a token of the kinship between art and medicine. The assembled shadows in the auditorium quietly continue waiting for the session to begin.

That morning, in a room at the Hotel Hakata Nikkatsu, a group of Japanese physicians had met with me to discuss the delivery of my lecture, which was to take place at 2 P.M. The lecture had been organized with all the precision of a combined operation. I would read my paper in English, and simultaneously the entire text (which had already been printed in English by the Congress just a few days before this meeting) would be flashed on a huge screen in Japanese. The audience thus could simultaneously follow my gestures, hear the lecture in English, and read it in Japanese. This method not only prevented their missing any part of the lecture but also helped them to practice English, which they are always anxious to do. Furthermore, a distinguished Japanese physician was to stand near me to translate into Japanese anything I might wish to say impromptu and he would also translate my comments on the colored slides for my lecture, which would be projected on a second screen on the stage. They even coached me on the correct pronunciation of the Japanese names mentioned in my lecture and on the names of those Japanese physicians present on that occasion whom I wanted to cite. The elaborate arrangements were truly impressive and a unique lesson in efficiency, courtesy, and consideration. They had thought of everything possible to facilitate matters for the speaker and to make the lecture proceed without any difficulties or snags—evenly, smoothly, pleasantly. And it did. The audience listened in a silence that was almost religious, and when I finished they rewarded me with a warm, affectionate ovation. I was moved and overwhelmed.

Before delivering my lecture I had the opportunity of chatting at length with various colleagues from Fukuoka and from other Japanese towns, and also of touring this up-to-date, industrious city.

The streets of Fukuoka are modern, noisy with traffic, and bustling with commerce. Everywhere there are signs of great prosperity. The people work six days a week, and a skilled worker earns from one hundred to one hundred and fifty dollars a month, and in addition, receives numerous fringe benefits. From my window, on the fourteenth floor of the hotel, I could see a river, a great factory district that could very well be Pittsburgh or Manchester, and endless rows of small dwellings, most of which have television antennas. On television, which is becoming increasingly widespread, the Japanese can listen to political speeches and see *Kabuki* dances, baseball games, and Hollywood Westerns that feature cowboys who wield six-shooters and speak in Japanese. But move away from the center of the city, in the direction of the lovely beaches nearby, where my kind colleagues took me on a never-to-be-forgotten walk, and you will see golden rice paddies, flowering meadows, and peasant huts with many-colored paper carps tied to the posts, which serve to indicate the number of male children in the family and also to invoke the gods of fertility.

Aside from Fukuoka's great technical industry, the chief industry is dolls, which I found very charming. I saw them all over the city, millions of them, and two of them now adorn my office in New York. They are the famous Hakata clay dolls, which reproduce to the smallest detail the venerable figure of an old man with great *satori,* or philosophical wisdom, or the lotus-like beauty of a geisha taking shelter from the April showers beneath her parasol, like a flower beneath the branches of a willow tree.

The sessions of the Congress are being held in various places in the city: hotels, hospitals, and this magnificent twelve-story building with its numerous rooms, completely up-to-date television installations, loud-speakers, and intimate rooms where tea, bean cakes, and almond cookies are served by kimono-clad Japanese girls, who walk with the mincing steps of a timorous fawn in the woods.

124

Tuberculosis, unresolved by antibiotics, is still Japan's national problem. Because the Japanese diet is rich in fish and rice, which are practically the only foods peasants and fishermen eat, the incidence of arteriosclerosis and heart disease is low. Tuberculosis, on the other hand, continues to decimate the Japanese, who, because of malnutrition and poor working and living conditions, are traditionally prone to it. The new generation of physicians has no confidence in antibiotics and chemotherapy as the sole combative measure against the terrible white plague. They prefer an adequate diet, rest, exercise, and sun and fresh air, the same measures prescribed more than two thousand years ago by a kindly physician in the shade of a plane tree on the Island of Cos.

Japan entered into modern medicine in 1854, when Commodore Perry's memorable visit opened Japanese ports to the West. Dutch physicians had previously dominated Western medicine in Japan, under the rule of the shoguns. Only when the emperor regained power did first English physicians and then German physicians influence the Medical College of Tokyo University. To the work of the Dutch must be added that of the Protestant medical missionaries, which was followed by that of a score of Japanese medical societies, created at the end of the nineteenth century, and by the medical interchange between Eastern and Western scientists. This collaboration produced such prodigious results as the discovery of the infectious agent of bubonic plague by Kitazato and Yersin, and the isolation of the causal germ of syphilis in cerebral tissues of paretic patients by Hata, a collaborator of Ehrlich and Noguchi. A martyr to science, Noguchi died as a result of an accidental inoculation in the course of his studies of yellow fever.

Following Marco Polo's romantic adventure in the thirteenth century, Portuguese traders were the first Western visitors to Japan. Their deadly firearms so excited the admiration of the Japanese, who had never seen firearms before, that they promptly reproduced and manufactured them. The dispensers of material possessions were soon followed by the disseminators of enlightenment, the missionaries. St. Francis Xavier and the Jesuits—initially received with affection, and later expelled from Japan—engaged in medical and surgical work among the poorer Japanese.

Their work was continued by the physicians sent by Philip II, then ruler of the entire Iberian peninsula. These doctors left behind them a pharmacopoeia of plants, which they themselves had ploddingly compiled from Nipponese flora. The heritage they left laid the groundwork for the Dutch physicians, who reaped the harvest of half a century of the good works of the Portuguese. The Dutch fought the isolationist policy of the Japanese toward Western medicine; the Japanese government prohibited the study of Dutch by the people, although a few were taught the language so that they could fraternize with Dutch physicians and thus transmit information about new drugs and surgical instruments.

Traditional Japanese therapies, such as acupuncture and moxibustion, existed side by side with new therapeutic methods. Soon after, the Japanese began to develop their own medical genius, and the first great native physicians created their own medicine, emancipating it as much as possible from the Chinese doctrines that had originally inspired it. For Japanese medicine had begun by emulating Chinese medicine, holding illness to be an impure thing whose chief method of treatment, in accordance with Shinto beliefs, was purification by ritual, followed by empirical and psychotherapeutic measures. Moreover, during the Han dynasty, indigenous Japanese medicine, which according to legend was of divine origin, had become imbued with Chinese culture and, a few centuries later, Buddhism—by way of Korea, that perennial intermediary bridge between China and Japan—and the Chinese method of treatment was added to Shinto methods. Cosmogonical anatomy and physiology, which the Japanese adopted from the Chinese and which are based on the interdependence of the Yin and Yang principles and the torture therapy of acupuncture and moxibustion, became the basis of Japanese medicine and have continued to form part of it to this day, depending on the fluctuations of history, political vicissitudes, epidemics, and Japanese relations with China. Since the beginning of the twentieth century, however, Japanese medicine has been rapidly assimilating the best of Western medicine, without abandoning its own rich medical and folklore tradition developed from Chinese roots.

But the venerable professor from Kyoto has now finished his kind, warm introduction of me. There is applause from the attentive shadows. The spotlights execute a few dance steps on the stage and again focus steadily and brilliantly upon me. I take off the chrysanthemum and carefully place it on the lectern. I stare at the seated shadows, trying to "feel" their mood. There is definitely an aura of good will. And I begin my speech to my Japanese fellow physicians:

"My friends, it is a great honor to have been invited to Fukuoka to address this distinguished Congress, and it is a great privilege to speak to you as a colleague and brother-in-arms in the field of medicine. I am here to learn from you. My modest person is only a symbol of the many physicians who, across thousands of miles of the Pacific Ocean, live and work in America and who, regardless of nationality, share, as colleagues and as men of good will, your hopes and your dreams. Our being here together testifies to the universality of Medicine, which recognizes no frontiers in time or in space. Such universality has often made possible a creative exchange between Japanese and Western medical scientists, for instance, between Shibasuburo Kitazato and Alexandre Yersin, and between Sahachiro Hata and Paul Ehrlich.

"Ever since the beginning of my acquaintance with Japan, first through my readings, later through friendship with Japanese colleagues, and now through this visit to your beautiful country, I have felt that yours is a land well known to my heart. The reason for this is that, besides the Japan of the lovely cherry blossoms, there is also the Japan of dreams, which I met and promptly loved when I first studied your literature and your art, when I looked at the exquisite paintings in the style of Yamato-e, and by Korin, Kobayashi, and Honami, and when I read the inspired pages of Lafcadio Hearn, who later became Koizumi Yakumo, and who is buried here in Japan, the land he so dearly loved.

"There is reason for the greatness of your destiny. Countries like Japan forge their greatness not only with magnificent collective achievements, but also, and above all, with many individual wills to greatness, even though some of these may not have been fulfilled. For the effect of these wills is never totally lost when enough work has been put into them.

"One of the reasons for which I greatly admire your country is that you combine an age-old tradition of wisdom with a modern urge for action. In the last century you have been 'in a hurry' to do great things in medicine and in science. And I, personally, love haste, a deliberate, prudent haste, the *festina lente* of the ancient Romans, the haste to fulfill a duty promptly but well. I love the haste of those who, like you in

129

Japan, work fast because there is a great deal to be done and so little time in which to do it. For the road of science has no end. One should hurry to do things in order to be able to keep on doing more things. That is why haste is creative. He who makes haste is he who longs to do something great in the brief span of his life.

"I regret that I do not speak your beautiful language. I am most fortunate that you understand mine. All men of science, however, have a language that transcends mere words: the universal language of science, a language that recognizes no frontiers and that unites all physicians the world over in a universal crusade for humaneness, truth, and the progress of mankind.

"When a physician, whatever his nationality, speaks to a foreign colleague about medicine, any semantic difficulties that may exist between them are overcome by their intimate brotherhood, their goals, their ideals, and their dreams.

"That is why I believe that every time physicians from different countries gather together, as we have done here in Fukuoka, they are weaving the splendid tapestry of the medicine of tomorrow. At meetings like this, language is not only the flowery tunic of thought, but also the chisel with which we carve new cornerstones for the ideal shrine for the medicine of the future. For just as ancient vases enclosing the heart of great heroes symbolized gallantry and noble deeds, so does this scientific gathering symbolize the scientific

130

hopes of the physicians gathered here in search of truth. Scientific congresses like this one are the heartbeats of Medicine, and only by listening to these beats—the scientific congresses—can one diagnose the condition of Medicine. . . ."

THE IVORY FLOWER IN THE MUSIC BOX: THE GEISHA

AFTER RIDING PAST A SECTION of the city in which the housetops look like stacked oysters, we reach Masa, the best garden restaurant in Fukuoka, on the island of Kyushu. On the way here, the President and the Secretary of the Japan National Congress of Tuberculosis, charming, jovial Dr. Katsumi Kaida and the forever-cheerful Dr. Masuo Mori, had been as high-spirited as schoolboys on a holiday, laughing constantly and making us (an American physician,

132

Dr. Arnold Rich, who had by then devoted forty years to bacteriology, and myself) laugh either at their jokes or simply because their spontaneous, childlike laughter —a laughter typical of the Japanese—was irresistibly contagious.

The night is cool and clear, and the stars sparkle in the sky like silver spangles on the azure mantle of a *maiko.* Several lovely waitresses in embroidered kimonos welcome us at the gateway and then precede us up the path to the restaurant, walking backwards, facing us, bowing reverently all the way, as though we were Buddhas rather than physicians.

At the door of the restaurant we are greeted by the headwaitress, a woman of singular beauty. She looks so fragile that she must have been created in one single brush stroke. Her luminous smile and the gay symphony of her *geta,* on the unpainted wooden floor, accompany us all the way to the room where dinner will be served.

The room is spacious, even more so when a waitress slides open one of the *shoji.* A soft light pours down from the ceiling. Beautiful *tatami* cover the floor, and a low square red- and black-lacquered table stands in the middle of the room, with cushions stacked around it. The room has no other furniture. My American colleague and myself sit down with our backs to a *tokonoma,* a niche for a *kakemono,* or other art object, this being the place of honor for guests in both homes and restaurants. This particular *tokonoma* is adorned with a piece of green jade, the kind called "congealed mutton fat" jade, and a lovely floral arrangement: three tall slender stems, with a single flower perched like a butterfly atop each stem. The three sprays are arranged according to tradition: one points toward the sky, another toward the ground, and the third toward man. Behind them there is a scroll painted with a scene of wild ducks sweeping across a sky of oxidized silver.

My American colleague and I try to sit in the traditional Japanese fashion, with legs crossed under, much to the amusement of our Japanese colleagues, who magnanimously grant us permission to stretch our legs every now and then or to change position. Waitresses, as regal-looking in their embroidered kimonos as princesses, dash in and out with much pattering of their *geta,* always bowing before entering and upon leaving. They serve us green tea first and then set the table, without flowers, of course, for the food itself and the vessels that hold it are all the adornment needed. Warm sake from little porcelain jugs is served into thimble-like porcelain cups.

Quietly the headwaitress walks in and slides aside a large wooden screen. The room is suddenly filled with that miracle that is a Japanese garden. The moon rims everything in silver: willows, towers, pagodas, a rock lantern, a miniature Mount Fuji, and the circular stone slabs that form a path leading to a pool in the center, where the moon is reflected as one more circle of stone. With long invisible fingers, the wind plucks the strings

134

in the orchestra of plants. There is a live duck in the pool, but its feathers look as if they are made of silk, its beak of bamboo, and its eyes of emeralds. The alluring magic of the Japanese night quietly creeps through the slumbering garden, while the moon glides overhead like a great lady visiting her velvet dominions.

At a signal from the headwaitress, who now wears a balloon-shaped linen headdress, the procession of succulent dishes begins. The table is soon transformed into something out of the *Thousand and One Nights*. It is a gala dinner, a "three-tray" dinner. Red and gold lacquered bowls hold rice seasoned with vinegar; tiny plump pink fish repose like odalisques on white porcelain dishes; large bowls, of so fine a china that they are transparent, hold steaming white rice, each grain like a chip of ivory, and colored lacquered wooden boxes contain various meats, vegetables, and salads. There is much laughter and teasing from our Japanese colleagues as we struggle to capture with our inexperienced chopsticks bits of food, which prove to be as delicious to the palate as they are beautiful to the eye.

"And now," commands Dr. Katsumi Kaida, "have the geishas enter."

Like a kindly magician in a fairy tale, the doctor makes a signal and the room is suddenly transformed into another garden.

The screen facing the outer garden was now shut, and our room is closed on all sides, yet six human flowers have suddenly burst into bloom within it. They are geishas hired by our hosts.

They had rushed in, a torrent of laughter and color, their faces white and soft as magnolias, fragile and smooth as a smiling Ming porcelain, their dark eyes sparkling and gay, their raven-black hair combed into towering beehives, gleaming with chrysanthemum and camellia oil and smelling of exotic flowers.

The unreal look of their faces is heightened by their make-up, which is intended to make their skin appear stark white, enchanting masks such as are never seen on Western women. Their ears are white butterflies perched alongside their cupolas of black hair; their lips are painted scarlet, orange, or pink; their waists are like flower stems. Looked at as a whole, they are as ephemeral as a ray of moonlight upon water. Some of them wear golden flowers in their hair. All wear silk kimonos heavily embroidered in gold and silver with flying dragons, butterflies, birds, and flowers, creating a frame of enchanted nature for their slender bodies. Wound around the waist they wear a fifteen-foot-long obi, which ties into a delightful huge bow at the back, accentuating their butterfly look. ("The obi," one of them tells me, "is our tie.") A gorgeous brocade sash encircles their swanlike necks. As all who are knowledgeable in these matters know, when undressing they remove their clothes as a rose drops its petals, for Japanese women never wear clothes that come off over the head.

136

When they kneel, white ankle-length socks are visible above the little wooden bridges that are their sandals, and peeking out above the socks is a *naga-juban,* a long garment worn underneath the kimono.

One of them, as she bows in front of us, reveals atop her lacquered hair, combed in momoware, or half-peach fashion, a beautiful assortment of flower-shaped hairpins called *hanakanzashi.* Another one has placed among the roses embroidered on her neck sash a fresh rose, which she dreamily smells from time to time.

They have come to the *o-desaki,* the place where they will do the entertaining, and have entered the *o-zashiki,* or the room where the guests are seated, which is separated from the *o-desaki* by a sliding screen, without knowing who the guests are, for such is the custom. Thus they are compelled to improvise the entertainment, which they are expected to adapt to the personalities of their patrons.

They greet us and seat themselves around us, not brazenly but in ladylike though alert fashion, six angelical visions that provide an advance glimpse of the Japanese paradise.

To be able to understand the nature and social position of the geisha, one must first know their history and the psychology of the Japanese woman and the Japanese family.

Geishas first made their appearance in Japanese history several centuries ago, when the shoguns and the daimios felt the need for women to whom they could both tell their feats and pay homage, without the formal obligation of marriage. The precursors of the geishas were the *shirabyoshi,* or wandering female troubadours dressed in white who, in the old, traditional, chivalric Japan, went from village to village singing and performing pantomime acts.

Thus began an elite of women whose prime attribute was perfect beauty and who also had to comport themselves at all times as the unattainable feminine ideal, women who dressed like legendary princesses and had the manners of a *grande dame,* the discretion of a diplomat, the ingenuity of a comic actor, the gracefulness of a ballerina, the intuition of a wife, the demureness of a bride, and the solicitousness of a Samaritan.

The first school for geishas—a word meaning an accomplished person—was created in Kyoto, the spiritual capital of Japan. Generation after generation, parents at first sold and later reared their daughters to be geishas, for this assured them a place in the best society, fame, power, wealth, and sometimes matrimony, but in any event economic security and social protection.

The best geisha schools, the *kaburenjo,* are still in Kyoto. There, fifteen-year-old girls start out as *maikos,* or geisha apprentices. Three years later they are graduated as geishas, having been taught all the arts that constitute the secret of a geisha's charm. They are taught to dress with fairy-tale lavishness and elegance. The embroidered kimonos of the famous Sumiya school date from the seventeenth century, are worth hundreds of dollars, and weigh as much as sixty-six pounds. Geishas are taught to speak Japanese, and sometimes English, with grace and decorum and in a soft but deep voice, which is achieved by having them sing outdoors in wintertime; to perform graceful, traditional dances; to play the *koto,* or zither, the samisen, and the *shakuhachi,* or flute; to make beautiful flower arrangements; to manipulate a fan so that they can entertain for hours with it; to serve a table with graciousness and finesse; to flatter, compliment, and make the patrons, who are their lords and masters, happy, and also make them feel that the geishas are as God ought to have made all women but did not.

The geishas—there are almost thirty thousand licensed geishas in Japan—live in quarters from which they are summoned, generally in groups, to entertain at banquets, usually of men only, and are paid by the particular restaurant or hotel at an hourly rate of so many hundreds of yen. The geisha is an artist, a highly decorative figure, who provides strictly artistic entertainment during dinner and conversation after dinner and then, unlike the fake loose geishas abounding today in Japan, retires to her home.

Often, from the moment she becomes a *maiko,* at the age of fifteen or sixteen, a geisha has an official protector, usually a wealthy merchant, an industrial magnate, or a politician, who considers it an honor for his protégée to become famous and be much sought after. Sometimes, though rarely, such men marry their geishas. Many geishas, whose charms increase with the years as their experience and *savoir-faire* increases (in fact, there are geishas forty to sixty years old who are much more sought after than those of twenty), accumulate enough money (some of them earn more than two hundred dollars a month) to buy a geisha house or a restaurant. This last goal is reminiscent of the ambition of most Parisian demimondaines at the beginning of the century to save enough money to open a *bistro* in the provinces.

But until such a time arrives, a geisha never stops learning how to entertain her clients. Japanese women always know when their husbands are going to a party where geishas will be present, and they often help make the arrangements. Geishas are used by businessmen, politicians, professionals, and other wealthy people in Japan to help entertain visitors and business clients. It is common to read in the newspapers that a high public official has given a party at which he had fifty geishas.

Today the geisha is the one who perpetuates the great artistic, romantic tradition of Japan. In a Japan where girls are beginning to wear slacks, bleach their hair, indulge in free love, play baseball, dance rock-'n'-roll, go to American-style coffee houses and American movies, drink whisky, ride on the back seat of motorcycles hanging on to their boy friends, who like Marlon Brando wear leather jackets, and speak more American slang than a Broadway chorus girl, the geisha from her artistic island keeps alive the Japan of chrysanthe mums, lotuses, and cherry blossoms, the Japan of Pierre Loti and Lafcadio Hearn.

Japanese wives have ambivalent feelings toward the geisha tradition but are powerless, lacking the right to fight it. The Japanese home is patriarchal. Japanese society as a whole, as mentioned before, is like a family, with the emperor as the father, and the Japanese family is simply a smaller social unit in which the father is emperor. So deep-rooted is this family-like society that even gangsters call their leader *papasan,* and their leader's woman *mamasan.* Everything in Japan is organized in a pattern designed to preserve family unity and continuity.

I have spoken to many geishas whose lives are exclusively dedicated to their work and to caring for ailing parents and supporting their homestead. For without the latter, family unity is inconceivable.

But historically and socially, the well-to-do Japanese (whose marriage is usually arranged by his parents, bride and groom as a rule never meeting before the betrothal) divides his life and affections between his wife and children and the geishas, who in the evening help him dispel his fatigue, worries, and problems, and send him home, rested and content, to enjoy peace with his family.

The Japanese are married at a Shinto ceremony in which bride and groom, facing a *tokonoma,* share three different sized cups of sake three times. This is the only ritual required, and it is performed by a Shinto priest who pours the sake for them each time, while waving a beribboned bamboo wand that resembles a fly swatter. Usually, the wife will never again in her entire life go out with her husband. The home, according to Japanese tradition, must never be left alone, and when the wife goes out shopping, for instance, she must leave other members of the family home.

Her wealthy husband, on the other hand, when he finishes his day's work, meets with friends to drink sake or is entertained by geishas in a private room, arriving home two or three hours later, happy and relaxed. His wife and children greet him on their knees, their foreheads touching the ground. They then help him to his bath, wash and rub him before he gets in the tub, then wait on him while he relaxes in the hot water, and then help him into a kimono. He dedicates the remainder of the evening to dinner and to listening to his wife or children play musical instruments in the living room, which is enlarged by the removal of some of the paper partitions. Indeed, in many Japanese houses there is no bedroom. At night, mattresses are pulled out of closets and placed on the floor, to vanish once more into closets in the morning, leaving the house neat and uncluttered.

It is a joy to be a child or an old person in a Japanese household. Children are allowed to do as they wish, and babies are nursed whenever they cry, or, when older, they can eat whenever they wish, and sleep in their parents' bedroom. On the other hand, a child who dies before reaching seven years of age is considered to have performed an act of disobedience toward his parents, since he will not be perpetuating the family tradition, and consequently, instead of being cremated, as older children and adults are, he is buried in the country. The old people are loved and respected by family and friends. Old age is a delightful, creative period in Japan. Old men are listened to as though they were oracles and are free to devote themselves to poetry, painting, music, fishing, or their favorite pastimes.

Between infancy and old age, during a man's youth and maturity, the geisha fills the vacuum that would otherwise exist in his life if he had only wife and mother, both of whom are confined to the domestic world of *tatami, karakami,* and *bonseki.*

It was Lafcadio Hearn, the Irish-American fantast and poet, who described as "perishability" that quality inherent in Japanese civilization. After being in Japan for a few days, one realizes how apt his summation was. Everything physical in Japan is fragile, delicate, replaceable. Sandals are made of straw, the standard capes they wear are also made of straw and fall apart before washing; chopsticks are discarded after eating; *shoji,* the sliding screens that serve as doors, walls, and windows, are repapered twice a year; and the straw *tatami* that cover the floors are replaced every autumn. Everything is temporary, impermanent, replaceable—perishable. The very houses are like little unpainted wooden domino boxes, a type of architecture undoubtedly adopted to reduce to a minimum the effects of the frequent, devastating earthquakes.

Even their food is light, dainty, delicate, a delight to the eyes and to the smell and touch. Our thick steaks and other meats, the strong, heavy odors of Western dishes are unknown to the Japanese. French and Italian cuisine are the clamor of a martial band; the Japanese cuisine is the trill of a magic flute.

Perhaps it is this innate perference of the Japanese for the ephemeral, the transient, the perishable, that leads him to seek, instead of the deep, strong passions of the Westerner, the light-hearted carefree game he plays with the geishas and the loves that, like cold flames, never grow hot. It is also possible that the Japanese are never gay, frivolous, or romantic in their homes, as they are with the geishas, for fear that it might impair their authority and prestige.

Burdened with this dual personality, the Japanese outside his home is like a fun-loving, warm-blooded student, but, as soon as he takes off his shoes to enter his home, he becomes a serious, though affectionate, stolid patriarch. The world of the geishas is a delightful artificial paradise for him, from which he emerges warm with sake and flushed with the geisha's compliments, which make the inevitable household problems more tolerable.

In turn, the geisha, aware that her beauty, charm, grace, and artistic skills are her only means of security, devotes herself to acquiring a loyal, steady clientele in anticipation of the day when other younger or more captivating geishas might alienate her clients' affection. But let us return to the geishas who are gracing our dinner with their beauty and talent.

The room is brightened by six constant smiles and six thousand fleeting laughs, by the starlike flight of their hands, as they serve us sake, choose the choicest morsels for us, ever watchful of the clumsy efforts my colleague and I make to pick up such difficult things as tiny round scallions or peas with our chopsticks. And all the time they chatter like parrots in Japanese and some of them in English, their lips blowing the syllables into the air like soap bubbles or sucking them in like asparagus, asking us a thousand questions, and venturing a thousand answers. From time to time, like prim, fastidious Angora cats, they nibble on a morsel that captures their fancy.

One of them, seated near me at one end of the table, speaks little, but when she says something, in Japanese, the other girls are convulsed with laughter. She is the oldest and the most interesting. Her face is a replica of the faces on Japanese prints of old dancers, an elongated face with the skin so tight across the cheekbones that it looks like polished bone, a lovely, heroic face worthy of being immortalized in jade and bronze. Another geisha who speaks a little English tells us that in her *tokonoma* at home she has a big, blonde doll from New York that someone gave her. The *tokonoma* can be used as a family altar with pictures of departed relatives, as a religious altar, as a pagan altar with fruits and flowers, or simply as a place where mirrors, figurines and other cherished objects are kept.

Another geisha, almost a *maiko* in age, is like a figurine that has escaped from under a glass dome on a mantelpiece. She has three little red spots painted on the nape of her neck and, according to custom, uses lipstick only on her lower lip. Together, the geishas look like a flower arrangement fashioned by the gods; individually, they are half flower and half bird rather than women.

As the dinner progresses, the geishas tell stories, perform juggling tricks, make us play *ya-ki-pu,* and stir up a cooling breeze around us with their fans, which wine and food have now made a necessity. With their fans they also trace charming stories in the air, in which one can easily detect the flight of birds, swimming fish, the patter of rain, and the warmth of the sun. Later, they teach us some Japanese words: *domo arigato,* thank you very much; *chotto matte kudasai,* one moment, please; *daijobu,* O.K.; *ashita,* tomorrow; *watakushi,* I. They play games with a pack of cards engraved with flowers and poems; they improvise poems with our names; they pantomime a *karate* fight, the fearful fighting method that employs the edge of the hands pounded to the hardness of steel by many years of training. With fluttering hands they evoke the beauty of Fujiyama, and they tell us a hair-raising tale of a man who turned into a human chair and a story about mirrors, both by the Japanese Edgar Allan Poe, Edogawa Ramp.

They also congratulate me warmly because my lecture to the physicians at Fukuoka fell on April 8, a great national holiday, Buddha's birthday.

When I offer one of them sake, she takes a few sips from my cup, which tint her porcelain face coral, and then she wipes off the Lilliputian cup with her finger and immerses it in scented water. I also offer her cigarettes, but this makes her sad, for there are only four cigarettes left in the pack and the number four (*shi* in Japanese) means death (number nine is also bad luck and, as in the West, so is number thirteen, or the sum of four and nine). They also consider the age of thirty-three to be unlucky for women and forty-four for men.

One of the geishas asks us what we see in the moon, and when the American answers a man and I say a woman (Americans see a man in the moon; Spaniards, a woman), they laugh heartily because what they themselves see is a little rabbit grinding rice in a mortar.

Another geisha praises my ears. They are "the ears of a rich man," she tells me, and if she had them her jade drop earrings would show off to much better advantage!

After dinner, they sing and dance. One after another, the geishas display their talents, playing the samisen and the *koto,* performing the April shower dances and

147

the *sakura* or cherry blossom dances, beautiful religious and pagan dances in which the vigorous, almost fierce, movements of the valiant samurai with his sword alternate with the gentle swayings of a young girl in love.

They then teach us some geisha dances. For a few gay moments we four physicians in our stocking feet, under the guidance of the geishas, are transformed into fishermen or peasants in a forest trying wholeheartedly, in an attempt to please the enchanting nymphs, to imitate the flight of cormorants or the swiftness of little fish.

Thus the geishas slowly cast their bewitching spell over us. Between unpainted wooden and paper walls, a magical world is gradually born, echoing with the music wrung from three-stringed samisen, the sound of which floats and falls like drops of rain from a tree.

From Masa we go to Waksamushi, The Red Shoes, and two other night clubs, where, in a dimly lit hall, *sakura* music is played on the piano and the samisen, and geishas dance or converse with the guests.

One of the most precious memories I have brought with me from Japan is that of the geishas. I went to several tea parties given in my honor at which there were geishas, and I was always captivated by their innocent charm. My host at one of those parties in Tokyo was Juzo Uyeno, a leading businessman who is also known as an authority on the art of arranging stones. Together with Japanese gardens, the geishas best symbolize that marvelous, luminous soul of Japan, the country of beautiful, bewitching things: jade, bronzes, lacquered and ivory objects.

Yes, it would have been beautiful to love and be loved one hundred years ago, during Japan's romantic period, by an ivory-skinned geisha with the elusive torso of a Hakata doll, who lived in a sunlit doll house with toy-like furniture, a miniature tea garden with rocks and sand, lotuses, willows, and water lilies, who wore kimonos as regal as an empress's mantle and had all sorts of little lacquer and bronze chests and boxes—to listen to her at sunset as she played *sakura* songs on her samisen, to gaze into her gemlike eyes and touch her mouth as red as a cherry freshly split in two by a greedy swallow, to watch her smile, that strange half-porcelain, half-jade smile, while she plucked off a cherry blossom far less delicate than her own hands. . . .

I remember Rubén Darío's golden verses on the geisha in his poem "Divagación" (*Prosas profanas y otros poemas*):

Amame, japonesa, japonesa
Antigua, que no sepa de naciones
Occidentales; tal una princesa
Con las pupilas llenas de visiones,

Que aún ignorase en la sagrada Kioto,
En su labrado camarín de plata,
Ornada al par de crisantemo y loto,
La civilización de Yamagata.

149

JAPAN

Love me, oh Japanese girl, Japanese girl
Of old, who knows naught of Western
Nations; like a princess
Her eyes dreamy with fantasies,

Who still dwells unaware in holy Kyoto,
In her carved silver chambers,
Decked with chrysanthemum and lotus blossoms,
In the civilization of Yamagata.

HONG KONG

A TALE OF TWO CITIES

HONG KONG IS OFFICIALLY
British, but if one were to look at an X-ray picture of
its chest, one would soon realize that its ribs may be
English, but its vital organs are Chinese.

So run my thoughts one bright Sunday afternoon in
April, as I stand on Victoria Peak, the highest point
on Hong Kong Island.

Two hours earlier we had made an incredible landing at Kai Tak Airport, on a narrow eight-thousand-

foot-long cement runway surrounded by water. The jet plane that brought me from Tokyo—one of the more than a thousand planes that land there each month—had descended at an awesome speed, as if, overheated by its flight, it craved a cool bath in the waters of the bay. Observing the tense expression on my face, my neighbor, a silver-haired Englishman, who, while puffing at a volcanic pipe, had been methodically leafing through the stock-market quotations of the *London Times,* smiled and said: "I have lived in Hong Kong for twenty years, yet every time I return here from a trip I always feel the way you do now. It seems impossible to land on such a short narrow strip of land." He paused. "But they never miss. They won't this time either. The pilot was born in Manchester. So was I."

By a divine miracle and Manchesterian technical skill, we landed safely and soon after passed through customs, most of the officials being Chinese. My luggage was not even opened. Already one could sense the presence everywhere of the waters of Kowloon Bay and catch a glimpse in the distance of lofty blue mountains, Victoria Peak among them, veiled in a pale mist. From the airport I drove to the Hotel Miramar in Kowloon, one of Hong Kong's most modern hotels, although I had wanted to stay at the Hotel Peninsula, Hong Kong's equivalent in classical tradition to the Raffles Hotel in Singapore. Unfortunately, it is invariably filled up. I reached the hotel hot and weary from the trip (a four-and-a-half hour flight from Tokyo punctuated by the inevitable frequent meals, including the classic "flight breakfast" of the Orient, ham omelette and steak with potatoes) and craving only one thing: a bath as prolonged and hot as a medieval bloodletting.

My room, decorated as the rest of the hotel in that impersonal modern style common to the great international brotherhood of hotels, was, fortunately, air conditioned. Quickly stripping off my clothes, after firmly pushing out the horde of officious Chinese "boys," who under the slightest pretext kept irrupting into my room, and locking the door, I rushed into the bathroom, jumped into the tub and, recalling painful past experiences, turned on the cold-water faucet first. Nothing came out. I then turned on the hot-water faucet. Again nothing. Puzzled, I got out to summon one of the boys. A sign nailed to the bathroom door suddenly glared out at me: "Water is available only between 4 and 8 P.M."

Such is the prevailing situation in Hong Kong. Many homes never have water. Even during the rainy season, hotels have water only twice a day, three hours each time. At other times the water service is limited to three hours every second or third day! Rainwater collected in reservoirs is the sole source of water, which explains its scarcity during the dry season and in periods of drought.

It is amusing to observe how at 4 P.M. every day hotel residents, regardless of where they may be, drop everything and dash off to their hotels to soak in their tubs while they read, telephone, write letters, or have tea and pastries.

Soon I myself was doing the same thing. At four o'clock every day I would dart back to the hotel, jump into a tub full of water and, luxuriating in the feeling that I was having one of the most precious things in Hong Kong, I would write, read, and compile my notes on the previous day.

Hong Kong is encircled by the sea, but its fresh water is limited. As a consequence, to maintain the city's pulse beat, it has to impose drastic controls on the consumption of water, which makes the precious liquid a luxury for the rich and a terrible problem for the poor.

Another habit I soon acquired in Hong Kong was to fill every vessel I could find in my room with water —the bath tub, the wash basin, flower vases, the water bottle, glasses, including the toothbrush glass, thereby trying to compensate for the fear of being left without water indefinitely.

On the day of my arrival, lacking the much desired bath, I did the next best thing: I went out to see Hong Kong. My destination was to be the top of Victoria Peak, where I would see the city of Victoria spread at my feet.

It is impossible to describe the life and physiology of a country without having a knowledge of its anatomy, that is, its geography. The first thing I learned was that the colony of Hong Kong comprises the island of

Hong Kong, which contains the capital, Victoria, usually referred to as "Hong Kong," and which is about thirty-two square miles in size; the peninsula of Kowloon, located directly across the bay from Hong Kong; the New Territories, connected to Kowloon by a railroad and mountain roads that extend to Canton in Red China, and one hundred and ninety-eight other islands, most of which are uninhabited and deserted. Altogether the colony comprises about four hundred square miles of land and is inhabited by ninety-nine per cent Chinese and only one per cent white people. Most of the Chinese speak Cantonese, with some Mandarin (a word derived from the Portuguese *mandar,* to command), the Shanghai or other dialect, depending on whether they are from southern or northern China. Most of the English residents speak only English, naturally. Many Chinese speak pidgin English (business English, the word "pidgin" being a phonetic deformation of the word "business"), a barbaric language combining English, Cantonese, and Mandarin words. Educated Chinese speak impeccable English. A common denominator unites all of these people. They all live in Hong Kong for one of four reasons: they were born there, they have fled from another country, they are in the civil or the diplomatic service, or they want to make money fast with no questions asked. Hong Kong is a blessed refuge for the majority, and a golden granary for the few.

Since the Hotel Miramar is situated on Kowloon

Peninsula (on Nathan Road, a street that leads into Taipo Road and eventually into China), I went by taxi to the pier where a ferry took me across the bay to Hong Kong Island. The center of Kowloon is a veritable paradise of shops (I shall return to them later), but on its outskirts there is an unbelievable area where millions of Chinese refugees huddle together like beasts without a lair.

In the city of Victoria on Hong Kong Island on the lowest, or bay, level are the great shipping companies, which are the financial core of the island, the business buildings, and many modern shops. On its outskirts are the Chinese quarters, which although terribly poor are generally in better condition than the refugees' quarter in Kowloon. Chinese policemen, with whistles and helmets, and Hindu policemen, with beards and turbans, are everywhere. The middle level of Victoria Peak is devoted to British government buildings and to recreation parks. The upper level, which extends right to the summit of Victoria Peak, contains the mansions and luxury residences of the English.

So vast is the difference between British Hong Kong and Chinese Hong Kong that, barring their physical proximity, there is no point of contact or similarity between the two. They are truly two cities, the two cities described by Plato: that of the rich and that of the poor. The only relationship between the two is their forced proximity, against which the British have reacted by keeping the majority of the Chinese down in the

158

lower zones, while they themselves have sought to escape Hong Kong's horizontal sordidness by taking flight up the mountain, to their mansions, situated at heights which only eagles would dare contest.

In Hong Kong one must resign oneself to spending considerable time each day crossing the waters between Kowloon and Hong Kong Island. Some great hotels, as well as many shops, are in Kowloon, but the travel agencies, the business offices, other excellent and newer hotels, elegant shops make it necessary for one to go to Hong Kong Island. However, crossing the bay affords one, for about four American cents (twenty Hong Kong cents), about ten minutes of sheer enchantment. The view is magnificent, for the bay, after that of Rio de Janeiro, is the most beautiful natural bay on earth, and its waters contain as much of the spume of romance as they do salt; the novels that have been written about it and the films made here are numerous.

The bay of Hong Kong makes one feel as if he were in a fairy-tale setting, on an immense, softly rippling lake (except for those rare instances when it is lashed by violent winds), with waters that can be emerald green, metallic gray shot with shades of copper, or, though not often, blue. On hot days, when the haze of heat descends heavily upon them, the waters, frightened, turn into a gleaming sheet of white-hot steel.

I have now ascended about one thousand eight hundred feet up Victoria Peak—more than a mountain, an English pudding—in the Peak tramway (sixty Hong

Kong cents), a cable-drawn, funicular-type tram that for seventy-seven years has been making the climb from lower Hong Kong to the top of the mountain.

There are lofty mountains everywhere; when one stands on Victoria Peak, it seems to dwarf the mountains on Kowloon and even the distant mountains of China. In addition to the ferryboats that incessantly ply the bay, looking as though they were suspended from the pale sky on the chain of smoke rings that pour out of their smokestacks, there are junks and sampans, barges, fishing boats, luxury yachts, skiffs, motor boats, battleships, sloops, ocean-going liners, regatta boats, and numerous freighters that look more like rafts than boats and are so weighed down by crates, sacks, barrels, and bales that their decks are practically at water level.

There is a constant surge of sound, fed by the noises from the boats, the echo of human voices, the lapping of the waters. But from the Peak, this auditory rumor is transformed into a visual perception. One senses, rather than hears, the noises of the bay rising through the mist, which floats in shreds over the waters, as if the white robes of the angels had been hung out of heaven to dry.

It is a hot day, and the breeze atop Victoria Peak brings little relief. The sky looks as if it were covered with ashes, and the bay glimmers as if its waters were sweating. In the distance below, even the largest boats look like toys, but even from here one can hear the shrill sound of their whistles and see the streams of smoke pouring out of smokestacks and soaring above the batlike sails of the Chinese junks.

Fanning out along the mountainside are white mansions with beautiful gardens planted with British exactitude, blossoming parks, and the tower of the great White Pagoda. Farther below, government buildings and office skyscrapers stand out like domino pieces. It is another London, with English flags flapping like handkerchiefs in the air, as though waving good-by to the boats in the bay. Here thousands of Britons live in an opium-like dream, in which nostalgia for Victorian colonial imperialism and for the comforts of London life are combined, all seasoned with the spice of danger. For at their very doorstep dwells the fearsome Chinese colossus, which has already awakened from its centuries-long sleep.

Standing at the top of Victoria Peak, a symbol of the golden age of British colonial imperialism, facing the blue mountains of China, I evoke the historical tapestry of Hong Kong. A knowledge of its past is absolutely essential in any attempt to understand present-day Hong Kong and to foresee its future.

All roads in the Orient lead to China. All the history of Southeast Asia, regardless of which country may be under analysis, has been influenced by China—in bygone eras that influence flowed from China's culture, religion, and philosophy; in the future it might be from Chinese industrialization and their hydrogen bombs.

Following the upheaval caused by that human earthquake, Genghis Khan, Southeast Asia during the last seven centuries was, by comparison with Europe, relatively calm. Until the last world war, it underwent very few important political, social, or cultural changes, despite the fact that the Asiatic countries have less in common with one another than do the countries of Europe or of the Americas. The heart of Asia has always been China, which, historically, developed as a decentralized society without any integrating or centralizing nexus. It was simply an agglomeration of small villages and towns grouped around a square with a market place. For a long time it had few large cities. The emperor, the Son of Heaven, was often a symbol rather than the actual ruler. China was governed by petty princes, trade guilds, and the family, which was the *social* unit, under a patriarchal system that fostered a sense of collective responsibility and ancestor worship among the people. Moreover, the worldly, sophisticated philosophy of Confucius provided the people with an intellectual tradition, a code of ethics, and the aspiration to good government.

With regard to the outside world, China had early had commercial relations with Imperial Rome, which it provided with beautiful Chinese silks. Later in the fourteenth century, China also traded with the Arabian merchants, who established a small colony near Canton; with the Nestorian Christians, who had dwelt on the edges of the Chinese empire for many centuries after 489, when they fled to Persia; and with the Jews. After the Crusades, Europe turned its eyes toward Asia —and Asia toward Europe. A bloody bridge from Asia to Europe was soon laid, a bridge of corpses and smoking ruins left in the wake of Genghis Khan and the "golden hordes" of Batu Khan, his great nephew.

Then, in the thirteenth century, a trading mission arrived in China and included the bold Venetian adventurer, Marco Polo, who subsequently took the silks and philosophy of China back with him to the Piazza San Marco. The China of that time was immensely advanced in culture, technology, science, and politics, far more so than any European nation, a fact that is all too often forgotten. Until the Middle Ages, China was a beacon of culture and technology, of refinement in living and subtlety in thought, a beacon that shone with far greater radiance than France, Spain, Italy, England, or any other country of the then known world.

In the sixteenth century the first Portuguese navigators and tradesmen arrived in China (the same Portuguese who under Don Affonso de Albuquerque conquered the settlement of Malacca a few years later) and still later came the Dutch and the Spaniards, who attacked and terrified the inhabitants of China. These Europeans traveled to China, among other reasons, in quest of spices. They were followed shortly afterward by the missionaries, who introduced both the cross and the Inquisition. At that time the Jesuits succeeded in found-

163

ing centers in both China and Japan. In the late sixteenth century, the Italian missionary Matteo Ricci
introduced into China Italian erudition and science.
By the eighteenth century, England, France, Holland,
the United States, and Russia had limited commercial
relations with China. The Europeans were forced to
trade through an officially designated group of merchants, the Co-hong merchants in Canton, and the
Russians succeeded in obtaining a commercial treaty
utilizing a resident trade mission of their own in
Peking.

In this historical cavalcade, the history of Hong Kong
begins with that magical poppy that from time imme-
morial has made man dream—opium. For the history
of Hong Kong originated in the history of opium.

At the outset, the Dutch used opium, mixed with
tobacco brought from the Philippines by the Spaniards,
for the treatment of intestinal disorders. Opium, which
had been used to some degree in China from the time
of the Tang Dynasty, was increasingly introduced into
China, via Formosa, by Portuguese traders. The English subsequently displaced the Portuguese in the smuggling and sale of opium to the Chinese, who used it
at first for medicinal purposes. Within a short time the
Cantonese opium trade was in English hands. For a
century the English openly sold the lethal poppy to
the Chinese, despite the heated protests of the emperor
in Peking. The opium traffic, which initially consisted
of two hundred chests a year, slowly increased until it

164

reached forty thousand chests a year, according to some authors, and six million pounds of opium according to others.

The British opium traders, voracious for this easily obtainable medium of exchange for China's tea, silk, cotton, and silver, continued increasing the shipping of opium from India, the use of which became a deadly national vice, one the Chinese found irresistible. In 1800, the importation and cultivation of opium in China had been prohibited by imperial edict, whereupon the English East India Company, which the British had founded in 1600 for the purpose of trading with the Orient, even as the Dutch in 1602 founded the United East India Company, continued purchasing the plant in India and exported it in merchant ships to Macao, from where it was then smuggled into China, until the East India Company lost its monopoly in 1833.

Many nations, besides the English, participated in the remunerative illicit traffic, receiving in payment for the opium Chinese silks, tea, and silver. This went on until 1839 when the Chinese High Commissioner, Lin Tse-Hsu, appointed by the emperor to suppress the opium trade, had a shipload of six million dollars worth of opium destroyed. The irate British withdrew from Macao to Hsiang-chiang, a small barren island situated at the mouth of the Pearl River, to await the arrival of their warships. (Hsiang-chiang, meaning "fragrant harbor," was the property of the aristocratic Tang family, which had won the island during the Ming Dynasty.)

Thus began the Opium War, which ended in 1842. After Chinkiang on the Yangtze had fallen into the hands of the English, the Chinese, who even tried disguising themselves in tiger skins to frighten the British artillery, signed a peace treaty, the Treaty of Nanking, granting the English an indemnity of twenty-one million dollars for the destroyed opium cargo and other damages, plus innumerable privileges, including the right to traffic in opium and to trade and reside in the ports of Canton, Shanghai, Amoy, Foochow, and Ningpo.

In this same onerous treaty, the English demanded perpetual ownership of the barren rocky island of Hsiang-chiang, which they had occupied during the Opium War. The English anglicized the name of the island to Hong Kong, by which name it was incorporated in the lands belonging to the British Crown. Then, in 1860, just over one hundred years ago, the Chinese granted England the peninsula of Kowloon (meaning the "Nine Dragons," after the shape of its eight hills plus the emperor of China, whose symbol was the dragon) and on Stonecutters Island in Hong Kong Bay in perpetuity, and in 1898 they leased the so-called New Territories, or the lands plus one hundred and ninety-eight islands adjacent to Kowloon, to the British for ninety-nine years.

Such is Hong Kong's history. Barring therefore the holocaust of nuclear war, which might put an end to the world, Hong Kong will undergo an historical change in 1998, thirty-two years from now, upon the expiration of the lease on the New Territories, at which point the English, in the best of cases, will have to withdraw to Kowloon and the island of Hong Kong.

As an aftermath of the Opium War, an ever-increasing friction developed between China and the Western powers, most of which, including the United States, had previously had official trade relations with the Chinese. The Chinese continually attacked foreigners in the streets and also destroyed their property. Meanwhile, the traffic in opium flourished, as did that in Chinese coolie slaves, whom the English and the Dutch shipped to the Caribbean islands. This tragic human cargo was picked up in Macao, which became a piracy center, and crated like wild beasts in the bowels of cargo ships.

In 1856 France and England unleashed another war against China, which lasted four years. Only the advent of the Chinese Revolution of 1911 put an "official" end to the production of and traffic in opium, which today is practiced only clandestinely in Macao, Hong Kong, and in Asiatic countries.

Hong Kong therefore is the product of an act of piracy on the high seas of History. The Chinese Communists could have occupied Hong Kong at any time after they came to power. They have not done so because it is far more advantageous for them to preserve this valuable outpost of international trade and, above all, of intrigue and espionage.

From the summit of Victoria Peak, I take one final look at the bay of Hong Kong. The eye can encompass the seventeen square miles of the bay and, beyond Kowloon Peninsula, the New Territories, and the Mountains of Kwantung in China.

Later, when I am more rested, I shall take a long walk. I am curious to see this miraculous British feat, the transformation of this rocky cliff, the ancient empire of sea, wind, and sea gull, into a colonial miniature of England, with its green carpeted lawns, its city bustling with bankers, its banks as solid as the empire once was, its elegant mansions ablaze with blossoming gardens, its verdant parks forced upon the rock by the hand of man, the tall vine-draped walls that protect the sacrosanct privacy of the British homes, the squash and tennis courts, the golf greens, the statues of the royal family and, even more symbolic, the tall red-brick tower topped with a huge four-faced clock of a type that can be seen wherever the British rule (I would swear that this is the same tower I saw in the little square near the harbor in Nassau in the British Bahamas!), the official residence shrouded in an isolating silence, the cemetery looking like another garden, the Christian missions, and countless de luxe automobiles. Rule, Britannia!

More than three and a half million people dwell in the colony of Hong Kong (seventeen thousand per square mile), including the island proper, which is eleven miles long and two to five miles wide, and the territories around the bay. Of these, only twenty thousand are English and eight thousand are of some fifty other nationalities. The remainder are Chinese, who multiply at a rate of seventy-five thousand a year, and this figure does not include the million refugees (the number varies from author to author and year to year) who infiltrated from China between 1950 and 1961. Some two and a half million Chinese live in the thirty-six-square-mile urban area of Hong Kong; of another eight hundred thousand, one hundred and forty thousand live permanently on junks and sampans in Aberdeen, and the remainder (chiefly the Cantonese, Hakkas, Hok-lo, and Tanka) live in the New Territories and on the one hundred and ninety-eight smaller islands of the colony. This brief deluge of statistics clearly indicates that the British constitute a very small minority. The steadily increasing Chinese population must, no doubt, be making the official British mantle that cloaks them burst at the seams.

The English—government officials, soldiers, diplomats, ship owners, bankers, journalists, merchants, financiers, assorted professionals, and the rich and idle—live in a world of their own within their city, a world that grazes that of the Chinese only by sheer accident, in the fleeting contact of bodies in the streets, shops, and ferryboats.

The English divide their time between making a living, playing golf and tennis, fishing, swimming at the paradisiacal Repulse Beach—a gleaming stretch of platinum, rather than of sand, for the privileged few who have access to it—drinking whisky or gin and tonic at their clubs and playing bridge and poker. The women look after their homes, ruling their Chinese servants with an imperious hand, go shopping, play bridge, and gossip over tea.

Curious to learn what is sold in Hong Kong, I visited many shops in both Hong Kong and Kowloon. Since Hong Kong is a free port, no duties are paid on imports, with the exception of cigarettes, tobacco, and liquor. Luxury items from all over the world can be purchased here at prices lower than anywhere else in the world.

Shops are ruled by one interest only: to sell—to sell everything and sell it quickly, in order to bring in more things, sell more, and make more money. Display windows, unbelievably vulgar, reflect this hustling spirit, which animates all merchants in Hong Kong, regardless of nationality. The same window will display gold watches from Switzerland, Japanese cameras, and movie cameras from Germany, English hides, Indian silks, stoles from Thailand, nylon stockings from the United States, and ties from Paris, alongside an assortment of dishwashers, refrigerators, bicycles, riding saddles, tires, television sets, china, and bathtubs!

Crammed chaotically with these and a thousand other objects, each shop window reflects the aggressiveness of its owner, who spends his whole day at his shop. European proprietors keep their Chinese or Malayan clerks running back and forth. Chinese proprietors sit in shirt sleeves at the doorway of their shops, sipping tea, fanning their ever-perspiring Buddha-like bellies with little paper fans, and waving away the flies with a bamboo reed that has thin strips of cloth fastened at one end and looks like a cat-o'-nine-tails.

A large amount of Chinese merchandise is manufactured in Hong Kong in more than eleven thousand factories, where masses of half-starved Chinese toil long hours, turning out, like machines, embroidered linens, silks, wools, teak, camphorwood and sandalwood chests, rugs, toys, rattan furniture, leather wallets, shoes, suitcases, and small lacquered boxes. This merchandise can be brought into the United States if accompanied by a certificate guaranteeing that it was made in Hong Kong. Other items, such as embroidered tablecloths, brocades, ceramics, jade, chess sets, *mah-jongg* sets, and ivory figurines, which come from China, will not pass the United States customs.

Also obtainable are Hong Kong's famous silk suits, inexpensive and elegant, which any one of the four or five thousand tailors in Hong Kong will make to order not, as advertised, in less than twenty-four hours, but in four or five days, if you wish the seams of the suit to survive the first cleaning.

One day I went to what the English refer to as "Thieves' Market" and the Chinese as "Cat Street." It is an extremely steep, narrow street, cut into steps all the way to the top, where little curio and antique shops

171

are lined up one behind another like school desks in a classroom. Nothing they have is of much use to the American tourist, for they sell Chinese goods, half of which would be confiscated by the United States customs.

But what is remarkable about Cat Street is the street itself, a veritable microcosm of humanity. Chinese men, young and old, sit on rickety chairs right in the middle of the street, while barbers shave their faces or crop their hair, leaving only a few tufts on top of the skull, like dried-out clumps of shrubbery on a rock. There are busy shopkeepers everywhere, restoring an icebox, scraping furniture, inflating bicycle tires, mixing mysterious medications that they bottle in the open air in little crystal bottles or in glass demijohns, mending used clothing, repairing shoes, fixing locks and electric plugs, cutting, hammering, chopping, sewing, sawing, perforating, polishing, varnishing. Hundreds of children crowd the gutter, shouting, laughing, jumping, fighting, or licking sweets as ominous looking as the bowls of noodles or the fried meat rind that old men, seated on the ground, eat with their fingers, sucking in the noodles noisily.

But my thoughts while standing on Victoria Peak have taken too much time. It is growing late. I fear I shall miss my four o'clock bath. The English must be getting ready for their five o'clock tea.

Once again I take the Peak tram, this time to descend the 1,890 feet that separate me from Hong Kong. In the

still waters of the bay the *wallah wallah,* or motor
launches, make their eternal rounds. Rickshas trot by
taking some Englishmen to their five o'clock tea.

I have taken a richsha only twice, once in Macao and
again in Hong Kong, both times out of sheer urgency
and when almost forced to do so by a policeman, for
the idea of human horses deeply distresses me. Asiatics,
on the other hand, sit inside the rickshas with an imperial air, staring at their two-legged human horses
without seeing them.

Of the eight hundred and fifty licensed rickshas in
Hong Kong, I understood that only about two hundred
were operating then. The rickshas are usually stationed
near the ferries, their litters painted red or green and,
sometimes, canopied with a striped awning. They line
up like taxis, one behind the other, but this does not
mean that they are waiting their turn. Instead, the drivers besiege every prospective passenger, clamoring and
pushing one another violently.

It is claimed that, although seventeenth-century Japanese drawings portray a vehicle similar to the ricksha,
the first real ricksha did not appear until 1871. An
American, Jonathan Goole, who served under Commodore Perry at the time the latter opened Japan to the
West and who subsequently became a missionary, and
went to live in Yokohama with his invalid wife, wishing her to be able to go out for fresh air, gave a Japanese
carpenter a design based on an illustration of a pram in
Godey's Lady's Book and had him build the first rick-

sha, short for *jinrikisha,* which in Japanese means a man-drawn carriage.

In the beginning the rickshas were made of iron with wooden wheels and had side panels painted with chrysanthemums and cherry blossoms or with the owner's coat of arms. Later, wire wheels with tires were used, many of which were manufactured in New Jersey! The rickshas spread from Japan to China, Indochina, Thailand, Burma, India, Ceylon, Africa, and wherever human horsepower was cheap.

Rickshas became so popular that they succeeded in eliminating sedan chairs, palanquins, and howdahs from the streets. But today their use is declining. The coolie who pulls a ricksha earns only about nine cents for every five minutes of running and pulling and sweating. He has to trot a thousand miles a month to earn about a hundred and fifty Hong Kong dollars, the major portion of which is kept by intermediaries and exploiters. It is painful to watch them lying, exhausted and perspiring, in the sun, or cooling off too quickly in the shade, or hastily devouring messy-looking concoctions from a metal pan, or sucking noodles that look like worms from bowls. For these unfortunate creatures, very short indeed is the road to malnutrition and tuberculosis.

When I finally descend from Victoria Peak, following the instructions of a policeman, of whom I had asked the way to get to the ferry, I take a ricksha. The coolie, blatantly ignoring my orders, breaks into a trot in a direction opposite to what I have given him. Whether he is motivated by malice or by stupidity, I do not know, but once a ricksha is in motion the vertiginous traffic of vehicles on all sides, including huge double-decked red buses that the rickshas elude with Olympian indifference, makes it extremely difficult, if not impossible, to jump to the ground.

Exasperated, I begin to stamp my feet on the floor of the ricksha until finally the coolie turns the ricksha around, retraces the ground we had covered, and drops me near the ferry. He then demands twenty times the amount quoted to me by the policeman. Paying no heed to the commotion he raises, I place on the ricksha five times the amount I should have paid, plus a tip, and walk away. Screaming at the top of his lungs, he follows me, until he sees me approaching a policeman. When I retrace my steps toward the ferry, I see him squatting on the sidewalk, sharpening a butcher's knife with a blade as big as a guillotine's. He looks like a jackal about to attack. I pass him just at the same moment as does a Chinese family coming from the opposite direction, whereupon he yells something to them that makes them look at me and laugh. Fortunately, the incident ended there. I reach the hotel after tea time, but still in time for a bath.

The Englishmen by now would be gravitating toward their clubs or homes, where probably a thick slice of roast beef, a bottle of ale, and a piece of Stilton await them. The coolies, squatting on the sidewalks, would be pecking at their noodles and rice with their chopsticks.

The two cities of Hong Kong eat and sleep at the same hours, but the chasm that lies between them, the orderly British city and the motley Chinese city, is wider and deeper and far more dangerous than the green waters of Hong Kong Bay.

FIVE O'CLOCK TEA ON
VICTORIA PEAK

W*as I really at that party,
or was it only a dream I had when I was in Hong
Kong?*

Five P.M. on Victoria Peak.

Mr. and Mrs. Fanslow Shaterbury's garden, where
the cocktail party is being held, is dotted with gerani-
ums as red as a fever rash. Balloon-shaped laurels fence
in the garden, and a second border of white, blue, and
purple flowers still glistens from the watering they were

177

given before the party began. In the middle of the garden, white water lilies and red lotus blossoms carpet the waters of a white marble pool.

Three wide glass doors lead from the garden into the mansion, as white and solid looking as a Scandinavian woman tennis player. Through the doors, one can see the interior of the house: crystal chandeliers, silver candelabra upon which the sun breaks its golden lances, a table aglow with fine white linen, silver, porcelain, and crystal. A Negro butler and two white-clad barmen stand behind the table, erect, grave, and alert, like three bullfighters facing a wild bull whose tricks are an unknown quantity.

Thanks to an American colleague of mine who introduced me to some of his friends, I have been invited to this party, affording me the opportunity, supplemented by information supplied by my friend, of peeking into the British microcosm in Hong Kong. For even as a single drop of sea water contains all the essence of the sea, so too this house and party embody some of the component parts of the English world that rules the destinies of Hong Kong.

Standing by a rosebush with dozens of little yellow faces turned toward an unpolluted blue sky, are three men dressed in natural-silk suits, made in Hong Kong, of impeccable English-type cut. Their hands, elegantly holding cigarettes from England and whisky from Scotland, are raised alternately, either to smoke or drink, or to emphasize their words.

"I've said so a thousand times," one of them complains, "but nobody's done anything. The situation at the club cannot continue. Yesterday at lunch I again spoke to Hawthorne. I have spoken to everyone on the admission committee. Hawthorne promised once again that they would look into the matter. But I'm afraid we must take direct action, call a meeting, force a decision by general vote."

"Cowan," the second man explains to the third, "wants the club to change its eligibility requirements for new members."

"Precisely, Dawson," Cowan interjects. "See here, Almsley," he continues, addressing the third man. "It's not just a question of the club being flooded with all sorts of undesirable elements. The excessive number of members is already doing great harm."

"What are the present admission requirements?" Almsley asks.

"Simply that the applicants be economically solvent, of reputed moral respectability, and permanent residents of Hong Kong. But that is not enough. The club already has a handful of Americans who have formed a clique apart. They don't show even the slightest interest in cricket, yet they're always raising a rumpus with their baseball discussions. And they drink too much and don't even care what they drink. Some of the members are more transient than resident and have no interest whatsoever in Hong Kong's economic progress. Others, although they could live on Victoria Peak, prefer to live in the city below. If all this continues, it will be impossible to maintain the club's high standards."

"I realize all that," Almsley replies vaguely, "but you said something about doing great harm. What do you mean?"

Cowan drains half his glass of whisky, puffs his English cigarette, and with a mysterious air approaches Almsley's ear.

"I'm going to tell you something in the strictest confidence. A few days ago I had a chat with Oswald, the barman. He told me something that's been worrying me ever since. You know the 1948 port that the club acquired and that we drink only on special occasions? Oswald told me that there are only fifty cases left and that when these are gone it's going to be deucedly difficult to get more. Such a dreadful situation! Between the droves of new members and the Americans, who practically drink the port from the bottle the way they do Coca-Cola—which is all they deserve to drink—it won't be long before all the port will be gone. We connoisseurs of fine port are going to see some lean days in the future."

Of the three men, Reginald Cowan is the oldest, but he carries his sixty-odd years with vigor and arrogance. He has the head of a bulldog. His hair, still thick, is flaming red. He is the president of a shipping company with offices in Hong Kong and Singapore. His cargo ships transport all sorts of goods, from lumber to glycerine. Some people add contraband tobacco and even, years ago, arms to Communist China to the long list of products he ships, but they do it only in whispers. Cowan has lived in Hong Kong for forty years and has the same proprietary air toward it as he has toward his ships and his family—a small, colorless wife, who next to his big towering frame is but a shadow of a woman, and two sons, who for the last few years have been members of Victoria's cricket championship teams.

Cowan knows everyone who is important in Hong Kong business and politics. He does not know, nor does he care to know, any Chinese other than those who deal with him and pay him well and promptly. He talks about Communist China with paternal disdain, much as he talks about club members who do not play golf as well as he. Many years ago he went back to London, but, when he realized that in his own country he was nobody and that his fellow countrymen were even greater snobs than he, he promptly returned to Hong Kong, where he could be a snob with hardly anyone to outmatch him.

Archie Dawson is forty-five years old. He is tall and athletic and dresses with refined elegance. Born in Hong Kong of a Liverpool family, on his father's death he inherited several thousand pounds sterling, which, in the hands of a competent financial advisor, has mounted to a tidy fortune. Today, Dawson has controlling shares in three Hong Kong banks and owns a highly successful investment firm. He is a bachelor and rumors circulate about his strange amorous predilections. He lives in a sumptuous mansion, high on the Peak, with a dozen servants, eight of whom are Chinese and the rest, including of course the butler, English, born in Victoria.

Dawson's obsession is to close Hong Kong off to all Chinese refugees. Whereas his friends regard the Red menace with indifference, he lives in mortal fear of what might happen if the day should come when China intervenes in the policies of Hong Kong or when the refugees, with Chinese support, rise up in revolt against the British. Dawson devotes most of his free time to various committees that work either openly or secretly toward one end: forceful legislation, implemented even more forcefully with soldiers, arms, and air and naval patrols, to close off the island and ship all refugees back to China.

It is said that Dawson's grandfather was a refugee from Smyrna who changed his name in England and adopted British citizenship. In trying to bar Hong Kong to all refugees Dawson, unconsciously, is simply trying to wipe out the shadow of a family past that he both hates and fears.

Lord Hugh Almsley is less than forty and of short stature, which he tries to disguise by wearing special shoes with secret, built-up heels. He came here from London about twenty years ago, at the end of World War II, after quarreling with his family over a minor scandal involving one of his mother's maids. He lives off the yearly income his family sends him and is having a wonderful time while waiting for his father to die and leave him his fortune.

Lord Almsley came to Hong Kong by accident. When he left London he vowed never to return to the world of Mayfair clubs, West End night clubs, wild duck hunting in the summer, the races and fox hunts in the fall. He was determined to become a great romantic figure in the Orient, to change from playboy into a forger of new glories for the empire. In Japan, however, the people did not understand him, nor he them; in India he found animosity and antagonism everywhere; in Singapore he felt completely disoriented. Finally, in Hong Kong, he found exactly what he was seeking: a world like that of London, but colorful and exotic.

Here he leads the same life he led in London, but with no restrictions, other than those imposed by his limited income, which he supplements with his winnings at poker and bridge, at both of which he is an outstanding expert.

In London, Lord Almsley had read Maugham's South Sea Island stories and Conrad's novels of the Orient. Here he reads only the gossip columns in the English newspapers and the racing results. He is vaguely irritated by all the agitation in the present world, as if it were a personal assault on his peace of mind. Toward Chinese men he has the condescending attitude of a feudal lord toward his vassals; toward Chinese women, he shows marked interest, especially if they are very young, although he is both abusive and niggardly with them.

Lord Almsley will leave no more trace on Hong Kong's life than a raindrop leaves on a windowpane.

Three women stand talking near the lotus pool. The sun transforms their hair, of one to a cap of polished gold, of another to pure silver, and of the third to glowing copper. Two of them are drinking tea; the other holds a tall carved crystal glass at the bottom of which the last sip of whisky sparkles in the sun like a happy glance.

"Life gets more and more complicated every day," says the golden-haired woman. "Years back, in London, there was time for everything. Now there is time for nothing. Yesterday I was counting the committees I belong to. Do you know how many there are? Twenty-two." She sips her tea and, hardly taking a breath, goes on. "This means about one meeting a day, excluding special sessions. Naturally, bridge and parties suffer. And I do feel miserable about it. Nothing gives me greater pleasure than being with my friends. But the committees must keep functioning. Actually there aren't enough of them for all there is to do. But one thing still comes first: the hairdresser. There I do set the limit. I wouldn't miss an appointment at the hairdresser for all the tea in China." Patting her stiff coiffure, she adds, "My other commitments are reduced to a minimum, so that I can attend all the meetings."

"What you say about the lack of time is quite true,"

remarks the red-haired woman. "Of course, no one gives committees as much time as you do. You are entirely too generous. Nor does any one give as many parties as you do. I know I never have enough time for all the things I must do, and yet I get up very early!" Eager to make her point, she speaks rapidly. "By eleven o'clock —well, sometimes noon—I'm already at Repulse Beach water skiing. That leaves hardly any time for cocktails and snack at the beach club before my afternoon round of tennis. And then I have to dash back home. One of these days I'm sure to crash my Jaguar on the road. At seven my friends call for me to go for cocktails, dinner, and dancing. I'm afraid they always have to wait for me, at least an hour. I wouldn't miss my bath or dress quickly even if Laurence Olivier were waiting for me." Her charm bracelets noisily punctuate her comments. "I barely sleep a few hours, never enough. Yet I manage to belong to a few committees."

"What committees, Miss Allingworth?" the blonde woman inquires icily.

"Oh, various committees." And Miss Allingworth, wishing to steer the conversation away from dangerous ground, quickly turns to the silver-haired woman. "Dr. Jimson, I don't suppose you have much time for committee meetings."

"No," smiles the amused Dr. Jimson, "I have no time for committees. I'm afraid I do what little I can outside committees."

The blonde woman is Mrs. Victoria Fanslow Shaterbury, mistress of the house and hostess of the party. She is forty-eight years old, but with the help of hair tints, massages, and clever make-up she contrives to look her age and no more. Her husband, Homer Fanslow Shaterbury, is one of the richest men in Hong Kong.

Mrs. Fanslow Shaterbury has three passions in life: committees, gossiping, and the hairdresser, exactly in that order. These leave her little time or love for her husband and her daughter. Committees and the hairdresser provide her with the opportunity to gossip, thus uniting her three great interests in life.

Her greatest passion, of course, is committees. The other British women belong to three, four, or half a dozen. She belongs to all those she knows about, suspects that there are probably many more, and eagerly searches for them. She punctually attends all the meetings and delivers more speeches than all the other speakers put together. Some committees have a clear, concrete function, such as the committees for the Bridge Society, the Christian Mission, the Horticulture Society, or the Association of London Women. But most of the other committees have such vague functions and such diverse activities that neither she nor anybody else knows exactly why they meet, unless it is to play cards and drink tea or cocktails. There are committees for the protection of the British Navy, for the Cultural Union of the Commonwealth Nations, for the Spiritual *Rapprochement* of English Mothers, for the Alliance of Western Nations, for the Philosophical and Economic Progress of European Nations. Oh, yes, she also belongs—it gives her, she thinks, a noble philanthropic air—to the Committee for the Spiritual Protection of Chinese Anticommunist Families.

Mrs. Fanslow Shaterbury's life would have no justification without a committee to fill every hour of her day. Her atrophied conscience is sometimes vaguely disturbed by the way her husband has made his fortune, and subconsciously, through her feverish activities on committees, she is trying to counterbalance her husband's business practices on the Lord's scale. Just in case.

Sandy Allingworth is thirty years old and her love life is as scarlet as her hair. She is tall, a Grecian Venus, with luminous green eyes, like the sun seen through a grapevine. She wears the chic-est clothes in Victoria— sport clothes by day and evening clothes by night; they are usually as snug as a bathing suit and in green satin, with plunging necklines. You see her on Repulse Beach or at the tennis court almost every afternoon, her red hair ablaze in the sunlight, her eyes shielded by dark glasses, her mouth as red as her hair. At night she invariably makes the rounds of night clubs or attends private parties.

She has no family, claiming that she is an orphan. She came from Singapore and has been in Hong Kong a little less than ten years. Rumor has it that her mother was an American servant in the employ of an English family who adopted Sandy on her mother's death and later threw her out of the house for stealing some jewelry.

Officially, Sandy is a free, happy, athletic girl, who has a little money of her own, and in Hong Kong questions are never asked about how one has made one's money.

More than two dozen rich men in Victoria boast in the privacy of their clubs of having kept Sandy Allingworth during various periods of her sojourn in Hong Kong. The women do not like her, but they accept her because their husbands insist that she is "a great girl," a fine sportswoman, and a brilliant conversationalist. In reality, the husbands secretly nourish the hope of some day joining the two dozen men who talk about Sandy in private with true knowledge. Those learned in these matters say that when Sandy periodically disappears—she claims she goes to London to look after her financial interests—she goes to Singapore and Kuala Lumpur to visit two wealthy Chinese merchants.

Sandy is really a parasitic but harmless adornment on the island. She is not even aware of the millions of starving refugees crammed together only a few yards away from where she lives, or of the danger lurking on the other side of the frontier. What she does know is that for at least a few years her laughter, her gay prattle, her company—if not her time—are worth money, and she is cashing in on them.

Doctor Alice Jimson is a graduate of the Medical School of the University of Edinburgh. Upon becoming a widow, she joined a medical mission to Hong Kong, where for thirty of her seventy years she has been working as a pediatrician in two Chinese clinics and a British hospital. She is tall, strong looking, rosy cheeked. Her beautiful gray hair is combed back severely, dipping only slightly in a haze of silver over pale pink ears. Her gentle eyes have the tired look of the doctor who works twelve or more hours a day. Her ears have heard a great deal and her eyes have seen even more. She is the only one at the party who has studied Mandarin and Cantonese and speaks both fluently.

Doctor Jimson lives with an ancient Chinese woman servant in a small villa in the lower part of Victoria. She drives a Daimler almost as old as Victoria Peak. The English respect her for her hard work and her professional skill, but they regard her as an eccentric who cares nothing for bridge games or even cocktail parties. Whenever she attends a party, as in this case, they always suspect that she is after another donation for her hospitals.

Like other physicians on the island, Dr. Jimson would like to see many things done to improve the condition of the Chinese, especially of the refugees. She is perpetually obsessed by what would happen if plague, cholera, or typhoid fever should suddenly descend upon the hundreds of thousands of wretched refugees crammed together in tin plate and burlap huts in Kowloon. Regardless of how much she does as an individual, she

189

realizes that it is a mere drop in the bucket against the prevailing paucity of social aid. The Chinese who know her adore her, and through her personal prestige she maintains alive in them a feeling of admiration for England, a feeling she would willingly trade for a little help in resolving an even more pressing problem than that of disease: how to feed the hungry multitudes of Kowloon.

The last group I approach is composed of three men who are drinking Martinis with lemon peels.

"The Malaysian problem grows more acute each day," says one of them who has the unmistakable air of a government official. "And I don't see how it can be solved. Our solution would create strong political disturbances, and theirs is unacceptable to us. After Malaysia, Hong Kong would be next. The Federation of Malaysia has three and a half million Malaysians, two and a half million Chinese, and a million Indians, Europeans, and other nationalities. Singapore has more than three hundred thousand people of varying nationalities, and a million and a half Chinese. So far we have resisted the demands from these Chinese to be allowed to form an affiliation with the Federation of Malaysia. But how much longer can we resist?"

"I agree," the host, Mr. Fanslow Shaterbury, affirms. "On my last trip to Singapore I discussed the problem with my business agents and with several bankers and merchants. The situation is more serious than people think. Chinese secret societies are mushrooming every day. A night does not pass without meetings of these societies in Singapore and in Johore Bahru. The Chinese are now permitted to work in Singapore, but they have no effective political representation. The day they are granted the right to participate officially in politics —that day all our business enterprises, including my own rubber plantations and tin and metal business, will suffer a mortal blow. We must at all cost stave off that day, and the only way to do it is to make those incompetent fools in London, who are so bungling our foreign policy, realize that it is *we,* and not they, who will suffer if anything happens in Malaya."

"You forget, my friend, that I am a government official," the other replies, softening the rebuke with a smile.

"I know, I know, Stenham. You are not only a faithful but a splendid official. But you live in Hong Kong. You know our problems inside out. This cannot be said about our friends in the government in London. You do not want the Chinese in Singapore to gain political power any more than you want the Chinese in Hong Kong to do so. But I am neither an official nor a politician. I am an honest businessman. I do not want the fruit of my labor snatched away from me. In the final analysis, we are all interested in living and letting live. But this rule must be applied to everyone if we are to keep what belongs to us. Don't you think so, Jackson?"

The third man smiles slyly as he smokes his cigarette.

"I agree that everyone has the right to keep what *rightfully* and *legitimately* belongs to him." The emphasis on the two adverbs is so pronounced that the host's face turns red under his tanned skin. "On the other hand, I'm afraid that no one can hold back the advance of history. Perhaps the day is not far off when not only will the Chinese of Singapore, who already control business, gain political power in Malaysia, but all of Southeast Asia and Hong Kong will be swept up by the same political surge."

The official interrupts.

"Pessimism, sheer pessimism, Jackson. You're now talking like a newspaperman trying to see both points of view. But don't forget that if something should happen, all of us whites will be affected, even you."

James Stenham is an official in Her Majesty the Queen of England's government. He is sixty years old and from the age of twenty has worked for the British government in Hong Kong. So did his father and grandfather, both of whom were also born in Hong Kong. Mr. Stenham is very proud of his family's three generations of faithful service to their government. He is a dried-up rather than thin man, has no sense of humor, and his face is as colorless as his thinking and his speech.

His wife and children, standing together in a corner of the garden, are, with deadly concentration, consuming ham and cucumber sandwiches, one after another. Mr. Stenham, with great nostalgia, recalls his grandfather's stories about the sumptuous life led in his day by high government functionaries. They had magnificent horse-drawn carriages, splendid mansions, hordes of Chinese servants, and grand parties—at which genuine *foie gras* from Strasbourg ("which one never sees nowadays," he will remark plaintively), caviar ("which today is rationed out grain by grain"), and the best vintage champagne in silver goblets—which formed a truly elegant background for the military's dress uniforms, the ladies' glittering diamonds, and the gentlemen's swallow-tailed coats.

When Mr. Stenham's grandfather died, his father, lacking the necessary mental equipment, failed to obtain the important post left vacant by his father. Life then became much more modest for the family, although in tune with the greater modesty of the times. Now Mr. Stenham holds a post even more modest than that of his father and nourishes no hopes of improving it. To such a situation he has reacted by always strictly adhering to all bureaucratic rules, without ever giving a thought to the possibility of improving his lot. Instead he stays close to Mr. Fanslow Shaterbury and does favors for him whenever he can, in the hope that the latter will reciprocate, as he has at times, with small gifts. Upon his retirement or demise, Mr. Stenham will exit from Hong Kong life in the same manner as he now leaves a room: with no one even being aware that he has been there.

The young newspaperman, Anton Jackson, was born

in Hong Kong of an American father and an English mother. He is short and stout and wears a perpetual sneer on his thick lips, which he makes no attempt to conceal. He dresses slovenly. He boasts of having many enemies, which is true. It is rumored that he is a Communist, which judging by the way he talks is probably also true. Those who have tried to make life difficult for him have lived to regret it, for through his newspaper column on social and political matters he manages to more than pay back all attacks, either by publishing unpleasant items about his enemies, or, worse still, by ignoring them completely in his column. He has an untouchable position, having inherited a considerable amount of stock in the newspaper for which he works.

Jackson harbors a secret hatred (it is not as secret as he believes, for dissimulation is not one of his gifts) against the society in which he lives, but he lacks the courage either to abandon it or reform it.

He thinks of himself as a Communist, but actually he is antisocial. Secretly he admires and applauds Russia's and Red China's policies, but his efforts are not so much pro-Communist as they are anti-British. He had craved fame as a newspaperman and writer in London, but he failed in both attempts. He now compensates for his frustrations and inferiority feelings by projecting them onto the people around him, which makes him feel superior to them. He widely advertises that he is involved in committees and projects on behalf of Chinese residents and refugees in Hong Kong, but his enthusiasm and philanthropy are merely a camouflage for his personal resentments.

The host, Mr. Fanslow Shaterbury, was born in Singapore of a Dutch family engrafted for so many generations onto English stock that nothing Dutch remains except their business acumen. He is tall and corpulent. His great mane of reddish hair, perpetually ruffled, gives him the appearance of a lion, which age and experience has rendered more dangerous. His eyes are forever bloodshot from too much drinking, yet no one remembers ever seeing him intoxicated. He approaches every glass of whisky as greedily as a baby approaches his warm bottle after a hungry night in a lonely crib.

He has business dealings all over Southeast Asia, including, of course, Hong Kong, but primarily in Kuala Lumpur and Singapore. His business enterprises consist of the manufacture and export of various goods, shipping, and, as everyone knows, wholesale smuggling. He is calculating and ruthless both in business and in his personal life. People in Victoria tolerate him out of fear of his economic power and his lack of scruples.

He is one of the best known of the English among the Chinese because he would trade even with the devil, even if the devil were both Chinese and Communist. Yet, with all his millions, aside from occasional contributions to charitable works and churches, from which he is careful to milk as much publicity as possible, he has never made any effort to improve the lot of the suffering people of Hong Kong.

The Chinese, especially those who trade with him, detest him. For them he symbolizes the type of Westerner who is responsible for the Oriental hatred of foreigners.

Mr. Fanslow Shaterbury looks upon his wife's committee work with approbation, for it surrounds his home—at least so he thinks—with an aura of respectability and philanthropy, a perfect screen for his business tactics and his elastic morality, a morality in which the lowest business ruses are mere rules of the game.

The great passion of this man is his thirteen-year-old daughter, a beautiful, willful creature who from the age of eight has ruled their Chinese servants as though they were serfs. What her father does not know is that this pup of his already despises her father, whom she regards as a vulgar drunkard, as well as her mother, whom she considers a vain, foolish woman.

The party is about to end. The final topic of conversation is a lady who has lived in Macao for many years with her husband, a highly respected businessman. Three days earlier, the husband had left in his automobile on one of his periodic business trips. His wife stayed behind in their elegant villa in Macao. The next morning the lady received a stunning shock. Her husband was dead. His car had crashed against a tree on a turn of the road.

But an even greater shock was the fact that her husband had been drunk at the time the accident occurred and that with him had been a half-caste girl from Macao, an ex-cabaret dancer, who miraculously escaped uninjured. Upon questioning, the girl revealed—and everyone in Macao immediately learned of it—that for ten years she had been the mistress of the highly respected businessman.

The widow, naturally, is overcome by shame. She is, above all, profoundly perplexed. For she faces a great dilemma: tomorrow at the funeral, should she display the grief befitting the wife of a man who until the moment of his death had enjoyed a spotless reputation? Or should she wash her hands of him who departed so disgracefully from this world?

For nearly two days she has been plagued by torturing doubts. But suddenly she has a brilliant idea. She would do what every good British subject should do in a foreign land when faced with a grave problem. She will ask the British consul.

ROSES AND TIGERS

A ROSE GARDEN AND TIGER heads.

I am at the resplendent villa of Dr. Li Shu-Fan, one of the few Chinese who live on Victoria Peak, the private grounds of the British colony in Hong Kong.

It was through the kindness of my distinguished American colleague, Dr. Seymour Farber, that I had the good fortune of meeting this celebrated Chinese physician, director of the Hong Kong Sanatorium and

198

Hospital in Happy Valley, Hong Kong, owner of White Jade, a multimillionaire's mansion perched on Victoria Peak, of another princely mansion called Green Jade in Kowloon, and of a yacht worthy of a famous Hollywood star, anchored in the bay of Hong Kong. All this, he is wont to say, was earned with two fingers, the thumb and the index finger on his right hand, the same fingers used in signing checks, but also the fingers with which a surgeon operates, for Dr. Li Shu-Fan is a surgeon, and an outstanding one. His story is a combination adventure serial and fairy tale.

When he was thirteen years old, Li Shu-Fan left Canton, where he was studying, for Boston where he was going to study. Stopping in Montreal on the way, the Chinese lad stood studying the works of a watch displayed in a shop window, when a criminal hand threw a stone at him, wounding his scalp despite the thick queue coiled like a snake around his head. Unconscious, he was taken to a hospital and his wound was stitched and dressed. When he arrived in Boston soon after, where his father, a merchant, was living, his blood-matted queue was cut off and the stitches were removed. And not only was the wound not infected, as he had feared, but it did not even hurt. The boy was astonished that infection had not set in, for in his country all wounds terminated in suppuration, which in Montreal had been prevented by the use of carbolic acid. Then and there the lad decided to investigate the mysteries of Western medicine. In 1908, in

Hong Kong, he received his medical degree. Dr. Li Shu-Fan then went on to Edinburgh, where he was also granted medical degrees.

After that he traveled by Trans-Siberian Railway to Manchuria, where he was ordered to report to the Viceroy, Chao Er-Suen, who subsequently appointed him Chief Medical Officer of the Plague Prevention Service of South Manchuria to fight the pneumonic plague epidemic that was then devastating that land. The aged Viceroy treated the young doctor with the highest deference, even removing his eyeglasses before bowing to him, a gesture of supreme respect. In reality, Dr. Li feared that he had been summoned only to be beheaded, the punishment meted out by the Manchu court to members of the Sworn Allegiance Party, Dr. Sun Yat-Sen's revolutionary party, to which he belonged and with whose army he was later to march in the conquest of Canton.

Before taking on his responsibilities as Chief Medical Officer, Dr. Li went to visit his family in Hong Kong. His arrival in Shanghai, enroute, coincided with the Chinese revolution in Wuchang and Hankow.

After the successful overthrow of the imperial government and when the Republic of China was established, Dr. Sun Yat-Sen from Canton in Kwangtung, founder of the Republic of China in the same way that Lenin was of Communist Russia, the man responsible for almost single-handedly conceiving the revolution, was elected President. Dr. Sun Yat-Sen, an ophthalmologist who was graduated from the Hong Kong College of Medicine, named Dr. Li Shu-Fan Minister of Public Health in the new government of the Republic of China.

I had the opportunity of visiting Dr. Li Shu-Fan—who always wears well-tailored Western clothes and has black hair and bright, merry eyes twinkling behind his glasses—at his hospital in Happy Valley, a spotless clinic with three hundred beds and wide windows facing vast rose gardens. The atmosphere is idyllic, more that of a rustic hotel than of a hospital. There, with the conscientious assistance of his staff, the eminent Chinese physician has developed a great clinical center with one great advantage over most Western hospitals: a cheerful atmosphere, a sense of almost musical harmony. There Dr. Li and his colleagues minister to Hong Kong's rich and poor alike. (Since my first visit to Hong Kong, Dr. Li's hospital has been expanded considerably; also, he has established a medical foundation for medical education, research, and charitable services.)

I had lunch in a private office with him, Dr. Li Shu-Pui, who is Dr. Li Shu-Fan's brother and who shares his medical responsibilities, and his nurse, Miss Pon, engaging in lively conversation as we were served delicious prawns, chicken curry with the ever-welcome boiled rice, and for dessert succulent mangoes, accompanied by the inevitable tea. Afterwards, my congenial colleague took me in his deluxe American car to White Jade, his mansion on Victoria Peak, where so

201

few Chinese have succeeded in rubbing elbows with the self-appointed British elite.

Dr. Li Shu-Fan's mansion reminds me of Dr. Axel Munthe's Villa San Michele in Capri and of Somerset Maugham's Villa Mauresque in Cap Ferrat on the French Riviera. What a remarkable coincidence that the three most beautiful villas I have visited in the world, each with a breathtaking view, belonged to three famous physicians who were also writers—Maugham, Munthe, and Li Shu-Fan!

From Dr. Li Shu-Fan's villa one can see the bay of Hong Kong, the city of Victoria, Kowloon, the New Territories, the islands of the bay, and the bluish mountains of Kwangtung in Red China. The villa is luxurious, combining exquisite Oriental features with the best that Western décor has to offer. But what impressed me most—even as I was startled by the bizarre mixture of costly, artistic Oriental objects of ivory, jade, crystal, precious woods, bronze, and mother-of-pearl, with all sorts of inexpensive American trinkets and souvenirs, including cowboy figures, sold in Times Square—was the combination in the library and throughout the villa of the owner's two greatest passions: gardening and hunting—roses and tigers.

In the library, botanical treatises and catalogues on rose gardening stand side by side with books on tiger hunting in Thailand, elephant hunting in Africa, leopard hunting in Java, and lion hunting in Africa. And both types of books acquire form and life in the trophy room and in the rose garden.

The doctor's entrance hall contains specimens of the wildest beasts on earth, killed by him and mounted by skilled taxidermists in positions more lifelike than those of life itself. The heads of elephants, leopards, lions, wild boars, rhinoceroses, and wild Cape buffalo gaze down from the walls with eyes that still seem to be staring at the hunter's rifle. Alongside them are pictures of the animals snapped at the moment they were killed by the physician-hunter and documents verifying the hunting feat. (On one of Dr. Li's safaris in Africa, in less than a month he bagged the Big Five: lion, leopard, elephant, rhinoceros, buffalo.) A tiger as large as a baby elephant and completely mounted almost fills an entire room, like a symbol of defiance. He looks so lifelike that one can almost smell his wet fur and see his glistening eyes, his mighty paws ready to lunge and his sharp fangs ready to sink into one's flesh: a symbol of animal force ultimately vanquished by man.

But directly on the other side of the trophy room windows is the rose garden. The garden, at an altitude of one thousand feet, overlooks the bay of Hong Kong. The perfume of the roses mingles with the soft light from the blue sky. There, more than two thousand rose bushes are cultivated with loving care by Dr. Li. In the center of the rose garden, in a beautiful pool covered with lotus blossoms and white water lilies, stands an exquisite marble nymph, the work of Conway Jones, an English sculptor of the nineteenth century. The *Lily Girl* is gazing at her naked image in the green waters of the pool. The setting is idyllic, complete with bees, butterflies, and rustling leaves that seem to echo the sounds one actually hears and those one imagines from the bay below.

In his capacity as Minister of Public Health in Sun Yat-Sen's China, Dr. Li Shu-Fan had all the lepers sheltered in a leper colony, whereas previously, under the Manchu Dynasty, they had been allowed to wander and beg in the streets. Subsequently, he tenaciously fought an epidemic of bubonic plague. He enforced the quarantine of all plague-stricken patients entering the port, instead of allowing them to return to their villages to die amid their families, as was customary. He had large iron tongs and metal receptacles placed at street corners for the daily collection of dead rats— from whose bodies infected fleas would leap onto the legs of pedestrians—and later the rats would be examined in laboratories to locate the centers of infection. He prohibited the sale of coffins without a certificate stating the cause of death. He demanded that the coolies remove the street refuse before 8 A.M., which set off a strike of these collectors. He required that the health inspector cut off the queues worn by the men (louse ridden, dangerous relics of the Manchu Dynasty), resulting in piles of cut queues at the city's entrances. He then systematized the Canton's water supply. Later, he reorganized the Kung Yee University Medical College in Canton.

Doctor Li, together with other colleagues, attended Sun Yat-Sen, who was afflicted with a cancer of the liver that was inoperable, at the hour of his death. When Dr. Li eventually returned to Hong Kong, he was asked to reorganize the hospital, now known as the Hong Kong Sanatorium and Hospital. He worked in Hong Kong during the Japanese invasion of 1941 (one century after the establishment of the colony), but after its capture he escaped, reaching Free China the day the Japanese were to have forced him to be president of the Sino-Japanese Medical Association.

Later, when he was en route to England for treatment of a duodenal ulcer (which my distinguished friend, Dr. Co-Tui, later treated and cured in New York), he was arrested in India and accused of being a Japanese spy, but freed as soon as the error was discovered!

Doctor Li leads an active life, traveling, hunting, caring for his patients, reading omnivorously in several languages, and writing his memoirs (published recently under the title of *Hong Kong Surgeon*), while still having a busy social life among both the Britons and Chinese. But nothing makes this hero of medicine and of life so happy as to spend several hours in the sunshine of his rose garden, where we both sat for a long while chatting about all those things that, because they are part of the elemental and the eternal, bring men close together, such as flowers, birds, the sea, children, books, and music.

Dragons and Drugs

This remarkable man and famous physician, however, is the exception in Hong Kong. The Chinese city is as far removed from the British city, socially and economically, as tigers and roses are in actual life.

The Chinese city spans the lower bay level part of the island of Hong Kong, Kowloon, the adjacent islands, and the New Territories.

In Hong Kong are located the indescribably poor quarters of the destitute Chinese, their winding streets forming an undecipherable labyrinth. These Chinese are neither Nationalists, as are those in Taiwan, nor Communists as those in China. In Hong Kong the Chinese are simply Chinese. They preserve therefore their fantastic, poetic traditions. One night I saw in the gutter of a Chinese street countless little fires glowing like will-o'-the-wisps. The street shone like a candle-lit altar. They were commemorating, I learned, Yu Lan, the Chinese Feast of All Souls. During the Moon Festival all the store windows display cakes and pastries shaped in bizarre forms in honor of the full autumn moon. Once a year, in celebration of an ancient legend, thousands of Chinese on the ninth day of the ninth month will climb to the highest peak they can find and spend the day there.

Some of the other charming festivals are: Chinese New Year; Ching Ming, the Chinese "Easter," dedicated to paying respects to the graves of ancestors; the Dragon Boat Festival, when rice cookies wrapped in mulberry leaves are eaten; the Maiden's Festival in honor of the goddess of love; and the festivals celebrated in Shatin, at the Temple of the One Hundred Thousand Gilded Buddhas.

Parallel to these festivals are the Chinese superstitions. Business fluctuations in Hong Kong are so unpredictable that they would make even the most consummate statistician despair, for the Chinese are ardent believers in lucky and unlucky days. Nothing can induce them to do business or go shopping on certain days because they are supposed to be unlucky. There are days when water, which in Hong Kong is more precious than aged cognac, is hardly consumed merely because these days are deemed to be unlucky for taking a bath. Suddenly one will see thousands of Chinese burying garbage that had been piling up, because, according to tradition, it is a lucky day for burying garbage.

Another superstition is known as *fung shui* and deals with the most felicitous position for a house. Experts advise proprietors on how, when, and where the house should be built, it being considered extremely lucky to build it in the highest part of a valley, overlooking water, for then the house is a sort of stopper for the bottle formed by the valley, with the luck-bestowing waters passing through the neck of that bottle.

Once, a syndicate, openly ignoring the customs of *fung shui,* built a bank with the front façade wider than the rear, which according to this superstition is unlucky, because this funnel shape is an invitation for both good fortune and money to escape through the back door. Eventually the bank had to close, because the people were afraid to deposit their money in it. Upon occasion, luck assumes the guise of straw umbrellas or of hats, such as the mushroom-like hats or wide straw hats, fringed in black cloth, of the Hakkas.

I wanted to see "the other face" of Hong Kong, and so I visited the Chinese quarters in both Hong Kong (including Wainchai, the microcosm where Suzie Wong lived and loved) and Kowloon. In the Middle Ages the last emperor of the Sung Dynasty sought refuge in Kowloon when the advancing Mongols entered southern China mounted on frothy-mouthed steeds (the same Mongols who used to eat raw meat pressed beneath their horse saddles) and brandished swords as large as a guillotine blade.

Forever disguised as a perpetual festival for the fun-seeking tourist, the Chinese quarters of Hong Kong and Kowloon, despite their daytime picturesqueness and their gay evening lanterns, still fail to conceal the filth and misery of their tens of thousands of beggars. The quarters are a combination beehive, stable, pigpen, and dung heap. And yet they have all the poetry of the exotic. A multitude of shops, flying pennants, and banners embellished with commercial signs, which to those who cannot read Mandarin look like calligraphic flourishes and musical notes, offer the bargain-hungry tourist everything imaginable, from hairpins to jade. There are old men who look as though death, too busy to collect them, had passed them by, and children who already have a millenary look stamped on their little faces. Everywhere, old and young, with chopsticks that carelessly touch anything and everything besides the mouth, eat loathsome looking black concoctions, boiled rice, or noodles (the latter possibly introduced to Venice by Marco Polo).

Food stores display the incredible assortment of ingredients that go into Chinese dishes: smoked ducks hanging in clusters from doorways, numerous jars with inky sauces, stacks of dry fish, sharks' fins, swallows' nests, thin and thick noodles, eggs in vinegar, and dark-blue, almost black, eggs that have been preserved in lime for about two months, a supreme delicacy in the Chinese cuisine. The clerks, clad in loose pajama-like pants and hanging shirts, sit round little wooden tables gulping down boiled rice with chunks of dried fish. The air is aflutter with the whir of electric fans. You know when you are approaching a pharmacy because it is heralded by smells as indescribable as are the contents of their windows: jars containing intestinal worms as large as the Loch Ness monster, flanked by advertisements of remedies that will instantly kill the monsters, colored vials of innumerable medicinal concoctions, jars with more herbs than one knew ever existed, and bottles that may contain the teeth of a "dragon," the tail of a lion, or other magical remedies. Indeed, should anyone doubt how lucrative the apothecary business can be among the Chinese, let him promptly visit the Tiger Balm gardens, where I had been the day before.

When I mentioned to Dr. Li Shu-Fan that I wanted to visit these gardens, he said with a smile that he would gladly send his car to take me there, but that he preferred to show me his villas. (In my later trips to Hong Kong he was again a perfect host whether aboard his yacht or at his magnificent villa Green Jade in Kowloon.) The Tiger Balm gardens are the fruit of the fortune made by one Aw Boon Haw, a Chinese shopkeeper who "discovered" a miracle salve called Tiger Balm. Actually it is nothing more than a mentholated ointment. But Aw Boon Haw's inspired charlatanism turned it into a gold mine. He invested the profits from the balm in several lucrative enterprises and today his family owns the English-language newspaper, the *Hong Kong Tiger Standard*. Ironically enough, when Aw Boon Haw was stricken with rheumatism, he had to seek Dr. Li Shu-Fan's medical assistance, for the much publicized power of his salve failed even its discoverer.

The gardens are fantastically bizarre. If a team of paranoiac surrealistic architects had combined their talents, they could not have improved upon it. They are

a combination of Disneyland, Coney Island, Copen-
hagen's Tivoli Gardens, and other amusement parks.
Aw Boon Haw's residence, crammed with priceless
treasures, still stands in the middle of the gardens. The
gardens are the work of a psychotic and translate his
disturbed mental world as scientifically as the ink blots
translate schizophrenia in a Rorschach test.

The Tiger Balm gardens contain innumerable towers
and pagodas, huge flying tigers, winged elephants, and
fire-spitting dragons, all of them rendered in plaster or
cement and painted in such outlandish colors that the
entire park looks like a Technicolor nightmare, or like
the mad drawings of the offspring of paranoiac giants.
There are also temples, castles, and huge boats standing
alongside supernatural people and jungle beasts, cowboys, a towering Uncle Sam, caricatures of political personalities, and choruses of angels and ballerinas. A
dream had warned Aw Boon Haw that, once he ceased
making additions to his gardens, he would die, whereupon the credulous shopkeeper kept on adding barbarous decorations and pavilions to the gardens until his
death.

But to the poor a visit to the gardens is a true festival.
In their childlike delight is combined their admiration
for the fantastic spectacle with their mystical worship
for the creator of the gardens. In the distant horizon
the waters of the bay glimmer quiet and serene in their
incandescent blue.

Symphony With Chopsticks

But it is time for me to have lunch. There are three main styles of cooking in Hong Kong. The Chinese cuisine of the north is famous for its Peking duck, which is roasted whole until the skin is golden crisp and crackling and is served with a white unfermented bread, and also for its Mongolian-style lamb, roasted over charcoal or on a spit. This is known as the Mandarin style of cooking and is preferred by many wealthy families.

In the south, the cuisine is Cantonese (and Fukien) style, which has become popular in the United States with its sweet and sour pork, egg rolls, egg fu yung, chop suey, and other dishes. The third style of cooking is Shanghai, which is lighter than the Mandarin and sweeter.

From among these varied styles of cooking, one can choose a Peking soup with mushrooms and fried rice, swallows' nest soup, chicken and mushroom soup, or a pork and cucumber soup. Among the numerous meat and fish dishes there are such delicacies as barbecued duck, Peking, Cantonese, or Szechwan style; diced chicken with nuts and fried peppers flanked by chicken livers; pork with green peppers; beef in oyster sauce; fried shrimp in hot chili sauce, Peking style; fried sharks' fins; fish marinated in vinegar; crabs and lob-

212

ster with egg; fried bamboo shoots with sautéed cabbage and mushrooms; or fried rice, Cantonese style.

A typical Cantonese menu offers soup (which figures on all menus), sliced beef in oyster sauce, fried chicken balls and vegetables, pork chops with bean sauce, fried *garoupa,* a local fish, or sliced pork with mushrooms. A Peking menu offers fried shrimp with chili sauce, sweet and sour pork with tomato sauce, abalone, stew with asparagus, a yellow stuffed fish in wine sauce, and pressed duck with mushrooms. A Shanghai menu includes fried shrimp, fried eel, grilled fishtails, diced chicken with nuts, and steamed pork and vegetables. A Szechwan menu contains sliced pork with green peppers, diced chicken with red peppers, fried shrimp with chili sauce, creamed Chinese cabbage, and four varieties of meat. And always the inevitable tea. The cooking is nutritious, with a variety of flavors that confuses the palate but is light, quickly and easily digested, and moderately priced.

There is a very appetizing dish called Beggar's Chicken, a specialty of one of the lesser known schools of Chinese cuisine. This dish is cooked in a unique way: a chicken stuffed with cabbage, water chestnuts, and other ingredients is wrapped in lotus leaves and coated with clay. It is baked until the clay turns black; then the clay is cracked open, and the succulent chicken, which has been cooking in its own juices, is removed intact, ready to be served.

For lunch I chose a colorful Chinese restaurant on

213

Queens Road. An elevator takes me to the third floor.
In a large square room some one hundred Chinese are
seated at wooden and marble tables. Most of them are
in shirt sleeves, for the heat is oppressive, some wear
jackets over pajama bottoms, others are completely clad
in wrinkled pajamas. All are busily devouring their
lunch. The noise is indescribable. Eating for them is a
noisy affair, almost as if the food were the score of a
military march and their lips, tongues, and teeth the
wind instruments.

The only women present are the waitresses, clad in
blue or black pajamas, and several young girls, fourteen years old or less, who, carrying huge trays laden
with covered serving dishes, weave their way among
the tables. I wait for half an hour before I am finally
handed a menu. The waitress' brow is beaded with
perspiration. On her young face, the eyes and mouth
are three straight narrow openings, like that in a coin
bank. She asks me several questions which I do not
understand. No one in the restaurant speaks English.
I decide to take direct action. I reach over to one of the
trays carried by a young girl, who looks like an angel
painted by a Chinese Murillo, and lift the cover off
one of the serving dishes. Steam pours forth as from
one of Beelzebub's ovens. A dozen roast squabs stare
at me with such reproachful eyes that I quickly replace
the cover. And now a troop of girls surround me, their
dainty arms sagging under the tremendous trays piled
with covered dishes. I serve myself some sliced beef

and duck, cubed roast pork, boiled prawns, and, from a smoking wooden bowl, steamed sea food. Automatically I am served green tea and a bowl of boiled rice.

Once again my relationship with chopsticks is resumed, and within a few minutes I am stabbing away at the meat and sea food. If only we Westerners would imitate the Chinese and bring the food bowls closer to our chins, the food would not drop from our chopsticks. The act, although hardly elegant, is extremely practical. The Chinese of Hong Kong, like the Japanese, always eat with chopsticks. Forks and knives are nonexistent on their tables. The Chinese, however, use porcelain spoons for their soup, instead of chopsticks, as do the Japanese. Later, in Bangkok, I would see people eating with little metal forks as well as with porcelain spoons.

For dessert I am brought a bunch of *litchis*, a subtle-tasting white pulpy fruit with a spiked reddish-brown shell. The bill is remarkably low. I leave deafened by the incredible noise, a combination of laughter, stentorious breathing, shouts, and the gunfire-like rattling of plates from the kitchen. Indeed, the most typical thing about Chinese dining is not the smells and tastes, but the sounds. The crisp, roasted skin of Peking duck crunches and crackles as you eat it. Moreover, the Chinese make every conceivable noise while they eat. In the presence of soup, rice, and noodles, they breathe heavily, swallow noisily, smack their lips, puff, whistle, snort, and blissfully gargle, as if they had discovered a new dimension in gastronomy, one unknown to Westerners: sound.

The Other Side of Kowloon

I go out into the street and cross by ferry to go to the poor section of Kowloon. I see coolies with bamboo poles slung on their shoulders at either end of which are balanced trays, bowls, plates, and teapots, containing food being delivered to homes, offices, workshops, and stores. Rickshas trot by, drawn by the calloused feet of coolies, their backs half covered with rags, their faces contracted with exertion. I see Chinese women clad in black pajamas, but scarcely any white people.

I see a shop where brightly colored paper cutouts are sold depicting everything that a dead man may need in the life hereafter. I watch several families buying furniture, rickshas, little houses, clothing, food, rice, and tea, all in bright cutouts, to be offered to their mourned departed ones. Very likely the deceased ones had been mourned for forty days by professional mourners clad in white-hooded robes; white being the Chinese color for mourning. The shop even sells fake Hong Kong dollars, and the families buy them by the millions to offer to their dead by the simple method of burning the money to make sure they will get it.

The dark-green streetcars of Hong Kong do not go to these quarters. This is a world that grows increasingly poorer with time—a world of hive-like dwellings, of children rolling in the gutter, of baskets of spoiled vegetables and rotting meats heaped upon stands in front of filthy shops, of beggars and rogues, a world with lots of noise but little laughter, of much movement but little activity, of many souls but wretched bodies.

At the extreme end of Kowloon are the dwellings of the refugees and of the poorest of the poor. These are the "homes" of those who have escaped from Communist China—about two million since 1949—and from other neighboring areas. (It is claimed that from fifteen to twenty million persons in all have escaped from China, North Korea, and North Vietnam.) These poorer sections are often described, in willful blindness to reality, as a world where people live in complete freedom, with no rent to pay, no obligations to fulfill. They neglect to mention that these people often have no roofs over their heads, nor food for their hungry bellies. The refugees arrived here by various means: swimming, hiding under sacks in carts traveling from Kwangtung, or under the boards of sampans, or holding onto a rope hanging from a Chinese junk. Their improvised huts are made of discarded wooden crates or of sacking, to which the more fortunate ones have added a small metal roof made from empty gasoline containers.

They are really hovels piled one on top of the other on the mountainside, holes in the rock as dark as caves, harboring not only numerous families so painfully visible to the eye but also invisible deadly diseases. When it rains, these houses become sponges drenched with the mud and filth that pours down the mountainside.

Sometimes these are not human habitations. They do not have the dignity and cleanliness of the shacks I have seen in the tropics, in Jamaica and Panama. They are dens and burrows that even animals would scorn. They smell of rot and excrement. From time to time, a fire destroys them (like the one on Christmas Eve of 1953, in Shek Kip Mei, which left fifty thousand refugees shelterless) and wood, sacking, cans, and trash must be collected again to rebuild these hovels. Inside the shacks spared by the fire, as many as twenty people sleep on a floor that can barely hold four. There are garbage and latrines everywhere and their stench permeates everything. Occasionally a family is lucky enough to find a job that pays a few cents, and then the smell of incense cones and of fried lard rises from their hovel.

This tragic world, of mothers nursing babies who are born looking a hundred years old; of lone old people who spend their days without moving, without seeing, waiting for death; of children fighting, with strips of tin can as sharp as blades, over a lump of rice that has been thrown into the garbage—this tragic world cannot even be seen by the fortunate ones from the aristocratic heights of Victoria Peak. Let me add, in all justice, that the government of Hong Kong conscientiously does as much as possible in a most humanitarian way to cope with an impossible situation, and subsidies are given to some of the poor. New apartment houses for refugees are continuously being built in Hong Kong, some of which can house two thousand people in a single building, but even in them space is still so limited that sometimes up to five persons sleep in one bed. However, the situation has been improving steadily through the welfare work of official and private organizations.

Continuing, I go on to the New Territories. Located here are Shatin Heights with the Sai Lam Monastery; Wan Fu Shan, a rock formation that looks like a mother carrying a baby on her back; Fanling, where the British have contrived to build a golf course; the walled city of Kam Tin with its little towers; the agricultural center of Yuen Long; and Castle Peak, its bay swarming with fishing junks and sampans. And twenty miles from Kowloon stands the border line of Kwangtung province in Red China.

The land along the border is bright green with rice fields and dotted with women in lamp-shade hats and men clad in loincloths. Occasionally the sunshine sparkles on the silver of a bracelet or an ankle band, for these peasants are more fortunate than the refugees. They are able to eat. The children sometimes wear a silver wire around their necks and the young girls have colored kerchiefs on their heads. The men and women work wooden plows drawn by stony-faced, gray-torsoed water buffaloes.

The Communist border line is a mere barbed-wire fence and a handful of uniformed soldiers. The red flag with the five gold stars flutters over their heads. The other side of the border does not look any different from the side I am on. Identical rice fields stretch into the distance, with men and women clad in indigo blue tilling the land. Nearly seven hundred million people inhabit this Cyclopean nation of China. There is a great deal of movement from incoming and outgoing trucks laden with goods from Red China or Hong Kong. Some old Chinese men, dressed in black silk and with an air of importance about them, cross the frontier, each carrying a pagoda-shaped cage with a spry little bird singing (in Chinese no doubt) cheerfully inside.

Night has fallen. The sky over Hong Kong is aglitter with stars. I return to Kowloon and from there slowly stroll toward the bay of Hong Kong. The Peninsula Hotel is as brightly lit as a Christmas tree. I am back again in the world of roses, the world of five o'clock tea and cocktails at seven, of garden parties and cricket matches, of dinner at the club and dancing until dawn.

But only half an hour away is a world in which thousands of human beings are relentlessly stalked by poverty even as a hungry tiger is stalked by hunters in the jungle.

The library of my Chinese colleague is symbolic: roses and tigers.

Atop Victoria Peak, beneath the pale glitter of the stars, the roses sleep their perfumed slumber. Close by, too close for comfort, the hungry tigers lie awake, perhaps sniffing the scent of the unattainable roses.

SHADOWS IN THE NIGHT
OF HONG KONG

NIGHT IS SLOWLY DESCENDING upon Hong Kong. Two young Chinese girls, one from Shanghai and the other from Canton, are my guides. Both are refugees in Hong Kong, where they have had the good fortune to find employment with a local tourist agency. One of the girls happened to be free this evening and decided to accompany the other. They are close friends and treat each other with intimate but respectful affection. Lena Chenn, the girl from Shanghai, speaks Mandarin, and Ling Chee, from Canton, speaks Cantonese. Unable to understand each other in their own languages, they have adopted pidgin English as their *lingua franca* for talking between themselves.

Lena Chenn wears a tightly fitted black silk *cheong-sam,* with a high neck and side slits up to the middle of her thighs. Her body, slight, ephemeral, vaguely formed, is that of a not fully developed adolescent. Her braided jet black hair hangs down her back, accentuating her sprightly, nervous air like that of an impatient pony. She is dark complexioned and has the smallest eyes I have ever seen, like mustard seeds, and a radiant smile that lights up her face like a festival lantern.

Ling Chee, tall and slender, is dressed in an amethyst tunic and black pants. The only adornments she wears are the metal agency badge, which her friend also wears, and a silver pin over her heart. Her hair is an ebony beehive high on her head. She is fair skinned and has a round, delicate face, with great, dark, honey-colored eyes that intensify her sweet smile. One of the girls is like a princess out of an ancient Chinese legend; the other, a yellow rose from an exotic garden.

There is nothing mystifying about China's language problem, one I witness whenever the girls try talking to each other in their native dialects. Although Mandarin, the language of the old Manchu court, is spoken in four-fifths of China, which means it is a language used by more people today than any other in the world, there are at least seven other Chinese dialects whose speakers cannot understand one another.

There are three varieties of Mandarin: Nanking, the southern; Chengtu, the western; and Peking, the northern. Since so many dialects are spoken along the coast of China, the first foreigners to visit there believed that a different language was spoken in every part of the country. However, there is no more difference in the Mandarin spoken in Peking and Kunmin, which are about a thousand miles apart, than there is in the English spoken in Texas and Alaska. And, fortunately, the written language is uniform throughout China.

We are on our way to Aberdeen Bay, where we plan to have dinner. The bay of Hong Kong lies behind us now, with its *paquebots,* sampans, barges, tugboats, and a thirty-thousand-ton transoceanic liner that looks like a giant swaying hammock. The first evening lights begin to flash red and gold upon the water. On the sampans, squatting Chinese women in flowing skirts and baggy pants are preparing the evening rice. My two guides, one of whom is driving the agency automobile, chat like happy little birds as the car speeds along the beautiful highway leading to Repulse Bay and Aberdeen.

Aberdeen, one of Hong Kong's many fishing villages, was named after its Scotch counterpart by some British traveler in a moment of jocularity, sentimentality, drunkenness, or perhaps a combination of all three. For this Aberdeen, in which some two hundred thousand Chinese (no one has counted them) dwell, is a floating village.

As in the legendary Isle of Lost Ships in the Sargasso Sea, formed of drifting ships from all the seas in the world, in Aberdeen thousands of junks, sampans, sailboats, and rowboats, none with a motor, are huddled together like a flock of sheep, forming a huge floating island in the quiet waters of the bay. In this floating village there are countless sea-food restaurants, junks converted into a paradise for those who relish watching their dinner leap, live and kicking, from the sea into the pot.

The car rolls swiftly and smoothly. Each time we make a turn in the road, now climbing, now descending the mountains, dazzling views spring up one after another, like pictures in an album: sprawling blue bays, beaches of platinum sand, sumptuous estates, tennis courts and cricket fields, blossoming gardens, and now and then people wearing immaculate white with tennis rackets or cricket bats under their arms.

In the past few days I have met many refugees with whom I promptly struck up a conversation, for anyone will talk to a foreigner, always in the hope of inveigling something out of him—money, a meal, a favor, anything—or even of robbing him. A few dollars or a stolen passport may well prove to be the redemption and salvation of a fugitive dependent on Hong Kong's dubious hospitality.

There exists in Hong Kong a transient population, mostly Chinese, although some are from other parts of Southeast Asia, ranging from Japan to Singapore, that

224

has not succumbed to Kowloon's poverty, to the wretched lot of those who live there like rabbits in their burrows. These are the people who came from well-to-do families in China and who have had a prosperous business, a good education, or a profession. There are some who still have a little money, which they watch over like a smart canary watching over his last seed. Many depend solely on their knowledge of languages, their good looks, if they are women, or their wits, if they are men.

Often these people lead a precarious existence, passing quickly from a temporary job to starvation and no roof over their heads, tricking innocent tourists, or exploiting other refugees. Many times they are driven to committing criminal acts—the law of the jungle prevails, the survival of the most cunning, the strongest, the cruelest. Some of these are the people who get tourists drunk at night in order to rob them, who, if necessary, will not hesitate to beat them up, cut their faces with a razor blade or a piece of glass, or fracture their skulls with a bicycle chain, a bottle, or a sand-filled sock. Once they have the victim's money, jewels, or passport, they abandon him in a dark alley or toss him into the bay.

All the impecunious refugees have the same attitude toward life. There is no hope or future. They cannot return to China, from which fear made them flee, the fear of being shot or imprisoned as anti-Communists or out of some personal vengeance, or perhaps they could not withstand the life of misery subsequent to the confiscation of their property or the loss of their jobs. They cannot leave Hong Kong because they have no passport or money, and because no country would admit them. They are loathe to remain in Hong Kong, partly in fear of the slaughter of refugees that will take place the day China might occupy Hong Kong, and partly because they can barely survive here from one day to the next, ever hungry and ever fearful. Their only hope is to get some money somehow or a passport that they can either sell or use themselves in order to be smuggled into America, Thailand, Japan, or some other country where they can try to start a new life.

Meantime, until this almost unattainable object is attained, refugees and fugitives comprise most of Hong Kong's nocturnal fauna. Nights in Hong Kong are not stars in the sky and lights on the ground. These are only the backdrop. Nights in Hong Kong are the human shadows that, filled with desperation, maraud in the dark.

Lena Chenn tells me that she was married to a Chinese merchant from Peking. With the advent of Communism, he divorced her for being anti-Communist and abandoned her and their only child. She shows me the child's picture. He has a ferocious-looking Mongolian face. According to her, he is the living image of his father. When Lena Chenn realized that she and her son were going to starve to death, she used the last of her savings to pay a professional refugee smuggler, who got them across the frontier hidden in a cart, under sacks of rice and cages containing pigs and ducks.

In Hong Kong Lena Chenn went through some very difficult times at first. Frankly she tells me that she had no other recourse than to offer herself to men. Through one of these men she had met Ling Chee, who was working in a tourist agency and helped her to get an occasional job as guide once she knew Hong Kong. Lena's knowledge of English and French, learned during happier times in Peking, proved useful in getting this work. She now shares a tiny apartment in Kowloon with Ling Chee, and her job allows her to send her boy to school.

When Lena Chenn talks about her future, her gay face becomes clouded. For her there is no future. The struggle becomes more difficult each day. One never knows when one will lose one's job and finding another is almost impossible. She earns barely enough for food, clothes, and her son's school fees. Once a month she and her son go to see an American movie, and she dreams about living in a country where the houses are tall glittering towers and the people drive cars as big as battleships. What an impossible dream! Hong Kong is a nightmarish mousetrap from which she can never escape.

Ling Chee is less pessimistic, but she has no illusions about leaving Hong Kong. She was a chemistry student in Shanghai at the outbreak of the Communist revolution. Her parents, wealthy, powerful, and enemies of the new regime, were assassinated in Shanghai. Greedy relatives had gained control of her family's property and had thrown her out on the street, fearing the regime's vindictiveness if they allowed her to live with them. Her ambition, now that she has a job (which she got through one of her male friends, whom she stopped seeing when his wife returned to the city), is to save enough money to resume her chemistry studies.

Ling Chee talks like a learned old man and is eager to meet a *chun-tzu,* Confucius' term for the superior being, the gentleman, the foundation of ancient China's ethical code. She is well versed in Taoism, the doctrine of Lao-Tzu, the path of quietism, and, like her friend, is a Buddhist. She frankly admits that if she lost her job, she would resort to the way of life practiced by most Chinese refugee girls in Hong Kong, although that sort of life terrifies her, because of its inevitable "occupational hazards": disease, pregnancy, jail, or being stabbed and then drowned in the bay. But, with luck, Ling Chee hopes to obtain a chemistry degree, get a job in a factory in Hong Kong, and some day make the leap across the Pacific toward the land of promise.

The Magic Bay

We cross the little streets of Aberdeen, which are bustling with Chinese buying food for dinner or bartering all sorts of merchandise, for bartering takes precedence over buying in this village. And, finally, Aberdeen Bay spreads out before us like a fan of lights.

The surrounding hills are cluttered with dark huts hanging from the mountainside, like the dishes and bundles from a coolie's pole. The blue-gray waters of the bay, greasy with oil and refuse, are set aquiver by the first evening lights. More than a floating village, this is a bay carpeted with boats.

As far as the eye can see there are sampans and junks of all sizes and shapes, a vast forest of masts, rods, and poles that soar upward past the sails of the junks. Such is the profusion of boats, which often are joined to one another by strips of wood, gangplanks, oars, ropes, or nets, that one cannot see the water; one can only visualize it. This village, however, is in continual flux. It is a fluid village, a fishing Venice with perpetually appearing and disappearing waterways.

The movement is ceaseless. Small boats, sampans, and junks are constantly trying to go heaven knows where, pushing and squeezing their way through the other boats, like a person pushing his way through the milling crowds in the lobby of a movie house.

Lena parks the car near the water. Many lights now dot both land and sea—kerosene and oil lamps, torches, and candles. The clamor and confusion are incredible. The air smells of salt and rotting wood, cooked fish, damp rope and sails, human waste, incense, and unwashed flesh.

We are accosted by a group of pretty girls wearing

colorful pajamas and big coolie hats and carrying long oars. They all clamor to take us in their sampans to one of the three big floating restaurants swaying to and fro on the far side of the bay. Laughing, shouting, and pushing one another, they take us by the arm and lead us toward their sampans. We choose one of the girls, as pretty as a flower, but as soon as we climb aboard her sampan, she, bursting with laughter, jumps back on the dock, while a disheveled old woman with a toothless smile grabs the oars and begins rowing toward the floating restaurants. Our pretty flower-like girl has rejoined the other pretty girls who are already searching for more customers. These girls never do any rowing. They are the bait used by old women rowers, who pay the girls a few coins for each customer they bring in.

Propelled by the ancient crone, who wears blue pajamas and a straw hat as wide as a baby's cradle, our sampan quietly glides between junks and boats, where, by candlelight, the fishermen's families are crowded together around the stoves upon which their dinner is cooking.

Each one of these sampans and junks is not a boat but a miniature world. The boats are the homeland of these people, for on them they are born, raised, married, bear children, and die, beneath the sun and the moon, the winds and the rains, in oven-like heat and freezing hurricanes. There, while still practically in diapers, they learn how to fish, and soon after learning

230

to walk on the deck they learn to row. There they are weaned from the breast to raw fish and crabs, and learn as children how to perform every one of the chores that make up life on the boats. As soon as they are old enough, they marry girls and boys from neighboring sampans, have children, work like oxen, and if lucky are loaned enough money by one of the big fisheries to buy a junk, on the condition that they sell all their fish to the fishery at low prices.

Entire families, including parents and grandparents, live aboard the junks, which serve both as cradle and deathbed. There, old people, grownups, young people in whose glands, and the rudders they handle, the future lies, and children live together with their hired seamen, all sleeping side by side on deck, sharing their food and often their families. Many of them have never been in Hong Kong, and their whole lives are spent beneath the sky, in a floating world on the sea, at the mercy of the angels of the winds and of storms.

We reach the junk restaurant and climb aboard by means of a rickety gangplank. The junk is something out of a Joseph Conrad novel, with huge sails and two decks. The hold contains the cabins of the owners, whose children are everywhere, playing with "atomic" rubber guns. The lower deck is reserved for the kitchen and the help. The upper one is the restaurant.

We now spend a delightful interval of waiting, watching Aberdeen Bay, whose waters slowly become spangled with the lights of junks and sampans while the

231

sky overhead is spangled with stars. We crack water-melon seeds between our teeth and sip jasmine and chrysanthemum tea while studying the menu. On the stern of the boat, several old Chinese men, squatting around low, square wooden tables, are playing *mah-jongg* with much clattering of the ivory pieces, and an invisible radio is playing music broadcast from Hong Kong.

We are now enveloped by the pleasant smell of cook-ing from the floating world around us. Each sampan is a platter of fried fish, a bowl of steaming rice, a cup of aromatic tea. The owner of the restaurant smilingly invites me to choose our own live fish from bamboo and rattan cages kept half-submerged in the water of the bay. We choose shrimp, lobsters, crabs, and eels, all of which a Chinese waiter promptly lifts from the cage and, in barely three deft movements of the hands, kills and cleans. They are then sent to the cook, who pre-pares a fish soup, an oriental bouillabaisse even more delicious than that of Marseilles. Steaming on the plat-ter set before us are shrimp stewed in their shells, fried crabs, fried fish of the day, fried *garoupa* and abalone, and slices of still another fish with mushrooms. We wash it all down with a warm, yellow Chinese wine, poured from porcelain jugs into tiny porcelain cups.

While consuming the succulent dinner, our eyes wan-der over the world around us, where two hundred thousand Chinese in junks and sampans are eating more or less the same food as we are, for the sea is democratic. Our dinner ends with tea and boiled rice, both food and ritual, followed by almond cookies and glazed sweets, which are not as sweet as the magic of the night silently hovering over the still unfurled sails and around the candles glowing, like the souls of children in heaven, on Aberdeen Bay.

The entire bay was bedizened with light, a brilliantly gemmed eve of a festival, with thousands upon thousands of lights softly flickering in the dark.

As a child, in my native Cartagena in Spain, I remember people filling bowls with water, pouring a finger of olive oil on top of the water, and then putting a round piece of cork with a wax wick inserted in it on the oil. When the wick was lit, it cast a soft light all night long.

And now, here in Aberdeen Bay, I am reminded of the *mariposas,* or butterflies, as those lamps were called because like luminiscent wings their light gently fluttered over the serene face of a saint on a wooden or canvas painting and on the angelical faces of sleeping children. Here they are before my eyes, hundreds of thousands of them like a child's fairy-tale dream. A sea of butterflies. I see them on junks and sampans, lighting the lined faces of women worn out from the day's work; the Buddha-like faces of old men asleep with their eyes wide open, pipes hanging from their emaciated hands; the faces of young couples sitting with their feet hanging over the water, dreaming perhaps of one day having a sampan of their own or a

233

little solitude, which they will probably never have;
the faces of children trustingly asleep on rolls of rope.
I see the lights illuminating now a sail, now a basket,
a heap of fish nets, an extinguished lantern, a bowl of
leftover rice swarming with insects, or an abandoned
toy. The thousands of flickering lights flutter like butterflies over the floating village, where poverty, disease,
and filth are for a few hours concealed behind the
nocturnal fairyland background.

Enchanted by the bejeweled night, I feel an urge to
associate myself symbolically with it. Taking a small
candle from a wooden box on the table, I light it. The
shadowed deck of the floating restaurant boat glows
with the scarlet radiance from the wax vesta. The tiny
flame shines for a long time. In a sampan nearby some
children suddenly stop playing with an old man clad
in white pajamas and stare fascinated at the sputtering
light. Suddenly the children, followed by the wizened
old man, begin jumping from boat to boat until they
reach my side. Their big, innocent eyes gaze at the
red-flamed wax light burning on my table. The old
Chinese mutters something to Lena who is standing
nearby chatting with the boat proprietor. I ask her what
he said, and in the words translated for me there is
distilled all the melancholy wisdom of his race.

"He said," Lena explains, "that from the distance
your flaming light looked like a fallen star, but close
up it is nothing but a burning candle in front of a
lonely man."

My little flame goes out, but those around me will continue to burn for several hours, until sleep overcomes man. And then the entire bay will repose in a darkness broken only by the stars in the sky. Finally, the pearly light of dawn will announce the supreme butterfly of all, the sun, heralding another day on Aberdeen Bay. Then, in unison, the junks and sampans will mobilize and set out to transport bales of cotton, cases of bottles, bundles of vegetables, sacks of rice, sugar and flour, crates of cabbages, drums of glycerine, and bolts of paper, or they will sail out to sea in search of fish, which is both food and merchandise. At sunset they will return, their nets bulging with fish flailing and flashing like thousands of broken fragments of mirror, the live silver of the sea.

My two charming guides, who for an evening have forgotten—at least partially—their problems, and I head back for Hong Kong. The lights of Hong Kong's bay twinkle like fireflies. The darkness accentuates the girls' Mongolian cheekbones, and their skin turns the color of honey. In the distance the glowing ferryboats silently glide across the bay.

Hong Kong displays like jewels its emerald, ruby, topaz, sapphire, and aquamarine lights. The girls are still cracking dry melon seeds between their teeth, a favorite pastime of the Chinese. More boats loom out of the distant bay, *wallah-wallahs,* cargo ships, tramps, cruisers. Their flags are invisible, but their lights trace colored mosaics on the still waters.

At this hour, thousands of refugees perhaps are being smuggled into the city. They are the backwash deposits from the regime of Mao Tse-Tung, fugitives from Communism. Between twenty thousand and one hundred thousand join the Hong Kong beehive each year, trusting, hoping, dreaming, anticipating, and always ready to do anything and to anybody.

By now I have explored not only the city but the night of Hong Kong and Kowloon. I have been to the night clubs, such as the Princess Garden, the Highball, the Mandarin, and the Faut Shau. I have also been to the Chinese harbor cafés where *mah-jongg* is played and where pale, tight-lipped, glassy-eyed Chinese offer you unspeakable vices in alien tongues. I have walked through the dark alleys of Kowloon and Hong Kong, their darkness punctuated by the even darker shadows that people them, and I have strolled along the shores of the bay, which are dotted with small cafés, as in Wangchai, from which pour the inevitable radio music, voices, and laughter that has not a happy but a sad and sometimes even sinister ring to it. During these walks I have spoken to many people, for at night they are more disposed to air their conflicts and neuroses, their problems and emotions.

On the streets one sees good-looking Chinese refugee girls cruising around like taxi drivers but in elegant private cars, offering passers-by their physical wares. Many accept, some only to awaken the following day in the gutter or an alley, wounded, penniless, and without a passport. Others never awaken and are fished out of the bay days later by vociferous Chinese.

Policemen are seldom seen, only men and women standing around, as though waiting for something, smoking cigarettes, their usually young-looking, waxen faces smiling diabolically in the glow from their cigarettes. Sometimes they stand in the doorways of the cafés, and the neon lights project a blood-red or arsenic-green glare upon their crafty faces. A coolie trots by, exhausted from dragging his cross—the ricksha—still hoping to find a passenger.

In the more modern night clubs, there are women dancing to American music on small dance floors, while at the tables there is a steady flow of Chinese wine and Scotch whisky. Amid the birdlike flutter of fans one sees there almond-eyed Annamese women, so small and slim that they are more like the stenographic counterpart of a woman; Indian women as impassive and sculptural as statues; Japanese women as small and fragile as little birds; and Chinese women, inscrutable looking and dignified, their tightly fitted, sensuous *cheongsams* split to the middle of the thigh. The men are mostly American businessmen or merchants from India, Singapore, Thailand, Cambodia, Laos, China, or Japan. There is an air of espionage, intrigue, scheming, persecution, plotting against enemies and friends in order to obtain information and figures that are later traded for gold, or for favors. A strange world dwells in these semi-lighted shadows, overlooking a bay that never rests.

237

Nighttime in Hong Kong is perhaps more pregnant with palpitating threats and invisible besiegers than in any other place on earth.

As in the jungle, where the hungering beast, fangs bared and claws alert, emerges at night to seek its prey, here too a sharp-fanged, steel-nailed fauna walks the night.

Night in Hong Kong is not a night of lights and stars. It is a night of human shadows.

238

MACAO

RED SAILS ON THE CHINA SEA

Seated before me are Macao's past and future.

The first is represented by an old man with a reddish curlycue beard, a big yellowish face, the color one associates with jaundice or malaria, huge tortoise-shell glasses, and teeth almost as large. Each time his head moves there is a blinding duel of flashes between his glasses and his gold teeth. He is dressed in Western style and is sipping a glass of Madeira as dark as a villain's soul.

241

The second, seated next to the old man, is a girl in the full April of youth, with an oval porcelain face that has that unique kind of Oriental beauty, and her hair is so tightly drawn round her head that its black lustre accentuates her luminous skin. She is dressed in the Cantonese style, a black silk tunic so tightly fitted that it looks as though it had been painted on her statuesque torso. The tunic is slit up one side, revealing a lovely, polished leg and part of an ivory thigh. She is smoking a cigarette and sipping hot tea, and smoke and steam shroud her as incense shrouds a goddess on an altar.

The old man speaks in a guttural language, which I finally recognize as Portuguese interspersed with Chinese. She answers him in Chinese sprinkled with Portuguese words. He is a Portuguese *fidalgo* and she is a young Chinese student. Macao's past and future are seated before me.

Today is April 13, and I am on my way to Macao aboard the *MV Tai Loy,* a ferryboat run by the Tak Kee Shipping and Trading Company of Hong Kong. I had been anxiously looking forward to visiting that fabled Portuguese peninsula—it is actually a peninsula and not an island, as it is still called in some novels— whose vast panorama of exotic humanity has inspired innumerable novels. It was 2:30 P.M. when I boarded the *MV Tai Loy,* one of three ferries, the *SS Takshing* and the *MV Fat Shan,* making the four- or, depending on the weather, five-hour trip between the British colony of Hong Kong and the Portuguese peninsula of Macao.

I had been welcomed aboard by a Chinese steward whose uniform at one time must have been white but was now like a painter's palette, colored by all the curries, soups, and wines that had been spilled on it. He escorted me to a small but clean stateroom, where I promptly dumped my suitcase and a stack of books, and then I climbed back to the deck to walk around the little floating island that would take us to Macao across the dark-red waters of the South China Sea.

It is a warm, humid day. The haze that habitually enshrouds Hong Kong has followed us, enveloping the *MV Tai Loy* like a cocoon enveloping a silkworm. Cautiously we get under way, skillfully veering around other boats like a taxi in city traffic. Behind, ahead, and on both sides of us there is land and everywhere there are fishing and coastal boats. The sea is awesomely still, the water dark and oily, and the sky as low as the ceiling of my cabin. The *MV Tai Loy* is from Hong Kong, but the surrounding islands belong to Communist China. The junks and sampans are primarily owned by Cantonese. Starboard, the coastal escarpment of that newly arisen colossus, Red China, opens up before us like an ominously mysterious fan.

Most of the passengers aboard the *MV Tai Loy* are Chinese and Portuguese who live in Hong Kong and work in Macao, or vice versa, or else people who have been visiting their families in Kowloon or Hong Kong, or spending a short holiday in the bustling city behind us. There are few whites, and they stand together discussing business. On deck, seated on canvas chairs or on the floor, Chinese boys and girls all huddled together voraciously read books that look like texts, or soiled newspapers that look as though they had changed hands many times. There are Chinese mothers nursing their babies, who stir restlessly among the rags that cover them, like suckling pigs on a bed of soggy leaves. A Japanese scribe, constantly dipping his little brush in a tiny bottle of black ink, quickly writes on a piece of rice paper characters that bear a strong resemblance to one of Miró's "magic" paintings or to a black and white abstraction by Mondriaan. Through the open door leading to the engine room drifts the pungent smell of grease and oil, which becomes mingled with the tantalizing odor of the crew's curry and rice.

The noise is the same one hears all over the Orient, plus the screams of the sea gulls that freely sweep through the air, indifferent to all political boundaries or to the variance in the color of the skin of men. Now and then, one of them swoops down like a diving plane and quickly ascends again, swallowing the silvery fish that was too slow to escape. There are many junks with sails like shark's fins, manned by entire Chinese families who are utterly absorbed in their fishing or in steering their boats, and also sampans with membranous sails and a necklace of iridescent scum around their prows.

I sit down in a spacious *salon* with wide-open windows, and it is here that I see the old Portuguese man with the Chinese girl, whose lovely legs are exposed by her *cheongsam* in that graceful and elegant manner, peculiar to Chinese women, in which the generous display of limbs is stripped of vulgarity. (The *cheongsam* is the second most seductive garment in the Orient, with its tightly fitted lines and side slits that reveal so much, exactly the opposite of the Japanese kimono, which is the most seductive garment precisely because it reveals nothing and therefore invites one to guess everything.)

There are many other passengers smoking, drinking tea, playing *mah-jongg,* computing figures on an abacus, or just fanning themselves with big fans made of fine, yellow palm leaves or with tiny *paipais* of heavy white paper.

I am traveling a variation of the route followed by the early Christians in the Orient, who from Macao went to Japan and then to Hong Kong. The nautical Portuguese, Magellan's fellow nationals, were the first great colonial power in the Orient. After having conquered what they first called the Cape of Storms, which they later renamed the Cape of Good Hope, and having discovered the sea route to India, the great Portuguese captains of the age of discovery and conquests turned their eyes toward the flourishing kingdoms of Cathay. The Portuguese had already penetrated the Malay Peninsula long before the English settled in Singapore, the "Lion City," an island that became attached like a reptile's tongue to the Malay Peninsula, just as Hong Kong became an English appendage to the Chinese continent. The great Albuquerque, as great a soldier as a statesman, had turned Malacca into a Portuguese possession. The sea captains, however, dreamed of reaching legendary China, where, it was said, the mandarins' palaces were covered with gold and the temples of silver, coffins were made of precious metals embedded with pearls, rubies, diamonds, and sapphires, the humblest servants dressed in the finest silks, and the cemeteries were filled with rare jade endowed with miraculous healing powers.

Two years after Malacca became a Portuguese possession, Jorge Álvarez, a Portuguese who made trading trips out of Freixo de Aspada à-Cinta, was the first to enter Cathay, after a daring voyage. He was followed by other Portuguese adventurers, such as Ferñao Peres de Andrade, who were lured there by gold and all kinds of legends. Thus, a chain of Portuguese trading posts was established along the Asiatic coast line extending from India to Japan.

The *MV Tai Loy* continues on its way, now pushing toward, now circling, the islands, which loom vague and unreal in the thick warm haze surrounding us. A missionary suddenly enters the room. Small and darkened by the Asiatic sun, he wears a habit that must have been brown before it faded. Large beads of sweat form a glistening wreath around his closely shaven

246

skull, and his small, tangled, russet beard looks like mountain underbrush. He sits down in a corner and promptly withdraws to his mystical isle of prayers. As I watch him, I recall another missionary, a brave Navarrese monk who sailed from his native land with China as his goal, only to die burning with fever on the island of Sancian, St. Francis Xavier.

That was the period of heroic missionaries, valiant captains of Christ's army, armed with no other weapon than their prayers. St. Francis Xavier served Portugal in life and attained sanctity in death in the Orient. From the Straits of Malaya he went along the Asiatic coast, defying all danger in his eagerness to reach China, which was difficult for foreigners to penetrate. But he was denied his wish, dying with what he believed was the promised land visible in the distance. He had dreamed of reaching Canton and preaching the faith of Christ to the pagans. But he died just as he had reached the threshold of his heroic destiny, in a primitive hut in Sancian, alone but for the native servant who buried him. Later, grateful Portuguese hands disinterred his body, which, according to legend, had miraculously not decomposed, and carried it to Malaya, and then on to Goa, where his remains now repose beneath the flag that he served with his faith and honored with his voluntary martyrdom.

The hands of my watch seem to be competing with our ferryboat in slowness. Finally, just as the Chinese girl and the old man seem to have exhausted their topics of conversation, voices and shouts are heard. We must be approaching Macao. The Chinese girl's long legs, beautiful as two Doric columns, vanish, with a graceful flurry of her silk tunic, through the door leading to the deck.

A Chinese, his face anonymous among all the other Chinese faces, asks me for my passport and then disappears through the doorway to the engine room. Only after he vanishes do I realize almost with panic that I had handed my passport to a stranger who wore no uniform and whose face I could not recognize in a thousand years. It being too late for regrets, I try to dismiss it from my mind for the moment.

The peninsula of Macao was incorporated into Western history years after the Portuguese Jorge Álvarez, reached an amicable agreement in 1513 with the Chinese, establishing trading relations in the port of Tun Moon between the island of Lin Tin and the city of Nan Tau, a focal point for boats going to Canton from Fukien, the Philippines, Borneo, what is now Viet Nam, and the Ryukyu Islands. His work was continued in Canton two years later by Ferñao Peres de Andrade. But it was not until forty years after Jorge Álvarez' trade agreement that the Portuguese captain, Leonel de Sousa, negotiated trade agreements in southern China and in 1557 established a colony in Macao.

The peninsula of Macao and the neighboring islands were at that time a paradise for pirates on the South China Sea. The unprotected harbors offered them open asylum after their audacious forays, ship boardings, kidnappings, and plunderings. The Chinese, terrified and helpless, were afraid to sail through the waters that rightfully should have been their own *mare nostrum.* Leonel de Sousa promised to vanquish the pirates forever, and for several years fiercely fought the pirates and finally succeeded in driving them from those parts. When the emperor received the news through the Viceroy of Canton, with whom Sousa negotiated, that the valiant Portuguese had succeeded in defeating the pirates with his arm and his sword, the Son of Heaven, from his golden throne in the Forbidden City, not only gave Sousa permission to settle in Macao but permitted the Portuguese to rent. And that is how it happened that the oldest foreign trading settlement in the Far East is Portuguese.

Of course, the name of the peninsula was not Macao then. According to legend, the unnamed peninsula adopted its original name during the Yuan dynasty, when a Chinese junk from Fukien was saved from a terrible storm through the intervention of a female passenger. It was subsequently discovered that this passenger was none other than the goddess Liang Ma, who had assumed the guise of an ordinary woman. The grateful sailors raised an altar to the goddess at the entrance to the harbor. Soon the goddess' name was affectionately shortened from Liang Ma to Ah Ma, and the place was referred to as Ah Ma Kao, or Ah Ma's harbor. The Portuguese adapted that name to their own

phonetics, calling it Amacau, which was later shortened to Macau, the Anglicized form being Macao.

I am aroused from my historical reverie by the boat
whistle, whose sharp-edged blast pierces the wooden
skies. Uneasily, I look around for the mysterious Chinese who had taken my passport, while all sorts of dark
thoughts flash helter-skelter through my mind. A passport in Macao, as in Hong Kong, is one of man's most
precious pieces of property. People will even kill for a
passport, which brings as much as ten thousand dollars
on the black market.

The timely entrance of the immigration officials puts
an end to the wild drama I am improvising. One of
them tosses a pile of passports and immigration papers
on a table, as if they were rotten fish. The passengers
mill around the table. The smell of humanity as niggardly in washing as it is generous in sweating increases. The shoving people put one on guard for one's
wallet. Next to me a Portuguese man, dressed in Western clothes and with no other indication of his Oriental
ancestry except his heavy-lidded Asiatic eyes, suddenly
tells me he is a secret police inspector in Hong Kong
and that he plans shortly to visit his son who is studying in Boston. During the trip, without identifying himself, he had spoken to me about the increase of crime in
Hong Kong. Now he assures me that if one is careful
there is no danger of being robbed or killed in Macao.
The Macao police have strict orders to shoot first and
ask questions later, when they see someone who looks

as if he were ready to commit a misdeed. Macao's justice, he insists, is instant, often at rifle point and without
a trial, and the destination of all those who persist in
challenging it is the common grave.

The passports are stamped by Portuguese-Chinese officials, immaculately dressed young men, all armed to
the teeth. One of them comments on my Spanish name.
Then the passports are left in a disorderly pile on the
table, whereupon the human mass surrounding it
swoops down upon them. There is a maelstrom of
hands, each passenger grabbing a bunch of passports in
quest of his own, tossing the others on the table when
he finally finds his, to the consternation of those who
have never seen this vital document handled in such a
fashion. On our return to Hong Kong the same pro-
cedure was repeated. It is after the passports have been
stamped that the greatest danger of losing them arises.

(Later, at Don Muang airport in Bangkok, something similar, in fact worse, happened. There the passports are collected by the authorities, who then leave
them by the hundreds in a big waiting room, placed on
open wooden shelves similar to those used to display
magazines in clubs. Each traveler picks up his passport
there at his convenience, and often, I imagine, he picks
up one that is not his.)

I go out on deck. Macao looms before us like an
island—that is what it looks like—green with many
trees and busy with many junks, sampans, and boats.
The sky has now turned a deep, clear blue. A golden

251

sun like a big bright orange shines overhead. I can already see the cathedral spire soaring above the city. As the *MV Tai Loy* skirts the stone jetty that separates the outer wharf from the inner one, I suddenly have the sensation that I am arriving at a little harbor in the Levant or in Andalusia. Narrow streets climb up the hillsides, the houses have grilled windows and doors, and flower pots hang everywhere. The coast line is called Praia Grande, and prominent on it is the Hotel Riviera, the best hotel in Macao, where I was later unable to find accommodations. The whole place looks heavenly and peaceful. It is not. When I later disembark and enter the city, I find myself right back in the same maddening noise that prevails in Hong Kong.

The pier is crowded with relatives, Chinese and Portuguese, of the passengers (the excursion to Hong Kong is a family event) and when we dock they all rush aboard. There are many children swimming around the boat, clamoring for coins, which they retrieve from the water and hold between their teeth. The pier is also crowded with Chinese dressed in their national attire, mostly grimy and ragged, rickshas with their half-Portuguese half-Chinese human ponies, and policemen in impeccable white uniforms, with pistols, rifles, or machine guns under their arms.

Carrying my suitcase, I descend the plank amid the shrill, gay multitude. I look back and in the distance I see many sails and red flags. I am told that it is a fishing fleet from Communist China. Macao is a point of entry to China and the sailboats with their red flags proclaim China's presence on the sea. We are completely surrounded by the Red colossus.

For more than four hundred years the Portuguese have made of Macao a sanctuary for refugees and an altar for Christ's faith. But we live in another era now. Alongside me, the Portuguese *fidalgo* descends very slowly, but his young companion, the Chinese girl, is already running down the wharf with the swift legs of an impatient greyhound. Macao's past is still aboard. The future has already reached its destination.

ONLY TEN STEPS—
THE THRESHOLD TO CHINA

TAK MENG LOOKS AT ME WITH
eyes that are soft and shiny, like two dark plums
in the sun, and with hands as quick as those of a magician he serves me my breakfast on the sunlit terrace
of the Hotel Bela Vista in Macao. He does not look like
a servant. With his bright, smiling face and his constant skipping around my table, he combines the
sprightliness of a Pekinese dog and the agility of an
acrobat. Tak Meng has been assigned to tend to my

needs during my stay at the hotel. He is a Chinese from Macao. Like all the other Chinese I have seen here, he looks about eighteen years old but seems to have the experience of one hundred and eighteen years behind him. He is the living incarnation of China's millenary wisdom, a wisdom, however, that now includes rock-'n'-roll.

I had been awakened early in the morning by a sound I had not heard in many years, a sound unfamiliar in New York, Tokyo, and Hong Kong: the crowing of roosters. The trills and whistles of tropical birds had promptly joined the choir. After the pin-sharp attack of the shower's icy needles, I dressed, went out on the terrace, and ordered breakfast. Tak Meng quickly brought it to me, a breakfast that seemed straight out of a New York hotel kitchen: orange juice—delivered daily from Hong Kong—corn flakes, and bacon and eggs.

The hotel is still asleep. In compensation, the banyan trees, teeming with birds, are singing in the sunshine, which does not illuminate so much as permeate the landscape with a soft, albescent light. The waters of the harbor at the foot of the hill on which the hotel is located are like a hot plate of steel. The sails of sampans and junks glide in the distance against a backdrop of misty blue. There are no other sounds. Macao is still resting from its long, rowdy nocturnal life.

Returning with me to my room, Tak Meng keeps up a steady stream of conversation. He can speak Portuguese but prefers Cantonese. He can also most amusingly torture and mutilate the king's English, pidgin variety. He informs me that part of his family works in Macao and part in Canton. He often crosses the frontier to visit them or even to do small, occasional jobs in Red China. When he sees me putting away my fountain pen, pocket flashlight, and some other odds and ends in one of the table drawers, he bursts into that staccato flight of laughter typical of the Chinese.

"No wolly about put things away," Tak Meng advises. "Chinese never touch." Laughing again, he adds, "Never touch little things. Only big things."

Convulsed with laughter, he bows and vanishes, leaving behind the memory of his white jacket and jet-black hair, a walking domino. At a later point in my sojourn in Macao, I shall recall Tak Meng's symbolical words.

Dinner the night before at the Hotel Bela Vista, which is three minutes from the harbor by taxi, had been undistinguished but plentiful. Vegetable soup, fried *garoupa,* a mixed dish of not very tender lamb and beef, canned pineapple, an ordinary Portuguese wine, and coffee.

But the view compensates for the food. From the dining terrace one can see the blue waters of the harbor, gently lapping the flanks of the hill, and the brown sails of the junks inflated by the warm breeze. The vast expanse of sky overhead, whether Portuguese or Chinese, is a deep blue. The hotel is just a short distance from the sea, on a hill lined with trees and spotted with red and gray roof tops. One can hear the birds singing —they know nothing of language differences and understand each other's songs come what may.

Near the hotel I spot a school, a worn old building with a large bare yard where I see a group of girls dressed in black school uniforms. Their uniforms are those of a Catholic school, but their faces are pure Chinese. Led by the nuns, the girls are chanting Catholic prayers in Chinese, and their nostalgic chorus remains hovering over the slumbering landscape.

I spend the day exploring the city on foot and by car. My chauffeur and guide, Tsang Kau, is a Chinese who speaks both English and Portuguese. He had proudly given me his card, which on one side bears his name, address, telephone number, and the number of cars he owns, and on the reverse side, the name of Wan Man, a healer (*curandeiro*) on the Rua dos Mercadores. Tsang Kau has a yellowish complexion and a hearty schoolboy laugh, and for fifty years has been struggling to earn a living guiding tourists and chauffeuring them around. He was recommended to me by Dom Joaquín da Costa Canavarro, the owner of the Hotel Bela Vista.

Dom Joaquín is a Portuguese *fidalgo* who learned the restaurateur's trade through extensive practice in Europe and Moscow. His seventy-eight years do not appear to affect him in the least. He speaks beautiful Portuguese and eight other languages, is shaved like an English lord, and dresses in the finest clothes, like a wealthy Coimbra nobleman. He loves Macao, where he came to live thirty years ago, and which he knows backwards and forwards. He showed me the view from the hotel—the Pearl River estuary, the ocean, the Praia Grande, the ferries, fishing junks, pleasure yachts, and little boats, the island of Lantao—with obvious pride, as if it all belonged to him. He is especially proud of the Macao lighthouse, which is one of the oldest European-type lighthouses on the China coast. Its scissors-like blades of light have been cutting the dark waters of the South China Sea for a century.

Tsang Kau shows me around the city and its monuments. I have an interesting conversation on Macao's history with one of the directors of the fine official information bureau. I then seek out St. Raphael's Hospital. A venerable, ancient institution, founded in conjunction with the Holy House of Mercy in 1569, reconstructed in 1640, and extended and modernized in 1939, the hospital is famous because through it Western medicine was first introduced to China, including the use of smallpox vaccine, which replaced the old Chinese method of variolation. The hospital was the scene of a decisive episode in Chinese medical history, when the first Western medical missionaries stopped here and treated its patients. They were the first Westerners to arrive after Marco Polo and with them they brought European drugs and medical methods. The Jesuits built São Paulo do Monte, whose mighty ruins, culverins, and bronze cannon, which have now been silent for centuries, are still standing.

My tour begins where Macao's history began, with a visit to the temple of Kuan Yin, the goddess of mercy. It has a red roof, three square portals with big-bellied colored lanterns on either side, large halls, and a main altar on which stands the goddess, with eyes modestly lowered and the tight-lipped smile of an Oriental Gioconda on her face.

Four centuries ago, fishermen's huts were huddled together around the original temple, a constant prey of pirates prior to the arrival of the Portuguese. It was in this temple, in 1844, that the Chinese Viceroy Yi and Caleb Cushing of the United States met, across a stone table built expressly for the event and upon which I am now making these notes. It was here that they signed the first treaty between their respective countries, countries that today suspiciously eye each other from opposite sides of the ocean.

Another monument of historical importance is the Leal Senado, located in the heart of the city, a building in the sober seignorial style typical of Portuguese mansions, once the seat of the government and subsequently the city's Municipal Building. It houses the oldest European library in the Far East, with thirty thousand volumes slumbering in beautiful wooden bookcases carved in the style of John V by Macao artisans, who were inspired by the library of the University of Coimbra. Many literary treasures of the sixteenth and seventeenth centuries are to be found here. Over a door inside the Leal Senado, there is an inscription proclaiming that Macao is the *Cidade do Nome de Deu não há outra mais leal* in commemoration of the loyalty shown by the Portuguese of Macao to the Portuguese crown from 1580 to 1640, during Spain's occupation of Portugal. From this time the municipal government was known as the Loyal Senate, because of Macao's devotion to the mother country, so firmly proved in the times of Philip II of Spain, when Macao refused to recognize the Spanish rule over Portugal and kept the flag of Portugal flying over the peninsula.

In the Renaissance and baroque book that is Macao's architecture, the *pièce de résistance* is the ruin of St. Paul's Church. The most striking thing about this church is the fact that all that is left is its noble façade, which, from afar against the blue sky, looks as if a child had cut it out of silver and gold paper and pasted it on blue paper. As one approaches the façade of what had been a monumental church, one can see on the lowest of the three tiers four statues of Jesuit saints, among them St. Francis Xavier. On the middle level there are statues of the Virgin Mary surrounded by angels, the fountain and tree of life, of a ship and a Gorgon, of an apocalyptic monster and a skeleton. And dominating it all there is a statue of St. Paul with the dove of the Holy Spirit and a cross of Jerusalem.

But behind this façade there is nothing excepting the blue sky, the winds, and the sun's sensuous caress on the ancient rock, as though angels had ripped the building out of the ground and borne it to heaven, leaving behind only the beautiful but spectral façade as a reminder of one of Christianity's great places of worship.

Missionary work went on all during Macao's heroic epic. In a book published by one Father Cardim in Paris in 1646, he says: "Macao is renowned throughout the Orient as a storehouse of gold and silver objects, silks, pearls, and other gems, in addition to all sorts of spices and perfumes from China, Japan, Tonkin, Cochin, Cambodia, Macassar, and Solor, but above all it is renowned as the seat of Christianity in the Orient."

This was the period that witnessed the religious celebration of the news that sixty-one people from Portugal and other countries, members of a mission to Japan in 1640, had been tortured and slain by the Japanese. The celebration lasted twenty days, proof of the religious fanaticism and love of martyrdom that prevailed then. For three weeks Macao writhed in the throes of a religious festival that reached feverish heights, with artillery salvoes, *Te Deums,* display of the Sacrament, and the tolling of bells, an impassioned challenge to the ferocious pagan hordes awaiting them only a few yards away in China.

In 1562 a stone and wooden edifice reminiscent of a stable was built, after the style favored by the Portuguese pioneers. This was the Jesuit College of the Mother of God. In 1594 the college and its church, St. Paul's, began to be constructed. They subsequently suf-

fered frequent fires, which the townspeople could fight
only with buckets of water. Eventually the church of
St. Paul's was rebuilt, of which only the façade now remains. It was designed by Father Spinola and built by
Japanese Christian artisans at a cost of thirty thousand
taels of silver. The façade of St. Paul's Church is a
masterpiece of Christian belief interpreted by Japanese
artists in an Oriental atmosphere. Feeling with one's
hands the heroic stone of the ruins, darkened more by
the years of sun than by the fire that destroyed it in
1835, one cannot but visualize with deep emotion the
cathedral that once stood there in all its proud baroque
beauty and that now, like one more martyred missionary, silently bares its stone stumps to the heavens above.

At the college, inspired by the life and death of St.
Francis Xavier, missionaries trained to practice their
ministry and to face an almost inevitable martyrdom in
China, Japan, Annam, Thailand, Laos, Cambodia,
Solor, Timor, or Korea. It was truly a seminary for
martyrs! These Catholic missionaries were followed in
1807 by the Protestant missionaries, such as Robert Mor-
rison and his wife.

My tour also includes a visit to the Fort of Guia and
its lighthouse, previously mentioned, whose original
machinery, built by the Portuguese of Macao, was completely made of wood. I then pass an endless procession
of churches, some as humble as an acolyte, others as
grand as an archbishop, little churches concealed by
flowers and ivy like a pious woman by her mantilla, big

churches with the proud arrogance of a Portuguese *fidalgo*. I see statues of the heroes, martyrs, statesmen, explorers, and poets of old Portugal.

Alongside the old section of Macao is the new city, which is rapidly being built over the old ruins: the municipal swimming pool, of Olympic proportions; the modern market places of São Lourenço, Horta e Costa, and Horta da Companhia; the municipal dog shelter; the new apartment houses; the magnificent Guia Circuit, an automobile racing course; the hockey field where Macao natives have won international fame in this sport; and the tennis courts and football fields. These places form part of the setting in which the three hundred and sixty thousand inhabitants of Macao and its two adjacent islands, Taipa and Coloane, eat, play, love, struggle, live and die, an area that measures barely six square miles, one of the most densely populated areas in the world, overlooking the Chinese giant, and forty miles from Hong Kong.

But now we are on a road that winds in and out beneath the pounding sun, a road on which I have seen an ancient bus stop to let pass a chain of carts drawn by even more ancient water buffaloes.

My car stops in the middle of a road bordered by dusty trees. I walk toward the frontier. There is no one around except a few children playing in a ditch, a stray dog, and further on, in the middle of the field, more water buffaloes, alongside which the small-sized peasants appear even smaller.

I reach the frontier, the threshold to Red China. It has a friendly, almost provincial, name: The Portas do Cerco (Barrier Gate)—the entrance way to Communist China, through which tiny Macao peers daily at her mighty neighbor and through which the latter comes in contact with the world via the interracial turnstile of Macao. Before me is an archway of yellowed stones, built a century ago, and on either side there are small sentry boxes that look as though they had been made for toy soldiers. Four Portuguese soldiers with rifles are seated in the shade of a plane tree, smoking and perspiring profusely in their faded uniforms.

A short stretch of road is visible on the other side of the archway, and farther on there are more sentry boxes. A group of Chinese soldiers armed with rifles slowly pace up and down the dusty highway. On this side of the archway the red and green banner of Portugal is flying; on the other side, the red flag with the five stars of Communist China. Nothing else.

Old cars come and go, laden with bundles and wooden cages, from between whose slats chickens and pigs peer out. This is Kwangtung's customs station, Pak Sa Leang. Should one continue in a straight line along the road on which I am now standing, one would reach West River Delta and Canton. Through this road the Chinese bring hogs and suckling pigs from China and return with fish from Macao.

On the other side of Portas do Cerco there is nothing except some rice fields and bleak stretches of land.

264

There are no wire fences or walls, no guards or soldiers other than those stationed at the gate. Anyone, it would seem, could sneak across this frontier. Nevertheless it is far from easy. There are invisible guards and invisible defenses. Actually, unless one has a pass, as do the hundreds of Chinese who go across daily, it is very difficult to penetrate the mystery of the Bamboo Curtain.

Enveloped in the heavy mantle of heat, I slowly walk back to the car. And suddenly I remember little Tak Meng at the hotel this morning. I remember him telling me that the Chinese never take little things. Only big things. And I realize that China need not bother to retrieve the little human pieces that manage to sneak out through the opening of that multiracial piggy bank which is Macao. The day China so desires, it will be much simpler for her to grab the whole piggy bank.

I take one last look at the frontier. The Chinese soldiers stand at the Portas do Cerco motionless, rifles in hand, waiting.

REFUGEES IN MACAO

SIXTY YEARS AFTER VASCO DA
Gama had landed in Macao, the port was still a haven
for pirates who roved the South China Sea. Macao's
historical tradition as a refugee's paradise began then
and continues to this day. From the beginning of Portuguese rule, while Macao's first harbor, shipyard, and
lighthouse were under construction, refugees from all
the neighboring regions began flocking there and continued doing so through the centuries to come. During

the Spanish domination of Portugal, the Portuguese protected the persecuted and hid them as well as they could. During the wars against the Dutch, Macao provided asylum even to the enemy. Through the centuries Macao has sheltered many famous refugees, but the most famous one in modern times was a Chinese surgeon.

I visited the Chinese hospital where Dr. Sun Yat-Sen worked in Macao. In this modest white building, the physician examined the eyes of thousands of Chinese and Portuguese; all the while he was laboring to remove the veil that clouded their vision he was dreaming of removing the veil that clouded China's historic vision. Later, during his exile in Macao, he was being sought by China's Manchu police, who were attempting to execute him. Here in Macao, amid the Portuguese, so near and yet so far from his native land, the Chinese doctor found his much-sought asylum. When visiting hours were over, he would walk across the gray dusty land toward the poor country road that could bring him into Canton in a few hours. Here in Macao, Dr. Sun Yat-Sen, the father of modern China, worked and simultaneously planned the Chinese revolution.

It is one of history's paradoxes that in one of Europe's most steadfast outposts in Asia, amid Portuguese Jesuits and other Christians, was incubated one of the greatest republican revolutions in history.

In exile, Dr. Sun Yat-Sen forged his republican revolution, just as Lenin had planned Russia's Communist revolution during his exile, and José Martí dreamed of Cuba's revolution against Spanish domination during his exile.

The majority of refugees who escape to Macao today, however, do not come to plot revolutions, but to flee them. Hundreds of Chinese gamble their lives and their savings in order to reach Macao, port of hope. The next step is to try to smuggle themselves into Hong Kong, where in all likelihood they have relatives. Since refugees cannot legally enter Hong Kong unless they have been in Macao for six months, they all strive to accumulate enough money—from twenty to fifty American dollars—to get smuggled, in the hold of a boat or at the bottom of a barge, into what they believe to be the promised land, a land in which they will live in hovels that are not fit for beasts.

Most of the refugees are peasants from southern China who are tired of too much work and too little to eat, who spend every one of their days plowing the fields and who live on bananas, rice, and potatoes reduced to a mush and doled out to them in meager portions. To escape this wretched existence, they sometimes steal a fishing boat at night and sail toward Macao, or they try to swim from nearby islands, often drowning in a storm—the best nights for escaping are the stormy ones—or being killed by a burst of Chinese machine-gun fire, thus finding the freedom of death in the dark waters of the South China Sea.

Macao shuts its eyes and shrugs its shoulders at the

incessant avalanche of refugees, but cannot help them. Many refugees spend years looking in vain for work or for some way of reaching Hong Kong. They can be recognized by the rags they wear and by the air of being lost, as of birds without a nest, that hovers round them as they aimlessly wander about the streets of Macao. Sometimes they find their way to the offices of Nationalist China installed here by Chiang Kai-Shek. There they surrender their Communist papers, which are of great value to spies of the Nationalist Army, and they try to answer the questions that the Nationalist Counterintelligence asks them, for which they receive twenty Hong Kong dollars.

The best sources of help for Chinese refugees in Macao are the Catholic organizations, which for a few days provide them with rice, noodles, powdered milk, and other food, and an organization for the aid of refugees established by Chinese businessmen, which provides them with some food, finds them a piece of ground to sleep on, and also helps them to find seasonal work.

Only the sick are granted permission to leave China. Instead of being killed, as they were in primitive societies, for whom sickness was an onerous burden, they are instead thrown out of China. But Macao, their haven of freedom, is only a small peninsula, with hardly enough government posts for the eight thousand Portuguese who dwell there. The remaining Chinese (more than three hundred thousand) and foreigners who live there are left to get along as best they can in business and industry. Macao's policy with respect to the hundreds of Chinese who take refuge there every month is the same as Hong Kong's toward the thousands who finally find asylum in that strange crossroads of races and religions.

In the Shade of the Poet at the Illuminated Grotto

At the present moment, I am on my way to the Camoëns Garden to visit the grotto where another exile, who also found asylum in Macao, worked on an epic poem that would bring him fame and recognition.

Camoëns Garden is spacious and beautiful, with vast groves of trees and many flowers. The landscape follows the gentle undulations of its hillocks, just as a flowered dress follows the curves of a lovely woman. Walking through the garden, parts of which retain their original enchanting wilderness with lizards scudding through the underbrush, butterflies flying about, and numerous birds conjuring up a golden canopy of trills, I come to a small stone grotto polished by rain and wind. It is Camoëns' Grotto. The cool interior is bathed in a bluish light. It was here that the poet sat and composed his verses of bronze and iron, verses that made his temples burn hotter than Macao's sun.

Luiz de Camoëns, Portugal's greatest poet, was born in 1524 of a noble family, and he grew up to an impetuous, even violent, youth, given to adventure seeking and

270

brawling. His early poems were already touched with genius. He fought in his country's army against Morocco and lost his right eye to a musket bullet. Disillusioned because his country failed to recognize his poetic merit or military worth, he embarked in 1553 for India, and in 1557 he sailed with the occupation forces from Goa, in Portuguese India, for Macao, where he had an official post. Political differences with his country kept him in exile in Macao. During all this period he had been composing his epic poem *Os Lusíadas,* extolling the greatness of his motherland, which though far across the sea lay close to his heart. On his way back from Macao, Camoëns was shipwrecked near the coast of Cochin, China, but he swam back to land using one arm, while with the other he held above his head his manuscript of *Os Lusíadas.* Upon publication of his poem in 1572, two years after his return to Lisbon, King Sebastian granted him a pension.

It is noon when I enter Camoëns' Grotto. The silence inside is profound and suddenly I am filled with a strange emotion that makes me recall another occasion in one of my other journeys. Once in Algiers I had experienced the same feeling in a grotto very much like the one in which I am now standing. There, it is said, Cervantes conceived of *Don Quixote,* while he and his fellow Christians, being held by the Turks, awaited the moment of liberation. Like Cervantes, Camoëns was a soldier; Cervantes lost an arm in battle, Camoëns an eye. Like Cervantes, Camoëns was at first denied recognition by his motherland, both as a writer and as a soldier; like Cervantes, Camoëns wanted to go to the Indies in search of better fortune, a desire he fulfilled but Cervantes did not. Cervantes wrote his masterpiece in the forced exile of jail, Camoëns wrote his while in exile in the East; and in a simple but epic style Camoëns extolled the historic grandeur of his country, just as Cervantes extolled the moral greatness of a great human being. Both ultimately achieved a well-deserved glory in their respective countries.

Plucking a yellow flower from a wild blossoming bush at the entrance of the grotto, I place it at the foot of the poet's bust. A golden flower, the color of medals. Mine, though, is not a military medal, for this man was a poet and in his exile he did not plot revolutions, like Sun Yat-Sen. Instead he composed a poem in praise of the country that had rejected him, a poem that added new luster to the *Cidade do Nome de Deus*. And I personally feel a greater love for poets than for soldiers; love for those who, while in voluntary or forced exile, with their pen weave subtle philosophies, as did Juan Luis Vives in Bruges, or great poems, as did Garcilaso de la Vega in Austria and Camoëns in Macao; love for those who have proved that the poet's winged word is far more lasting, and therefore mightier, than the warrior's sword. Camoëns symbolizes not only the worthiest type of refugee that Macao has ever had, but also the type of refugee that flourishes best in history.

We head back for the hotel. The façade of St. Paul's

Church rises before us upon the hill. Its windows no longer look into a church, but look instead into the greatest temple of all, the blue heavens. These paneless windows are a symbol of Macao. They are the windows of a cathedral that prefers the radiant light of the sun to the twilight of stained-glass windows. And today, by virtue of its Christian attitude toward refugees, the tiny land of Macao stands transformed into one vast cathedral.

POMBO ASSADO AND FAN-TAN:
NIGHT IN MACAO

T WO O'CLOCK IN THE MORN-
ing in Macao.

The street, onto which I emerge from the Central
Hotel, my ears still ringing with the clatter of fan-tan
chips on the gambling tables, is deserted. With practically all the lights turned off, the spell cast by the
multicolored signs is gone and with it the city's deceiv-
ing polychrome beauty. Instead, protected by a cloak
of shadows, poverty and dirt once again take possession

274

of the streets. And with them, in the wake of midnight, fear creeps up. There is no one in the dark, empty street, which only a couple of hours ago was an anthill of humanity, a rainbow-lit festival.

My hotel, the Bela Vista, is at the other end of the city, but I see no one to take me there or to direct me. In the dark doorways I do not see even the usual tightly skirted, sensuously hipped figures, or the furtive men with evil expressions on their faces. At night, Macao becomes a mysterious empire of shadows.

My nocturnal exploration of Macao has followed upon the heels of my daytime excursion of the city. It is all well and good to see monuments, but how much better to see cities, and the best way *not* to see a city is to get bogged down in its monuments. Monuments are a city's history and art, canned in stone containers, preserved in the form of churches, palaces, and museums. A city's living history, however, talks, breathes, and has legs that can swiftly move from place to place. And so, after my due ration of monuments, I decided to have a look into the life of the men and women who live and die in the *Cidade do Nome de Deus*.

Macao is Hong Kong in miniature, without the striking natural scenery of the latter and without the presence of England with her magnificent buildings and touches of colonial imperialism, illusory tokens of her past triumphs and glory. What Hong Kong and Macao have most in common is obvious. Both, to the traveler's eyes, are Chinese cities, but whereas in Hong Kong there is a sprinkling of blond, blue-eyed English-speaking men among the predominant Asiatic population, in Macao there is no such contrast, for the Portuguese through intermarrying have developed a close resemblance to the Chinese and physically are often indistinguishable from the latter.

When I first walked the narrow streets of Macao, my head burning with sun and my sport shirt damp with perspiration, I felt as though I were back in one of Hong Kong's quarters. The native part of the city has not been modernized, and, with the exception of the Portuguese constructions built several centuries ago and the big modern buildings outside the city, everything is Chinese.

The streets, flat and narrow, teem with bicycles and rickshas, and men and women scurry along in faded Chinese clothes, less fancy than those worn in Hong Kong and therefore more authentically Chinese. Gray, white, and black predominate, and there is a greater number of soiled, wrinkled pajamas than of ankle-length robes and tunics.

The air rings with the cries of vendors hawking all sorts of trinkets and foods swimming in inky sauces that look as though they might harbor an entire encyclopedia of infectious diseases. Fat men in shirt sleeves, seated in the doorways of their shops or leaning on their pushcarts, peddle their wares in a drab Cantonese singsong, punctuated every now and then by the golden flash, like that of a gold doubloon, of a Portuguese word.

There are shadowed arcades lined with small Chinese shops, over which rectangular strips of white cloth with red and black signs flutter in the hot breeze. At night these banners become beds for a multitude of flying insects. Many of the shops are as cavernous as grottoes, and the figures of the shopkeepers inside are barely visible as they wait, as silently as the spider for a fly, for a tourist to be trapped in their web of persuasion.

There are few Portuguese signs and the Western alphabet looks stern and severe alongside the merry dance of the Chinese characters. I read some of these Portuguese signs: *Barbearia, Sapataria, Restaurante, Jades, Fotógrafo, Livraria Tai Seng—Artigos de Escritório.* Occasionally one sees an English sign of surrealistic spelling. One barber shop advertises: "Especial plice for girl." The atmosphere is one of poverty, occasionally attenuated by a provincial bourgeois air, but a poverty that is spirited and at times even cheerful.

The great abundance of children of all ages is a sure clue to the favorite evening pastime of the poor of Macao. Practically as soon as they are able to walk alone, the children promptly improvise a counter with a discarded box, upon which they display bottles covered with the dust of time, like a vintage wine, containing tinted "drinks" in which death by infection quietly lurks. With a splendid indifference to the rest of the world, children satisfy nature's calls right in the middle

277

of the street, one lined up next to the other, often in front of their parents' shops, but more often, if they are not caught in the act, before their neighbor's. The smell of man's ignoble bodily functions mingles with that of cooking spices, which from early morning begins to drift through the air.

Women dressed in black from head to foot, as if they were in perpetual mourning (their somber clothes seem to intensify the heat), pour out from churches, where masses are held throughout the day, beginning at dawn, with the first bells of the Angelus tolling from all the belfries in the city. In Catholic churches, Chinese women, their heads covered with soiled black kerchiefs, kneel and pray to Christ in Chinese. Others say their rosaries in Chinese by the light of myriad candles, which like gleaming stars keep vigil over the congregation's pious rites.

Life in Macao is difficult. Salaries are low. To live decently, a government employee must earn five hundred *patacas* a month, of which almost half is spent on rent. The poorer people live in dwellings renting for ten or twelve *patacas* a month, and those who cannot afford even that often find themselves with the refugees and the beggars in charity concentration camps in Taipa or Coloane, two islands closely guarded by soldiers. At night one never sees people sleeping on the sidewalks because they fear deportation to the islands, but beggars abound in the daytime. Sometimes, in a desperate attempt to improve their wretched lot, they stow away in

278

fishing boats and eventually land in Hong Kong, where they display their sores or mutilations, much as they have previously done in Macao.

In the strictly Chinese sections, with their pebble-paved alleys, very near Avenida Almeida Ribeiro, Macao's Fifth Avenue, there are small Chinese shops in which the shopkeepers laboriously manufacture their own wares: bathtubs, stools, tables, chains, buckets, all made out of discarded wooden crates, boxes, tins, and old metal collected from all over the city. Many of the clothing stores sell used clothing purchased from refugees or inherited from them at their death. There are many little shops that exude an odor laden with the romance of China's legendary herbs, and pushcarts sell boiled rice, noodles, scraps of meat, tiny crabs, fish, strips of raw or smoked snake meat, and cakes and candies crawling with flies. Chinese and Portuguese signs hang from mysterious-looking boardinghouses and pensions, and the masklike faces that occasionally peer out from behind the dusty windowpanes evoke visions of sordid vices lurking behind the sun-baked walls.

In the centermost part of Macao are shops crammed with furniture, clothing, foodstuffs, and wines from Hong Kong and Portugal and marked at prices that would seem astronomical in the Chinese quarters.

The chief livelihood of Macao's more than three hundred thousand Chinese residents derives from its two national industries: fishing and the manufacture of matches and fireworks. Macao is the largest producer of pyrotechnics in the world. On the neighboring island of Taipa, there are five factories that manufacture fireworks, of which the largest, Kwong Hing Tai, employs almost three thousand Chinese refugees, ninety per cent of whom are women and girls. The smell of gunpowder hovers forever over the factories, and the girls who work there will never be free of the evil smell. It penetrates their skin, permeates their bodies, and even flavors their food. Barefoot, so as not to ignite the powder that forever covers the floor by the friction of their shoes, they work in units separated by thick, twelve-foot-high wooden walls, so that if an explosion were to occur the damage would be limited. The fireworks that will set the evening skies ablaze with shimmering emerald, turquoise, and scarlet lights and with cascading palms of gold and silver at Communist festivals in Shanghai or Peking, or at gala parties in Venice or Monte Carlo, are manufactured in Macao.

By evening, on my way from the hotel to town to have dinner, Macao has been transformed into a picture out of a fairy tale. The streets, especially the Rua da Felicidade, are iridescent tunnels beneath a forest of fluttering banners, colored lanterns, and restaurant and café signs. The arcades of shops are corridors brilliantly lit in the seven colors of the rainbow, and the pavements, which at this hour are always wet from the water buckets emptied out by shops and restaurants, are all aglow with the reflections from electric, gas, oil, and candle lights. It is now noisier than at noontime, but the sounds are happier in their discordance. Night and relaxation of parental vigilance has infused the children with fresh bursts of energy. Their little faces are tinted emerald, topaz, and amethyst by the street lights, their black eyes flash merrily, their hands avidly dart forward to beg for anything—a coin, a cigarette— and they skillfully dodge a smack from their mothers, give a dog a kick, or spit in the rice another child is having for dinner.

There are many policemen about, all meticulously dressed in white tunics and colonial-style shorts, wearing helmets, and heavily armed. At the corners, policemen sternly reprimand those who cross against the traffic, or punish an impatient cyclist who has tried to pass a light by making him wait until the light changes several times. Using whistles, shouts, and windmill-like motions of their gloved hands, they direct the bustling stream of humanity, which gaily ambles along on its way to drink, dine, play fan-tan, or pursue less innocent entertainment.

Fat Siu Lau, or the restaurant of the Laughing Buddha, is on the Rua da Felicidade at the corner of Travessa do Mastro. I cross the street, which glitters like a pagan altar. The gold shops, which by day are but dark holes in the walls, are now glowing furnaces, flashing jewel coffers, grottoes tremulous with the shimmer of gold. Rings, watches, necklaces, every conceivable jewel is sold in these little shops that are no more than cubicles. The camera shops display in overpower-

ing confusion all sorts of European appliances, in addition to kimonos, silks, lacquered objects, jade, pearls,
and sea shells. The air smells of sweating flesh and
spiced rice, of wax and incense, of lamp oil and cheap
cologne. Each street is not just a series of individual
shops and restaurants, but a vast colony of families who
know one another, talk to and shout at one another,
embrace and insult one another, who in the doorways
of their wretched shops share a glass of port or sake
or a bottle of Coca-Cola, while inside the shops thin,
haggard-looking women are being drained of years of
life by toiling over smoking, grease-smeared stoves.

The Laughing Buddha is an ugly old restaurant one
floor above the street. Its austerity does not relieve, in
fact it accentuates, its ugliness: four naked stained walls,
massive wooden sideboards, a fan that whirs and creaks
as if it were afflicted with rheumatism, a small radio
in a corner apparently broadcasting Chinese news, two
fat lusterless cats with a suspicious look in their eyes
lazily wandering around the place, and perhaps a dozen
Chinese couples and several families seated at the tables.
All are voraciously devouring the specialty of the house,
pombo assado, or roast pigeon, and rice, their faces
close to the rice bowls as their chopsticks swiftly move
from the rice to their hungry mouths.

There are two balconies, one facing Rua da Felicidade, and the other Travessa do Mastro. On the other
side of the street, I see liquor stores in which bottles of
arrack, whisky, Bordeaux, Madeira, and champagne

stand one next to the other. There are children everywhere, reckless bicycles that rest neither by day nor night, and pedicabs. Chinese women dart by with short, jerky steps, their wooden shoes clapping noisily on the pavement.

The *criado de mesa,* or waiter, a shriveled, mean-looking Chinese, brings me a wet towel for my face and hands. It is not a clean, hot, perfumed towel like the ones I was given in Japan, but cold, dirty, and foul smelling, like a criminal's conscience. The menu consists of *pombo assado* and Cantonese rice, preceded by *sopa de galinha e ovo,* or chicken soup with egg. A poor, slightly sour Portuguese *vinho branco* is served with the meal.

Roast pigeon is Macao's specialty. At the Macau Inn, the famous Portuguese chef, Angelo, prepares his pigeons, as well as chicken, African style, barbecued with an African sauce that includes Tabasco, paprika, wine, garlic, Portuguese olive oil, butter, bacon, cheese, milk, herbs, and spices, in secret proportions—a sauce he also uses on fish. He raises his own pigeons on the terrace of his inn. His bar is styled after an English pub and with the meals he likes to serve a bottle of Casal Gracia white wine. Pigeons, which are so favored by Macao gourmets, are raised locally from the best breeds imported from the United States and other countries.

But now, with the blinking lights of Chin Son Fong's *Loja de Vinhos* across the street blinding my eyes, I hungrily attack the pigeon that the waiter has just set before me. But suddenly my knife and fork stop in midair. On the plate, two bright eyes stare at me, wide open in accusation. The pigeon has been served with its little head entire so that I can suck out its brains and eyes, Macao gourmets' greatest treat. With one last look at the pigeon's plaintive eyes, I quickly walk out of the Laughing Buddha.

Slowly I stroll down the noisy streets in the direction of the Central Hotel, the tallest building in Macao where the only "official" gambling house is located. After centuries of permitting and living off this international vice, Macao now controls and limits it. People still gamble, get drunk, seek illicit love, and enjoy a thousand secret vices of which the Oriental is a master. But they say there is a mystery man, almost a myth, there who has control of every vice in Macao, allowing only the most inoffensive ones, such as fan-tan, to be seen, and aiding those who wish to indulge in the others, such as opium, gambling, and prostitution, to seek them out, take a risk, and pay dearly for them. In addition to these activities, his economic empire, which extends from Japan to Singapore, also includes traffic in gold. They also say that he presides over many charitable activities. Just in case, he is paving the way to heaven. If at best there is no heaven, at worst—who knows!—there may be a hell.

The Central Hotel is a six-story building with one hundred and forty-five rooms; there are restaurants,

cafés, and gambling rooms on every floor. The higher
the floor the more expensive, though far from elegant,
it is. I went through all the floors, peering into the
rooms that are open to outsiders, for there are others
mysteriously shut, with armed guards stationed in front
of the doors to "paradise."

Fan-tan, the game made famous in the West by
Sax Rohmer's novels about Dr. Fu Manchu, is played
throughout the building, although actually the gambling tables are only on the first and sixth floors. On
the first floor, Chinese in sweat-stained shirt sleeves
mill noisily around the tables; on the sixth floor, young
Chinese women serve as croupiers, the tables are quieter,
the *ambiance* more discreet, and there is a cabaret where
guests may dance. Sandwiched between the first and
the sixth floors is a labyrinth of rooms with huge round
openings on the floor, through which the gamblers
place their bets on the tables located on the ground floor.
The entire building is drilled with such holes leading
from one gambling room to another.

On the ground floor there are two huge fan-tan tables.
Circulating around the tables in two's and three's are
uniformed policemen, wearing Khaki shorts, black knee
socks, pistols in their belts, and rifles on their shoulders.
Some of them even carry machine guns. The look on
their faces leaves no doubt about their eagerness to exercise their authority. The rooms, despite the wide-open
windows, are hot and humid, and the naked electric
bulbs, hanging limply from the exposed wires, like

overripe fruit from a tree, only make the heat worse. The sordidness of the place is not mitigated even by the knowledge that one is in "exotic" Macao. In some instances even literature cannot redeem sordidness.

I approach one of the tables. The big table, made of cheap wood worn smooth by the fan-tan chips and the sweat and grease from countless fingers, has a square drawn on it divided into four sections and marked with numbers from one to four. The croupier looks incredibly old, as if death, pressed by more urgent appointments, has skipped over him. His head, bald, shiny, ivory pale, is but a skull on which the reflections from the lights fence with one another. His eyes, cold and hard as billiard balls, do not look at anything or anyone, yet see everything and everyone. His fingers are mere bones yellowed with age.

Once the players have placed their bets on one or several of the four numbers, the old man with a small stick slowly stirs a pile of button-like plastic chips and then covers them with a small metal bowl, thus isolating a group of chips under the bowl. Before lifting the bowl, he pushes away all the chips outside the bowl. With the stick, he then adroitly divides the pile under the bowl into groups of four chips each, until the final group contains from one to four chips. The number of chips left in the last batch determines the winning number; if four chips remain, the backers of number four win; if three, the backers of number three win, and so on. It is an absurd game, but one that consumes not only every cent of the fan-tan addict, but also his soul.

I play a few rounds from the third floor. The large opening in the floor is surrounded by a railing, with rows of chairs set around it. Through this sort of surgical amphitheatre I can see the fan-tan table on the floor below. Chinese girls collect the bets and place them in a little basket, which they then drop to the table below by means of a cord. The winnings are collected in the same way. In the interim the wait is relieved by the girls' wan smiles, smiles from which the tropical climate has sapped all joy, and the night life all color. From time to time little dishes of watermelon seeds are passed around, which the players crack between their teeth with resounding gusto, at the same time as they drink tea, beer, or whisky. I win two or three times, lose as many times, and then, bored, I go on to explore the upper regions of the Central Hotel.

On the sixth floor, the fan-tan tables are attended by Chinese women in black pajama-like pants. The players are few, and all are silent. There are heavy red curtains and mirrors, but even here I see the inevitable cuspidors, as big and ugly as urinals. The Chinese of Macao spit as much as those of Hong Kong. It seems as though something in their history has got stuck in their throats and they are constantly trying to expectorate it.

I move on to the cabaret. It is a large, rambling room with twenty tables, a band of five musicians who execute—in every sense of the word!—songs from Amer-

287

ican movies, a bar where the bottles are illuminated by invisible lights like images in a church, and a flock of hostesses, most of whom are Chinese. Seated in a corner, they quietly wait for the maître to call them. The maître approaches me. He is a Portuguese refugee from Canton and now earns a niggardly living as keeper of this bovine flock. He assigns a hostess to talk to me while I drink a beer.

Fen-Hui is Chinese and she bows to me as she sits down. She is extremely young, though one can never be sure about the age of a Chinese woman, has very black hair and very white skin, is dressed in Western fashion, and wears a lot of make-up. She only knows a few words of English, how to ask for a cigarette and order a Coca-Cola. Our conversation is limited, for once she has told me in pidgin English that she comes from Peking, that her family still lives there, that she has been in Macao for a year, and that she has no desire to return to China, everything else becomes progressively unintelligible. As if she were drinking champagne instead of Coca-Cola, her speech becomes increasingly difficult to my ears, and, finally, when she lapses into Mandarin, a total enigma.

Meanwhile, a few couples are dancing to the rhythm of the dissonant music. On the walls, neon-lit scoreboards permit the dancers to continue their frantic betting while they dance. For the first time in my life, I see young couples dancing who are far more absorbed in the scoreboards upon which are flashed in red the winning numbers than in each other or in the music. The waiters run back and forth with the dancers' bets. The Central Hotel is indeed a veritable gambling hive, in each of whose little cells the honey of money is casually distilled straight into the pockets of its fabulous proprietor.

It is two o'clock when I leave the Central Hotel. The hostesses are still waiting for customers. In their brilliant red, blue, green, and white tunics, they look like peacocks, but docile, submissive, utterly devoid of vanity, but peacocks just the same, waiting for their keeper's signal to display their beauty for a customer. Various sounds accompany me on my departure: the plaintive notes of a tango, the guttural shouts of the dancers placing their bets, the strident voice of my hostess arguing with the maître, who it seems has claimed a large share of the tip I gave her.

Out on the street everything is dark and silent. The *rua* is no longer ablaze with a myriad of colors. The lights have been extinguished. Only the heat of the dead bulbs remains hovering in the still air. I walk around for a while, looking for a taxi, a ricksha, a policeman, anyone. The side streets are equally dark and deserted. An occasional dimly lit doorway stands out in the darkness. Suddenly from one of these doorways a shadow silently steps out and stops in front of me. He is dressed in a long Chinese tunic of black silk. His face is an ivory mask. His eyes gleam like beads of glass. With a motion of his hand he invites me to enter the house. From the doorway, even before I look inside, I can smell what lies beyond. Opium!

Through the open door I see a small room. Eight or ten cots are lined up one above the other, like double-decked berths. Squatting in front of a tiny copper brazier, a Chinese girl, wearing a short jacket embroidered with red dragons and black pajama trousers, is immersed in the ritual of preparing the pipes. Impaling the little ball of opium, which she has just finished kneading, in a long copper needle she holds it over the will-o'-the-wisp-like flame of the brazier. Nearly all the cots are occupied by Chinese men. None is sleeping, but all are dreaming; none is dead, but all are totally sapped of the desire to live; none can see the frighteningly sordid room, only the visions and harmonies of the opium world, the miraculous multicolored *rua* that will eventually lead them to madness.

Thanking the man with a nod of my head, I continue my search for a vehicle to take me back to my hotel. The Chinese follows me closely, muttering in an insinuating voice words I do not understand. Suddenly, another shadow emerges from a corner, a noisy shadow with pistols. A policeman. The Chinese melts into the shadows behind me and the policeman, without even a glance in his direction, listens to my questions and in Portuguese tells me to follow him. A few minutes later we reach a street somewhat more brightly lit. A pedicab is parked on the sidewalk, and the policeman instructs the huge coolie with ropelike biceps, who is drowsing nearby, to take me to the hotel.

With the coolie's gentle, sustained pedaling, we traverse *ruas* deep in shadows, dimly lit *ruas, ruas* with adequate illumination, and again totally dark, deserted *ruas,* until we finally reach the avenue facing the sea.

The moon caresses the sea's dark tresses with her long fingers of silver. A breeze as light as a sigh gently rocks the tops of the palm trees and the banyans. No one is in sight. The coolie comes to a sudden stop at the foot of the steep ramp leading to the hotel. He refuses to climb up, and I cannot blame him. Slowly I climb the ramp toward the hotel, which looms huge, white, and shapeless amid the trees.

Everything is deserted and silent. The boy, Tak Meng, who apparently never sleeps, opens the door. Agile and mysterious, like an elf in a peasant fable, he leads me to my room. In an English made more guttural by the late hour, he asks me when I wish breakfast served and then leaves. I shut the door, but I do not hear his footsteps moving away. There is no doubt of it. He is still there on the other side of the door, silently waiting.

I wait perhaps one minute and then there is a soft knock at the door. Greatly puzzled I open it. Tak Meng's smiling face is transformed by the candle he is carrying into a mask of flickering lights and shadows. His smile broadens, and serenely he asks:

"You want a Chinese whore? Velly good family.

Velly good girl. Velly good whore. Twenty Hong Kong dollars."

I burst into laughter, thank him, refuse, and try to close the door. But he stops me.

"You want a whore from Macao? Not good family, but velly good whore. Only fifteen Hong Kong dollars."

My second refusal does not daunt him.

"A brothel. I take you. Young whores. Only ten Hong Kong dollars."

I am already closing the door, but Tak Meng quickly drops his last and easiest trump card.

"My sister, not young, but velly good whore. Only six Hong Kong dollars."

Laughingly but firmly I shut the door on Tak Meng's disappointed face.

Thus ends my exploration of nocturnal vice in the forbidden city of Macao.

BANGKOK

SEVEN IN THE MORNING IN
A VENICE WITH SAMPANS

WAT DI!" THE RITUAL GREET-
ing drops from Pen Phmim's lips with the ring of crystal against crystal, and her radiant smile sparks the
magnificent golden color of her cheeks.

Silhouetted against the earthy waters of the Menam
Chao Phya—Bangkok's smiling, Samaritan river—my
guide, Pen Phmim, seems even smaller than she actually
is. Her white silk pants and amethyst tunic accentuate
her incredible stalklike slenderness.

I approach the motorboat, which stands rocking at the quay a few steps from the Oriental Hotel. (In my later trips to Bangkok, I stayed at the Erawan Hotel, which is my favorite hotel in Southeast Asia.) At six-thirty in the morning the river was already dotted with sampans skillfully propelled by tiny women with oars as long as telephone poles. Suddenly a red flower on the hotel lawn takes flight. It is a beautiful bird. The first jarring sounds of automobiles, bicycles, tramways, and *samlors,* the motorized tricycles, begin drifting from neighboring streets. Opposite me, on the other side of the Chao Phya River, glitter the refulgent towers of Wat Arun, the Temple of the Dawn.

There is no other city on the entire spherical breadth of this planet so exotically beautiful and utterly fascinating as Bangkok, the city that makes even the cities in fairy tales seem prosaic by comparison.

It is a city of more than four hundred glittering temples (there are more than twenty thousand in the country), one of which is decorated with fragments of broken porcelain dishes from a shipwreck; a city of gold-leaf-covered pagodas; of palaces of Siamese design built with bronze, Italian marble, and Chinese glazed tile; of sanctuaries that shelter jade, emerald, or golden Buddhas, some of them more than a hundred yards high and most of them guarded by the towering figures of gods, men, birds, serpents, and demons, sanctuaries with walls of their compounds hung with thousands of little bells that keep tinkling under the breeze's invisible fingers. The capital of a country that still has elephants descended from the king of Siam's legendary white elephants, gold-leaf-covered royal barges, and mother-of-pearl altars, Bangkok, with its network of canals, is a Venice with sampans. It is also a city with jungles inhabited by tigers and rhinoceroses, crocodiles and leopards, *seladangs,* tapirs, serpents, and peacocks in colors as brilliant as the saffron-yellow robes worn by the Buddhist monks who populate this magical city.

With my mouth still savoring the cherry-colored papaya, nacreous bananas, and other tropical fruits in such vivid colors that breakfast had been like eating off a painter's palette, I set out to visit the *klongs* on the other side of the river, where thousands of Thai dwell in sampans or in huts mounted on stilts embedded in the water.

We cross the river. The lush green banks provide a sharp contrast with the new white buildings. Beyond the buildings, towering over them, hundreds and hundreds of wats, or Buddhist temples, gleam in the young sun like palaces of gold and glass in a mythical legend, their towers tinted in different colors: pink as the early sky, as green as sweet basil, or topaz, aquamarine, lapis lazuli, or malachite, the loosened gold leaf that gilds their walls quivering in the breeze like thousands of tiny golden tongues.

Slowly we approach the *klongs,* the canals that embody Bangkok's earliest history. One thousand five hundred years ago, Bangkok—the name outsiders give to

Krung Thep—was completely submerged beneath the Gulf of Siam. The gradual rising of the gulf bottom, along with the accumulation of mud deposits from the river, created a fertile delta. A handful of fishermen's huts upon the muddy banks eventually became a small village. Then, in 1782, the capital, which had originally been in Sukhothai, then in Ayudhya, and later in Dhonburi, was moved there. Man helped nature to make the city of Bangkok more habitable. Several of the kings, finding the Chao Phya River too long and winding a path to the sea, bored canals through the jungle. Through the years, the *klongs,* originally conceived as short cuts to the sea for the sampans, became a fluvial maze, a highly complex network of canals concealed by thick vegetation.

Subsequently, fishermen and farmers adopted the canals as their place of residence, anchoring their sampans all along the water. Later, to the collection of floating dwellings, other more enterprising individuals added wooden shacks that they built upon high stilts to protect them against floods. Today the *klongs* are home to thousands of people, as well as a fabulous floating market place where fruit, fish, and meat delight the eye and tempt the palate. It is claimed that the bottom of the Gulf of Siam is still rising, and that in another fifteen hundred years this Venice of Asia will be a dry, inland city, whose only access to the sea will be by train or plane. Fortunately, we shall not live to see that day.

A VENICE WITH SAMPANS

Our boat has left the main waterway and is now skimming along the *klongs*. Such sheer delight! At first we glide through narrow canals, veritable tunnels of solid vegetation that sets the water aquiver with green reflections. The walls of green are so thick that nothing is visible beyond them, but from time to time the foliage suddenly parts and dusky-skinned children with grinning faces peer through, their little bodies stark naked, like miniature Adams and Eves in a tropical paradise.

Through a clearing in the wall of greenery I catch a glimpse of some barges and sampans in an adjoining canal, their bottoms so level with the water that the people seem to be sailing on land. The air is filled with the fresh morning fragrance of plants and the sweet-sour odor of rotting leaves. Creeping through the vaulted foliage above our heads, the sun sheds patches of emerald and gold upon the water. Except for the soft hum of the motor, everything is still, like a fairy-tale journey to a hidden paradise.

Some of the canals are so narrow that the foliage hangs all around us like curtains and we have to part it with our hands. The water is overlaid with fallen leaves and the air is pungent with the smell of over-ripe fruit. Now and then the chirping of birds reaches our ears. Suddenly we hear the sound of voices and laughter, and at a turn in the canal, which our boat almost misses because of the heavy growth, we enter the market place of the floating city.

Only a few days before, in Aberdeen, Hong Kong, I had seen a floating city of junks and sampans where hundreds of thousands of Chinese dwell; now once again I enter a world afloat, but utterly different. The wide canal is bordered by houses mounted on towering posts, some of them built inside the water, others standing next to a jungle clearing, which serves as animal pen and kitchen garden.

The canal hums with the boisterous traffic of sampans, steered by little doll-like women in wide straw hats. With their long oars they deftly maneuver even those boats that appear to be on the verge of sinking beneath the weight of their cargo.

There is indeed a marked difference between Aberdeen in Hong Kong and the *klongs* of Bangkok. The people here are cleaner and, what is far more important, happier. To the Chinese in Aberdeen, the bay is but a waterway and an anchoring place for the vessels that serve as their homes. For the Thai of Bangkok, the *klongs* are more than a traffic artery; they are the recreation area of their homes.

I have never before seen so many smiling people, especially the children! There are hundreds of them, half or completely naked, cavorting like happy dolphins in a calm sea, leaping like baby seals in a pool, splashing happily in the mud along the banks like playful puppies, skipping and chattering like birds in the sunshine. The animal imagery employed here is justified, for these children have the noble, simple happiness of creatures who, like fish and birds, dwell within nature and are the happy masters of it.

Slowly we sail past a jungle of hundreds of little hands waving in the universal gesture of good-by, of little laughing mouths shouting hello in their own language and even babbling a few English words, of little heads with bright dark eyes happily staring at us from the water. This is the dream of all who love children: to see hundreds of them, and all of them happy. Of course, the water is dark and threatening, swarming probably with an invisible population of germs, though most likely contact with it from birth has immunized the natives for life. (A physician from Bangkok subsequently confirmed the immunity theory, with heartening statistics of the city's death rate.)

The sampans groan under the weight of huge baskets of exotic fruits heaped in architectonic pyramids of coral, emerald, and gold, wicker trays piled high with chickens already plucked, big joints of all kinds of meat, mounds of fish, lobsters, and other sea food freshly caught in the Gulf of Siam, eels, frogs, and cooked and uncooked rice. But what is most in evidence are huge pots containing curries, some of which are a fiery-red color and just as fiery to the taste, and others that are whitish in color and far kinder to the palate.

The smell of curry is everywhere. When one passes a sampan with pots of freshly made curry, the smell, which I find very pleasant, dominates everything. Not only can one smell it, but one can "feel" it, in the

tickling in the nostrils, in the taste that the air seems
to leave on the lips. Some curries are scented with
ground water bugs and wood insects.

Alongside the curry pots are others filled with salad
sauces, soy sauces, fish sauces, sauces with whole red
peppers as hot as Satan's cauldrons, and green peppers
in vinegar. The people of Bangkok combat the scorching heat outside with curries that ignite an even more
scorching heat inside their bodies.

Our boat advances cautiously amid sampans laden
with their fragrant or piquant wares, the aroma of the
fruit softening the smell of the curries. Swarms of children swim around us, begging for nothing, neither for
cigarettes nor pennies, showering us instead with the
gift of their smiles and their cries of greeting.

The wooden shacks on both sides of the canal have
spacious porches without doors. Their interiors are open
to all eyes: palm mats, home-woven wicker chairs, rustic
kitchens (a little burner and some pots), fishing tackle,
farming tools, clothing hung from thorns nailed to the
walls, palm fiber cots, and whole families engaged in
constant but quiet activity. Small childlike women
nurse their infants; others prepare curries, cook rice,
or clean the house. The elderly sit in the sunshine,
enjoying the ever-renewed, quotidian spectacle of life.

Life for these people is simple and free. They live
outdoors, in the shade of royal palms, surrounded by
tropical fruits and wild orchids. There is no lack of
rice, which despite its being husked and highly pol-

ished is the best tasting in the world. All these people have to do is extend their hands twice a day toward the canal and the jungle in order to obtain fish and fruit. They can cast their square nets into the canal and haul them in filled with the leaping silver of numerous fish, which, grilled over charcoal, bedded on mounds of rice, and sprinkled with sharp curry, provide excellent fare that never palls, supplemented by delicious fruits. Their vast rice fields yield them a rich booty of rice. Hot tea provides a happy finale for their meals that, in Siamese style, are eaten with a porcelain teaspoon and a little fork used to pass the food from the main serving dish to each person's bowl.

The canals vary in color, depending on whether moss or mud lines the bottom. At the same time as the ears reap a harvest of carefree laughter, happy shouts, playful splashing, and bamboo-flute music, the eyes capture a rich booty of fleeting images: a Thai doll-like figure, so fragile she looks as if she could break under the wind, propelling, with slender arms and a long oar, a sampan bearing pyramids of green and yellow watermelons; families, from morning on, performing the ritual of pouring the liquid coral of curry sauces over snowy mounds of rice; girls washing clothes, their bare torsos embroidered with gleaming beads of sweat; children in their birthday suits playing with big turtles; and women, hordes of women, in this happy Venice with sampans.

303

TIFFIN IN BANGKOK

Y<small>OU EAT CURRY AS THOUGH YOU</small> were a Thai rather than a Spaniard," Pen Phmim says to me.

We are having *tiffin*—as Somerset Maugham's characters loved to say in his stories about the East—in a Thai restaurant in Bangkok. The mere presence of the flaming-red curry on our table sets the temperature of the dining room soaring like a bonfire.

The Thai cuisine is not a cuisine; it is a pretext for consuming the hot curry sauces for which it is famous.

The daily diet of the poor people—the fishermen and the farm laborers who live on the *klongs*—consists of mounds of boiled rice, fish caught in the canals, and wild fruit. On special holidays they may have chicken and eggs, and, on rare occasions, meat. Their greatest delight, however, is varying the perennial rice menu with endless varieties of curry, the sharper, the better, which apparently has no effect on them other than to whet their appetite for still stronger curries at their next meal. People in Bangkok go to temple festivals, family gatherings, and other celebrations only in quest of a new and sharper curry, as divine an adventure for their palates as the bouquet and taste of newly discovered vintage wine is for the wine connoisseur or the freshness and consistency of the next container of caviar is for the gourmet.

I had been warned that Bangkok's curries are a burning culinary inferno and that I should proceed with the utmost caution. At the Palms Restaurant, at the Normandie Grill of the Hotel Oriental, at the Casanova Restaurant, at the Salinee, wherever I ate in Bangkok, I saw many a red-faced American tourist who had swallowed too hastily and choked on a spoonful of rice drenched in a hot curry sauce. The second error they commited was to try to douse the roaring fire in their mouth with iced water, beer, or whisky and soda. This merely increases the inflammation of the mucous membranes in the mouth and makes the burning worse. One soon learns that the best thing to do is simply to continue eating, including the curry, and, at most, to take a little sip of hot tea. If the burning in the mouth is such that the diner feels he is about to be consumed in flames, the paradoxical, classical Thai remedy is to gargle and rinse the mouth in the hottest water bearable!

Apparently my Spanish palate has had good training for hot foods. Thai friends marveled because not only was I not in the least affected by their sauces, but I always inquired which was the hottest and consumed it with great relish and with no ill consequences.

I find a pronounced difference between the hot curries of Thailand and the hot sauces I have tasted in Mexico and other tropical countries. Mexican sauces also burn, sting, and inflame the mouth, but they are utterly tasteless; they add no distinguishing flavor to the food. Thai sauces, however, are not only hot, they are indescribably delicious. I have tasted curries in Chinese, Indian, Arabian, and Mexican restaurants all over the world. I may have tasted sauces just as sharp as those of Bangkok but never any as delicious. In flavor, Thai sauces have no equal in the whole wide world.

Eating is culture and culture is eating when the act of eating transcends the mere consumption of food and is transformed into an art that appeals to noble senses. There are people who eat simply to feed themselves; there are others who eat to satisfy appetites more subtle than that for mere food, for whom satisfaction comes from the way the food looks, smells, and tastes, as well as the company, conversation, and atmosphere. For the harmonious provision of all these things, I would grant the Japanese a universal medal; they have indeed made a culture out of eating. And for flavor I would give second place in the Orient to Thailand, for their rice dishes with saffron, peppers, tiny cubes of meat, and curry sauces are a unique challenge to the palate and even to the spirit.

The Thai use a little fork for transferring the food from the serving dishes to their individual plates, and then a little porcelain spoon for eating, so that metal never touches the lips. There are no knives on the Thai table. Meat and fish are cut in the kitchen into bite-size pieces to fit into the tiny mouths of Thai women. Should it be necessary to cut something at the table, the spoon itself serves as knife, and, as in all of Southeast Asia, rice replaces bread.

Here are some of the Thai dishes I tasted, with their respective curries (one of whose ingredients is the powerful *pri-kee-noo,* a tiny green or red chili pepper, each inch of which contains the power of a megaton bomb): *kung tod,* fried prawns in a garlic and hot pepper sauce; *kao klug gapi,* rice with cubes of meat and fish; *kao pat,* fried rice with tiny crab, chicken, pork, onion, and egg, seasoned with saffron; *gang pet,* a strong curry of beef, pork, chicken, fish or prawns; a salad with coconut, mango, chili, and sugar; banana curries; a salad with cucumber, onion, cabbage, mint, and algae; tomatoes filled with inflammable extracts

307

that promptly soar to one's head; rice with fried chicken livers; beef fried in oyster oil with green chili peppers; sliced beef with cauliflower; an omelette filled with meat and peppers; and the famous "one-hundred-year-old eggs," black, gelatinous, the white garnished with amber-colored grass, the yolks soft and rank, a dish that, according to some, smells like horse urine, but which I found odorless with an elusive taste, melting in the mouth as though it were not an egg but the ancient soul of that egg.

The fruits are exquisite, especially the mangosteen, a small divinely sweet apple-like fruit, with skin the color of eggplant and flesh the color of mother-of-pearl, which, as if nature had declared it a fragile gem, grows encased in an outer rind that is the color of dried blood; and the durian, a large, prickly skinned fruit that smells like rotten cheese or eggs, but which when well refrigerated, has a wonderful flavor despite its smell. Two remarkable desserts are *sa rim,* soybean noodles with cold coconut milk and various extracts, and *ma prow sang-kaya,* a sort of custard made with egg yolks, palm sugar, and the essences of flowers. One can also go to Chinese restaurants, where Cantonese-, Shanghai-, Tai Chew-, or Fukien-style food is served.

Dinner ends with tea, served by quiet, smiling Thai waiters, who also bring you a silver finger bowl with rose petals floating on the perfumed water.

Dining in Thailand is a millenary culture, albeit a culture that sets the palate ablaze.

INTERMEZZO: TOUR ROYALE

SIX O'CLOCK IN THE EVENING in Bangkok.

The sun is descending on the green horizon as though it were about to recline on the hammock formed by the palm groves and go to sleep. The last scarlet reflections set fire to the gold three-tiered roof of the Temple of the Emerald Buddha, the Temple of the Dawn, and the more than four hundred other Buddhist temples, many covered in gold leaf beaten out long ago by the hands of loving artisans and now beaten by the incessant hammering of sun and wind.

I am pleasantly tired, as I had spent the day visiting medical centers, which was a most rewarding experience. At the Pasteur Institute I saw the spectacle of snakes being "milked" for their poison, which would be used for the preparation of antivenin. As it comes out, the venom looks like a beautiful drop of pure crystal.

From my balcony in the Oriental Hotel I can see the landscaped lawn where dozens of travelers, mostly English in sport shirts or jackets that fleck the green with bright colors, are seated at little white tables sipping tea as daintily as parakeets drink water from their cups, the steam from the tea reminding them perhaps of London's damp air. Other travelers sip cocktails that flash like rubies and topazes in the still ice-frosted glasses.

Further in the distance, the traffic on the Chao Phya River is already thinning. A few straggling canoes and sampans swiftly glide by, propelled as usual by tiny women with long poles. On the opposite bank of the river stand the temples, those wondrous marble, stone, and gold-leaf edifices in which saffron-robed bonzes forever kneel in prayer before impassive-faced golden Buddhas. Behind the temples I can see the *klongs*. The fishermen and their families are already squatting around pots of curries as hot as the contortions of a rhumba dancer.

Despite the air conditioning, the humidity in my room makes the air unbreathable. Besides, I feel the need for a change of atmosphere.

Some tourists I met on a flight to the ruins in Angkor have invited me to cocktails at the Erawan, Bangkok's most luxurious hotel and the gathering place for the elite among international tourists. I decide to join them.

Quickly dressing, I step into the foyer where the air conditioner, a gray rumbling elephantine-looking machine, blasts my face with gusts of hot air. Merely crossing the few meters of the foyer, an infernal oven compounded of motor and natural heat, is enough to make me emerge on the street drenched in perspiration, my fresh shirt converted into a wringing-wet rag in a few seconds.

The taxi ride to the Erawan Hotel brings no relief. Through the open windows swoop in blasts of hot air, such as must greet those condemned to Hell when they cross the threshold of that region. The taxi hurtles down the avenue and crosses the river at nose-dive speed, swinging through, passing, practically shoving aside the other cars.

On the sidewalks, fishermen, farm laborers, children, and women as tiny as dolls but as strong as panthers, judging from the mountainous loads on their shoulders or in their arms, glance at the traffic with eyes that have long grown accustomed to seeing fast European and American cars instead of slow white Thai elephants.

The activity around the Erawan Hotel when I arrive

is at its peak. In the swimming pool several girls are splashing in the green water like sprightly seals, their brightly colored bathing caps transforming the pool into a flower-speckled meadow. Dwarf trees dot the patio around the pool. An orchestra of three violins, a small piano, and a saxophone is playing Broadway melodies. The aseptic whiteness of the jackets worn by the "boys" serving cocktails and the steady splash of water in the pool give the patio an impression of coolness. This is a false impression. The necks of the women are beaded with the liquid diamonds of perspiration, and the white jackets of the men are stained dark with the water drained from their bodies by the oppressive heat.

I exchange greetings with several of the members of the Tour Royale, whom I had already met. A lady beckons to me and I sit down at her table.

Mrs. Wayne, an American writer of books on home economics, bears on stout shoulders sixty years of pink health and youthful vitality. She is a maternal type with concealed aggressions. Sipping a tall orangeade into which one could almost dive, she energetically fans herself with a palm fan bought in Cambodia. We chat while the music vies with the splashing in the pool and the tinkling of ice in the silver cocktail shaker of the barman, a Thai who perennially flashes upon one and all the snow of his smile.

Mrs. Wayne tells me her problems. She is traveling with the famous three-month Tour Royale, which left

California four weeks ago and has already visited Japan
and Hong Kong. There are fourteen persons on the
tour. They are now going to India, where it is said
the temperatures are utterly unbearable for all except
the natives. Mrs. Wayne is terrified at the prospect of
more heat. She cannot possibly endure another hot day.
She also can no longer endure her fellow travelers. The
members of the Tour Royale are already sick of one
another. Of course, their true feelings are properly concealed behind wan smiles, banal phrases, and little
courtesies. But there are still two more months to go!
And Mrs. Wayne is already on the verge of exploding.
Her fellow travelers are not beyond discrimination.
Such arrant hypocrites! Mrs. Wayne's capacious chest
is full of gossip and observations about her companions
and she proceeds forthwith to unburden herself of her
information. To what she tells me I add my own impressions, and amuse myself by conjuring up mental
pictures, my fabrications for fun, of the thirteen other
"fortunate," rich members of the Tour Royale.

Tom and Teresa Rensworth: he is a scenario writer
for a Hollywood studio; she is a model at a fashion
house in Beverly Hills.

Tom Rensworth wanted above all to be a fiction
writer, but when the magazine editors to whom he sent
his stories repeatedly shattered his hopes, he went to
work for a Hollywood studio, where as a chief scenario
writer he now earns a five-figure monthly salary. He
is a tall, gawky young man, with red hair and eyes the

color of gooseberries. He dresses as though not only his clothes but he as well had just emerged from the bottom of an overseas trunk. Frustration at not having become a famous author burns steadily within him, and he ceaselessly douses this inner fire with tall glasses of Scotch and soda, which he guzzles down as a thirsty child guzzles water from a fountain. Tom was henpecked into the Tour Royale by his wife, who gives all the orders in the Rensworth household, albeit with smiles and feminine wiles. From his trip around the world, Tom Rensworth will return to his world in Hollywood with no other gain than the hundreds of Scotch and sodas consumed at all the bars of all the hotels at which the Tour Royale stops. Everything else is nothing more than an animated post card, much less real to him than his studio sets. In revenge for his failure, Tom Rensworth is bent on destroying all the part of himself that might have been the writer and on liberating instead the glorified bureaucrat within himself.

At his side, Teresa Rensworth, a de luxe model, responds to the compliments of her fellow travelers as the sunflower responds to the sun. She is the belle of the Tour Royale, despite the frenzied efforts of two other women to win that privileged position. She has long, smoky blonde hair, enormous eyes that she always opens wide in an effort to hide her myopia, a mouth like a wild berry split in two by a greedy bird, a small, almost nonexistent bust, an elusive waist, and long sleek

legs with fleshless ankles. She talks a great deal and
always about the same thing—her clothes, her admir-
ers, how much everyone adores her. Her husband drinks
for two; she eats for half of one. Her meals not only
drive everyone to desperation, they give everyone a
guilt complex. In Bangkok, while everyone on the tour
was going into raptures over the delicious Thai curries,
she ordered a yoghurt and a Coca-Cola; in Hong Kong,
while everyone was gorging himself on the most
divinely crisp Peking duck, she had a cottage cheese
salad and a cup of Sanka; and in Tokyo, while everyone was stuffing himself on the most delectable sukiyaki until seams were ready to burst, she ate nothing
because she had had a malted milk in the morning.

Teresa Rensworth had somehow convinced the owner
of the fashion house where she works that the publicity he would derive from her being photographed all
around the world in his creations would be worth far
more than the expense involved. It was thus that she
had joined the Tour Royale.

Teresa flirts with everyone, but discreetly, not out of
respect for her husband, who is just another "contact"
in her world of advertising and public relations, but
because the only person she really cares for and loves
is herself. Teresa will return from the Tour Royale with
an album bulging with pictures of herself from magazines from all over the world, thanks to carefully
planned publicity. Years from now, while her husband
is being treated for hepatic cirrhosis, she will still be

showing everyone pictures of herself taken alongside a Pekingese dog in Nikko or surrounded by fishermen in Kuala Lumpur.

Joe Pilosero is an Iowa businessman who has made a small fortune in the manufacture of egg cartons. A widower for ten years, he is now sixty years old. Small, fat, and pink fleshed, when he joined the tour he looked exactly like an uncooked frankfurter. The Oriental sunshine has turned him into a cooked frankfurter. Joe Pilosero always wears the tourist uniform: a shirt, purchased in Hawaii, printed with half-naked girls gamboling in the waves of Waikiki Beach. He carries his passport clipped to the top pocket of his shirt, because he wants everyone to know that he is a tourist—and an American. Hanging from a shoulder strap, he carries a camera as big as a destroyer; three additional small cameras, several light meters, and other photographic gadgets hang from his belt like pistols from the belt of a nineteenth-century American desperado. He eats a great deal, but always with obvious dislike, because "all of these foreign dishes simply kill me." Only when he can get a thick steak, as bloody as he is accustomed to in Iowa, does he eat with gusto. He always accompanies his food with a tall glass of bourbon and soda, a glass that is never completely full or completely empty.

Joe Pilosero has come on this tour because his wife had always dreamed of their making this trip together, and before she died, in a sentimental moment, she begged him to make the trip alone for both of them. The promise he made is becoming increasingly difficult to fulfill. He feels alone and out of place in these countries which he does not understand and where he has to eat such strange food. He is tormented by the heat and has no one in the group he can talk to about trout fishing, his only passion in life. He is dying to return to his egg-box factory and to salmon fishing with his friends, who, like him, are all businessmen. Meanwhile he is kept alive by the business cables and letters, which he receives by the dozen, even as eggs are packed by the dozen in the cartons he manufactures.

He talked to me for a while, but as soon as he realized that I knew nothing about and had no interest in egg cartons or trout fishing, he lost interest in me.

Joe Pilosero will return to his home town from the Tour Royale convinced that in this big, wide world we live in, God chose Iowa as Paradise and him as its fortunate Adam.

The Stone family comes from the southern part of the United States. Father, mother, and their seventeen-year-old daughter. Sam Stone inherited from his father a cotton plantation which he has industrialized and converted into a money-making machine. He is more than fifty, tall, thin, but strong, with a closely shaven face that shines like a mirror under a perennial film of perspiration. He has cold blue eyes, which turn as hard as flint when someone contradicts him or something turns out badly for him. He is always dressed in a spotless white tropical suit and a white tie. His well-manicured hands look as if they never do anything except sign checks or hold a planter's punch.

Sam Stone has come on the tour to reward his daughter (she really demanded it, as she does everything else) for having finished high school. Mr. Stone regards the Oriental countries and their people with a mixture of benevolent superiority and scandalized surprise. For him there is no difference between the brown- or yellow-skinned Orientals and the Negroes on his plantation. He is revolted at the sight of dark-skinned people seated next to him in restaurants, trains, airplanes, cafés, or temples, but he is consoled by the sight of his daughter having such a wonderful time, for, after his plantation, his daughter is the most important thing in his life.

His daughter is named Georgiana: seventeen years of sex appeal, sensuous languor, unexpected bursts of dynamism, and exasperating fits of laziness. Georgiana is always too tired to climb the steps leading to the temples, or to go through the rooms of a museum, or to visit palaces. However, within a matter of minutes after her arrival at any place she finds out where there is American music and dancing and who the eligible American bachelors are, after which she promptly organizes wild rock-'n'-roll parties that last until dawn.

She has a fresh-looking, childish face, clear blue eyes, mustard-blonde hair, a statuesque body, and shapely legs that she displays with the pride of an Olympic champion displaying her cups and medals. She is arrogant with waiters and servants, and haughty with everyone else except her father. With him, she is simply despotic and tyrannical. She does not know anything about anything, but she thinks she knows everything about everything. The world to her is one more plantation, which some day will belong to her father. The only things that elicit her admiration or enthusiasm are usually things no one else cares for. When something pleases her, she breaks out into shouts, squeals, and exclamations, which invariably make her, as she intended, the center of attention. One day she will be a very beautiful woman. She will also be intractable and odious. All that Georgiana Stone will garner from her trip around the world will be a string of names of places with which to impress her boyfriends in Alabama.

Between father and daughter, or rather close behind them, there is always a small pale woman, white haired and sad eyed, a woman of few, soft-spoken words. Rather than a woman, Mrs. Stone is a mere presence.

Jim Saylor and Rupert Crawley are two young "geniuses"—thus they advertise themselves—from New York's Madison Avenue. Employed by an advertising agency, they earn impressive salaries, one as an account executive to a large soda manufacturing company; the other is in charge of the art work for the same company. At a memorable meeting, they managed to persuade the president of the soda company to send them around the world at company expense so that they could bring back enough photographic material and other information to stage a world-wide campaign introducing the company's beverage. In a moment of alcoholic stupor, following a lunch with too many Martinis, the president approved the project. Once he had approved it, he could not renege.

Jim and Rupert are only taking six weeks of the Tour Royale, having come by plane from New York to meet it halfway. Each young man looks like a mirror image of the other. They are both small framed and very thin, have delicate cameo profiles and softly waved hair; one is blond and the other brunet. Their speech is sprinkled with Madison Avenue jargon. They dress impeccably, the way travelers do only in the pages of *Esquire*. No matter how hot it may be, they never perspire, even though they wear tight-fitting trousers, silk shirts, printed scarves around their necks, and occasionally colored vests. They also wear the gaudiest and most complicated sandals to be found in those fancy little shops for men that have suddenly cropped up on Park Avenue.

Jim and Rupert often pull out of their pockets a picture of their dog Sandy and go into raptures over it, kissing it profusely. Sandy is wire thin, with curly hair meticulously pruned like the grass in a royal garden. His eyes are invisible behind his hair. Sandy has been left with a friend in the apartment shared by the two young men in New York.

Jim and Rupert are masters of rock-'n'-roll, which at first made young Georgiana Stone shriek with delight and later with indignation, when they chose to ignore her completely. In fact, they openly make fun of everyone in the group. They live in a world of their own, from which they emerge to make mysterious nocturnal excursions, returning at dawn with circles under their eyes and completely exhausted. The sun annoys them because of the havoc it plays with their cultivated pallor. They are utterly blind to the sensuousness of Oriental women, but miraculously recover their sight in the presence of slender young waiters.

Jim and Rupert will return from the Tour Royale with mountains of pictures, memoranda, and business addresses. They will also take back a secret file of furtive, sinful memories, which, in the intimacy of their apartment, they will share only with a small circle of friends, while Sandy jealously thrusts his pink little nose between their pale manicured hands, begging for another kiss.

Mrs. Jeanne Harris is the *femme fatale* of the Tour Royale. She is making the trip around the world to forget, she says, her recent divorce, which left her with a broken heart and alimony of fifty thousand dollars a year. She talks about her marriage and her ex-husband, a wealthy Texas industrialist, as if her matrimonial story were the most tragic in the world and also the most interesting. She does not mention, perhaps out of modesty, perhaps out of consideration for other people's feelings, that this was her seventh "official" marriage.

Years ago Mrs. Harris had been the winner of a national beauty contest. At the end of her short reign, having spent at a dizzy rate all the money she had earned, she launched on a matrimonial career. Her alimony has increased in direct ratio to her experience. Tall, slender, with flame-red hair, and always exquisitely dressed, Mrs. Harris can catalogue a man's financial bracket with one glance from her wide green eyes. She joined the Tour Royale in the hope of meeting her next husband, or at least a wealthy boy friend. But the Tour Royale, with its constant excursions to temples, museums, and ruins, has failed to provide this opportunity. Instead she has to content herself with exercising her seductive charms on her fellow travelers in general, a highly unrewarding occupation to the financially minded Mrs. Harris.

Mrs. Harris will return from the Tour Royale with the all-important knowledge that it is easier to find a rich man in the United States, which is a land of rich men, than in the poor countries of the Orient.

Peter and Sally Lawrence are newlyweds and have about them an aura of quiet passion and constant bliss. Sally's father owns the Consolidated Furniture Company in Baltimore. Peter, the assistant manager, fell in love with the boss's daughter and, as in movies with happy endings, married her. Both their ages together add up to forty years, for she is not yet twenty. Peter is a good, industrious boy, and Sally's parents saw in the marriage a happy solution to the problem of marrying off their daughter and retaining a hard-working assistant manager.

Sally is small, pink, and fresh as a rosebud sprinkled with dew. She has the lithe body of an athlete and the happy laugh of a school girl. She is studying furniture design, with a view toward working in her father's factory. Peter entered the company as an office boy and promptly worked up to a good position. Now his official family status assures him the post of future manager. He is tall and strong, has a sincere face and the alert eyes of a greyhound. Both Sally and Peter adore sports, and their honeymoon is punctuated with tennis games, wherever they can find a court, early morning swims, long days spent climbing the stone steps of temple after temple, and whole evenings spent dancing. They always smile at everyone, and seem to be living in a fairy tale, thanks to the generosity of Sally's father.

Sally and Peter will return from the Tour Royale determined more than ever to work hard in order some day to fulfill their dream: a house in Hyannis, Cape Cod, with three or four children, a tennis court, and a swimming pool. The vast world they are now visiting has only intensified their desire to create their own world within the confines of their home and live there ever after.

Major Mervin Alton and his wife are the cynics of

the Tour Royale. Thin, tall, with dried-up skin, their souls too seem to have dried up. They have money—securities, insurance, real estate—and a rank that he received during the war and to which he clings as if it were a medical degree from the Sorbonne.

They have no children. They have no friends either and do not want any. They live in an exclusive hotel in Palm Beach, Florida. In the summertime they go to New England. They look exactly like the two farmers, husband and wife, in Grant Wood's painting *American Gothic,* except that the painting symbolizes the austerity of work, whereas the Altons symbolize the cynicism of indolence.

The Altons have only one pastime: criticizing everything and everyone. They doubt everything and everyone, including themselves; find fault with the whole world and all its inhabitants; compare everything in terms of their own possessions, their hotel apartment, their restricted, select group of bridge partners in Palm Beach and canasta partners in New England. The world to them is only a setting for the farce of their cynical comments. The yearning for freedom of the Oriental countries revolts them, and so does the food. They find the weather detestable, and the people of the tour even more so. Nevertheless, once when a little Thai boy put his arms around the Major's legs and smiled at him, I saw their faces suddenly light up, but, with a furtive glance at each other, they quickly became serious again.

Perhaps behind their cynical masks they are saddened by unfulfilled dreams too intimate to be revealed.

Such are the traveling companions of Mrs. Wayne on the Tour Royale. Silently, in Bangkok's magic blue twilight, I watch them in action: sipping cocktails at nearby tables, dancing, diving into the pool, stopping here and there to chat.

Mrs. Wayne finishes airing her grievances. She is hurt because the group discriminates against her. She accuses them of putting on airs and acting arrogantly toward the whole world. Engulfing them all in a contemptuous glance, she suddenly leans close to me and whispers:

"Look at them. So elegant, so conceited, so arrogant. Each one thinks he is the center of the world. Well, let me tell you a secret. All of them, but absolutely *all* of them, have had diarrhea for two weeks!"

Without realizing it, Mrs. Wayne has just discovered the only common denominator, the true biological equalizer, among all the rich tourists on the Tour Royale, just as it is among all people.

BUDDHISM YESTERDAY AND TODAY, AND THE "OTHER" BANGKOK

The "OTHER" BANGKOK, which we are now crossing on a *samlor,* a motorized tricycle driven by a smiling, dynamic little man, is the modern Bangkok of which the Thai are so proud.

It boasts interminable avenues, with shops that imitate the selling techniques of American drugstores, piling up a motley assortment of cheap goods in their show windows. But there are also shops with the truly beautiful products of Thai handcraft: jewelry, silks, brocades, and bronze eating utensils with horn handles.

The streets with the best shops are New Road, which was "new" when it was built but is the oldest avenue in the city, even as the *Pont-Neuf* is the oldest bridge in Paris; Nakorn Kasem Compound, with its colorful bazaars; Ban Moh, with its silver shops; Sampeng Road, with its cutlery shops; Pahurad Road, where one can buy raffia tablecloths, sapphires, zircons, and the Thai specialty, *nielloware,* enamel ware with silver designs.

There is a deafening uproar of automobiles, buses, streetcars, taxis (which do not have meters but charge according to distance), and *samlors.* Modern buildings soar proudly into space, and there are many modern houses. But all one has to do is wander a little off the boulevards—where driving between the hours of 11 A.M. and 4 P.M. is sheer torture, for in the hellish heat each car is a red hot oven in which one is roasted in a few minutes—and one suddenly comes upon a canal, or upon peasants trailing after their water buffalo, whose impassivity remains unruffled despite the roaring scooters and motorcycles that have displaced horses and elephants as a means of transportation in Bangkok.

Modern Bangkok's Dom Mueng airport, an aerial crossroad for twenty-five air lines, is perhaps the busiest in Southeast Asia. During World War II, the Japanese had their prisoners of war construct a railway between Thailand and Burma; although it is still used by the Thai, it does not reach Burma. The modernity of Bangkok, which is the seat of the general headquarters of SEATO, is attested to by two television stations, almost three hundred radio stations, thirty-two newspapers, stadiums, pools, concert halls, and important banks, where you can find secretaries as beautiful as princesses, and where Thai bahts and satangs are exchanged for Australian pounds, Burmese kyats, American dollars, Hong Kong dollars, Indian rupees, Japanese yen, Laotian kips, Singapore dollars, Philippine pesos, Cambodian riels, English pounds sterling, and Vietnamese piastres.

The Bright Saffron Robes

The sight of some Buddhist monks on the way to their monastery reminds me that it is time to visit the temples and see Thai religion in action.

The religion of the Thai is Buddhism. The Thai, a word which means "free," originally came from the Yangtze River Valley in China. In the thirteenth century they emigrated southward, settling around the Chao Phya and Mekong rivers. Today there are twenty-eight million Thai (almost two million of whom live in Bangkok) in a country that is smaller in size than France. Most of the people till the land, producing the best rice in the world. They also produce preserved fish, salt, corn, tapioca flour, tungsten, teak, tin, and rubber. The country, which originally was called Siam by outsiders, a word derived from the Chinese *siam lo* (the country in the south), and was ruled by princes, today proudly calls itself Thailand, "the land of the free," and is a constitutional monarchy with much power held by generals. The oldest pre-Thai city, Lopburi, still exists, but the ancient capitals of Sukhothai, Ayudga, and Dhonburi have been replaced by the city outsiders call Bangkok and the natives Krung Thep, "metropolis of the deities," a name that designates admirably the city of four hundred temples.

En route toward Bangkok's temples, we pass Buddhist monks everywhere, clad in flowing robes of a color that varies from a brilliant orange through an orange-yellow to a vivid saffron. One sees them left and right, alone or in groups, with their shaved heads, many wearing sunglasses, and often carrying stacks of books under their arms.

Those monks are not like our professional clerics. Religion is Thailand, and Thailand is Buddhism. The monks are the people; the people are the monks. Bangkok, with its profusion of Buddhist priests, is one great sanctuary. It is customary for every male Buddhist in Thailand, including even the king himself, to become a monk for at least three months of his life and profess in the temple closest to his home, either as *samanera,* or novices, before coming of age, or as *bhikkhel,* once they have come of age. It serves as a valuable apprenticeship for their future lives. It teaches them a lesson in humility, which is as important as Buddhism itself.

One of my guides is a young law student. He will

soon finish his studies and will then enter a Buddhist monastery. He will leave his affluent family (his father is a judge), will shave his beautiful wavy black hair, don the saffron-yellow robe, rise every morning at dawn in the temple, eat only a bowl of rice every day before noon, drink water only between noon and sunrise, pray, meditate, and study Buddhism. Today he is relieving the semifast he has already started with cigarettes, betel, and Coca-Cola.

The monks obtain their food from any home in their path, for every single house has a daily supply of rice —adorned with a lotus blossom—in readiness to be given to the Buddhist monks who come by. I have seen them, impassive, dignified, silent, with heads high, stopping at the door of a house, not to beg for the bowl of rice that will sustain them for the day but to give the people the opportunity of performing an act of merit. These monks therefore are not really begging, and they express their thanks simply when they have been given their food.

The Buddhism practiced in Thailand is the pure, mystical Hinayana Buddhism of the south, or Pali Buddhism, which predominates also in Ceylon, Burma, Cambodia, and Laos, in contrast to the more complex Mahayana Buddhism of the north, of Viet Nam, China, Japan, Korea, Mongolia, and Tibet. Hinayana is the same form of Buddhism that was preached in India twenty-five hundred years ago by Gautama Buddha as the way to salvation and as a protest against Brahmanism.

Its basic concepts are reincarnation, or the belief that life, whether of men or animals, is a phase in a cycle of incarnation; and karma, the belief that every action elicits another compensatory one in the present or future life. It was Buddha's conviction that all forms of life, with their inevitable physical and moral sufferings, should be lived in such a way as to attain nirvana. Toward this end, he taught, man should strive to eliminate the causes of his future reincarnation by suppressing every act that entails such a consequence. This method of suppressing man's unsuitable acts constitutes the very core of Buddhism and the secret of its renunciations.

Salvation can be attained only in isolation from the world and from maya, the phantasmagoric phenomenal manifestations of the real world. Buddhists therefore originally grouped together in small bands of mendicant monks, who through solitary meditation and inward concentration strove to escape rebirth, that is, reincarnation after death.

Buddhism differs from other religions in that it lacks ritual and sacrament. It is a system of thought. All one has to do to be a Buddhist is accept this system and work out one's "own salvation with diligence." It is a religion without a God; paradoxically, it is an agnostic religion.

Once nirvana, or supreme enlightenment, is attained,

Buddha can no longer act on his disciples' behalf, and the disciples can only follow his teachings and venerate his greatness and his relics.

Looking now at some Buddhist monks immersed in prayer, I am reminded of Catholics praying, but there is really no comparison. Only the external attitude of immersion in prayer is similar. In reality, true Buddhists do not pray, nor do they give thanks to Buddha —whom they do not regard as a supernatural being but rather as the ultimate attainment of the Self, not a god, but a man who began like themselves—nor do they express their devotion to him. They simply express their desire that the merit they may have acquired in the performance of a particular action, or in refraining from a particular action, may produce, in accordance with the laws of karma, the desired results. But the people's innate animism tends to convert prescriptions for meditation into prayers, and images of Buddha into relics endowed with magical powers.

PORCELAIN ROOFS AND
GOLD BUDDHAS

Following Pen Phmim's lit-
tle steps, I enter a true fairy tale: Bangkok's temples.
I have seen many places of worship in the world. I
have been in the Egyptian temples where, in the mam-
moth shadow of the pyramids, death reigns supreme;
in the basilicas of old Byzantium in Istanbul, overlooking the blue waters of the Golden Horn; in Italian
churches, in whose mighty statuary the glory of the
Renaissance has survived; in the Gothic cathedral of

Chartres, whose stained-glass windows have perpetu-
ated the Middle Ages; in Shinto temples, Japanese
sanctuaries with vestiges of paganism; in Lebanese her-
mitages where the humility of the Holy family still
lingers; in Spanish cathedrals, bulwarks of Catholicism
in the Europe of the Reformation; in the Protestant
churches of Oslo and Berlin, which still reverberate
with Luther's words; in the ancient churches of Macao,
where Christ is prayed to in Chinese; in the temples of
Peru, where Indians pray in Quechua and make offerings of grain and flowers to the Christian God. Yes,
I have seen many places of worship throughout the
world. But nowhere have I seen temples like those of
Bangkok, temples that are fulfilled dreams, that are
religion transformed into fairy tale.

The wats cover one fifth of the entire city. Wherever
one may be, the wats with their many splendors relieve
the uniformity that is inevitable in any Oriental city
undergoing Western-style industrialization. Everywhere
there rise glittering towers, cupolas, columns, and
arches, overlaid with gold, tiles, mother-of-pearl, or
porcelain. At sunrise, almost four hundred lucent temples transform the city into a wondrous jewel chest
with the jewels spilling out in all directions.

The Grand Palace, encircled by a high-walled compound and bordered by pink lotuses and scarlet flowers,
has great beauty. More than a palace, it is a walled
city (it occupies more than one of the city's sixty-eight
square miles), with its intricate web of white and pink

government buildings, temples with courtyards paved with pebbles and *chedi* adorning the entranceways, a gold pavilion with overlapping triple-tiered roofs, luxuriant trees, and green lawns.

Thailand's sovereigns used to live in the Grand Palace, amid vast halls with crystal ceilings, marble stairs, silver statues, and pagodas with pointed spires. Symbols of the regal pomp of the past are the great royal barges, overlaid with gold leaf, as slender as swans. Now they stand in dry dock, but once, at great festivals, they bore kings whose vesture of gold glittered like a fulfilled dream.

Each temple of Bangkok is a coffer filled with new and marvelous revelations. There are no two identical temples, nor any two temple pavilions that are alike. The Wat Phra Kaeo, or Temple of the Emerald Buddha, is perhaps the most beautiful. Guarded by gigantic, fierce-looking demons made of brick overlaid with tiles, it contains a *bot,* or main temple, reserved for congregations of monks; a vihara for the public, which comes here not to pray but to venerate Buddha's memory; stupas, or bell-shaped memorial columns, containing the remains of deceased persons or a relic of Buddha. The walls are decorated with scenes from the Ramakian, the Thai version of the Ramayana.

It is a labyrinth of gilded *chedi,* altars, sacred flowers, and images of saints, gods, kings, demons, and mythological animals. Outside, bronze lions keep guard against walls covered with blue flowers and gold designs, and there are friezes adorned with Garudas, or birds, with men's faces (the national emblem), *kinnara,* or semigods, with human heads and birds' bodies; *singh,* or stylized lions; *chofa,* or gable moldings, in the form of serpents; and Nagas, the semihuman serpents who are genii of waters and rain.

The range of colors is comparable only to the assortment of construction materials: gypsum, bronze, wood, brick, tile, porcelain, mother-of-pearl, copper, silver, and gold in all forms (plain, carved, solid, plated; beaten into sheets or leaves; or molded in ingots). Outside the temple, thousands upon thousands of little gold bells in the shape of *bohdi* leaves tinkle night and day in the gentle breeze.

Inside the temple at the top of a pyramidal altar, within the mysterious penumbra cast by his gilded canopy, stands the Emerald Buddha looking down upon a veritable forest of little silver trees and rows of life-sized gilded Buddhas carrying golden parasols. These last were presented by and portray various kings.

The Emerald Buddha, carved from one single block of green jasper twenty-one and a half inches high, is attired in a robe and headdress of pure gold and precious stones, which are changed three times a year, in the hot, rainy, and cool seasons. It is said that the statue, which was originally believed to be of marble until the gilded overlaying fell off, came from India or Ceylon by way of Laos and that it has been presiding over the spiritual destinies of its worshipers here beneath the

336

temple's red and gold ceilings for almost two centuries.

Filled with admiration, I leave the temple accompanied by the tinkle of thousands of little bells trembling in the breeze. Outside on the temple walls, the gold leaf, rent by many past winds, hangs in thin strips, which in the breeze look like the darting golden tongues of sacred serpents.

Wonders do not cease. Wat Rajabopitr has Chinese glazed tiles and a luxuriant tropical garden; Wat Rajapradit has two marble towers from Cambodia; Wat Benchamabopitr is of Italian marble, with Chinese tiles, black- and gold-lacquered windows, rows of stone and bronze Buddhas, marble lions, and brilliant tiled roofs, all of which make this temple the gem of Thai art.

Wat Arun, the Temple of the Dawn, on the other side of the river, has a colossal *prang* or tower, more than two hundred and sixty feet high, as well as four smaller *prang;* the five *prang* are supported and decorated by angels, giants, monkeys, white elephants, deities, and mythological beasts. Giant demons guard the small chapel of the novices. From a distance this temple looks as if it were made of carved marble, but upon climbing the tower one can see that the walls are solidly overlaid with hundreds of thousands of bits of china and porcelain, which gleam in the sun as if the temple were made of snow. It is said that a ship with a full cargo of china and porcelain was shipwrecked in the Gulf of Siam and that the ingenious temple artisans broke the cargo into tiny pieces and used them on the Temple of the Dawn.

Wat Kalaga houses a mighty Buddha; Wat Saket includes the Golden Mount, or Phu Khao Thong, which contains one of Buddha's bones; the Wat Sutat, a Buddha twenty-six feet high, in addition to another smaller Buddha who presides over an assemblage of eighty life-sized painted figures of his disciples; and Wat Po, the biggest and most richly colored of all, with its tile roofs, golden nagas, and lofty spires, has a *bot* or temple with three hundred and ninety-four Buddhas and mother-of-pearl doors depicting scenes from the Ramakian.

In Wat Po there is a reclining Buddha entering nirvana, a figure one hundred and fifty feet long, built by Rama III, and made of gilded brick and plaster. The Buddha is supporting his smiling, enigmatic head on his right hand, his left arm is extended along his body, and the soles of his enormous feet, inlaid with mother-of-pearl, are inscribed with dharma signs, the wheel of the law, and the one hundred and six signs associated with Buddha.

As I leave the temple I find the huge courtyard bustling with activity. It is the eve of a great Buddhist festival. There are lines of monks dressed in glowing orange robes, waiting to pay tribute to the reclining Buddha. There is cymbal and flute music, peasant men and women dressed in white cotton pajamas, children playing and laughing like well-trained circus dogs, stands selling all sorts of trifles, and everywhere there are great cauldrons of bubbling hot curries, some scarlet, others green, ocher, or purple, fragrant with spices and sunshine, into which the women keep throwing handfuls of red and green hot peppers, and all sorts of other strong condiments.

Olive-skinned Hindus, golden Thai, and ivory-skinned Chinese mill around the stands buying sausages, dried smoked bats, boiled eggs or rice, and crisp roasted duck skin. Other stands sell incense cones and offerings for the Buddha. Little trees made of colored paper strips, inscribed with prayers and incantations in honor of the dead, wave in the breeze. String and bamboo instruments sound here and there. The smell of frying foods, boiled rice, and seasoned curry are noted along with the noise of the children and the chants of a line of monks who look like great bright-orange peacocks. In a little open-air theatre Thai dances are being presented. The first candles of evening are lit and glow like fallen stars. And just to make everything complete, there are Coca-Cola and Pepsi-Cola stands, and machines where, for a coin, one can play a sort of football with little toy figures, the Thai version of American pinball machines.

Inside the wat, in the narrow pavilion that encases him like a snug garment, the reclining gold Buddha keeps on smiling upon his believers from nirvana.

SIAMESE DOLLS

Ⅰ‌T WAS MY PRIVILEGE TO BE IN-
vited to the home of Dr. Chamlong Harinasuta for a
splendid Thai dinner. A young physician, he is a most
dynamic force in medicine in Thailand and one of the
most interesting medical personalities in Southeast
Asia. In addition to having an extensive private practice, he is the Dean of the School of Tropical Medicine
and Secretary General of the University of Medical Sci-
ences. He has done brilliant research in the fields of

filariasis, helminthiasis, and malaria. His lovely wife, Tranakchit, who is also a physician, assists him at the School of Tropical Medicine and in his private practice. Before dinner they took me on a moonlight tour of their garden, which contained all kinds of plants with splendid blossoms, from sunflowers to orchids. The wonderful meal included a variety of hot curries that were the best I had in Bangkok, in addition to many native delicacies.

After dinner I went to a dance recital at the Pakhavali Institute of Dance and Music in Boripat Road.

Siamese religion has inspired both Siamese art and theatre. Classical Thai dancing, like all Thai theatre, takes inspiration from the dramatization of scenes from the Ramayana, the great epic poem of India. The stage is generally small and dimly lit, and the music is light, with rhythms that are strange to Western ears and have an hallucinatory, hypnotic effect. The action is slow, the costumes are elaborate, the miming is fascinating. It is a theatre of ideas, rather than of action, each spectator dramatizing in his own mind the struggle between good and evil that is being represented on the stage by the actors' pantomime.

The ballet program I saw included *yu-ngid,* a classical dance; *krabot mai,* a rice-harvest dance done with the long poles peasants use, balanced on their shoulders, to transport things; some classical Thai fencing with swords and wooden sticks; *sat jatri,* a classical dance of the South; some dances with drums; and a dramatization from the Ramayana of a battle between giants and monkeys.

The dancers, exquisite dolls with faces of golden porcelain, wear elaborately embroidered costumes that weigh many pounds. These costumes, composed of several layers of silk, satin, velvet, brocade, and gold and silver gauze, embroidered with colored spangles and shimmering stones, are worn so tight that they have to be sewn directly on the dancer's body before each performance.

The dance, accompanied by bamboo, wood, metal, and shell instruments, is slow but fascinating. The almost rigid immobility of the stemlike bodies, punctuated by occasional sudden leaps and turns (reminiscent of the Japanese dances I saw in Tokyo), contrasts with the constant subtle movements of the hands, whose spread fingers transform them into fleeting stars, and with the intricate gyrations of the feet, dramatizing moods, passions, the entire mysterious chemistry of the human spirit. These foot movements of the Thai dance are not to be found in any other dance in the world.

Instead of dancing, these ballerinas appear to be sighing. They do not turn round and round, they float, they glide, like the moon upon the waters of a river. When they have finished, they bid the audience good-by with the lovely Thai bow, the palms of their hands together in a prayerlike gesture, slowly moving backward until they disappear, not, I am convinced, into their dressing rooms, so that their garments, which must to them

342

weigh tons upon their tiny bodies, may be unstitched from them, but into the hands of a giant, who gently lifts them by their waists and, with great care so that they will not break, puts them back in their resting places, perhaps a music box or a layer of cotton in little doll boxes.

KITES IN THE SKY OF THAILAND

Toward evening Pen Phmim takes me to Pramane Esplanade, near the Grand Palace, above whose gilt and pink cupolas a discreet but elegant sun still glows.

"We Siamese love sports," Pen Phmim explains to me, "but for many centuries we did not know Western sports. You will therefore find sports here that are completely different from your own. On Sundays, although it is illegal, there are fish fights, at which people bet heavily. *Takraw* is also very popular. The players toss a wicker ball back and forth, and it is permissible to use the elbows, knees, head, or shoulders. And there is Thai boxing."

I had already seen a Thai boxing match one hot afternoon, made even hotter by the enormous crowd that filled the stadium and by the strident music of the bamboo flutes, tambourine-like instruments, and drums that accompany these matches.

Thai boxing is the fastest, most dynamic sport in the world. The fighters are allowed to hit not only with their gloved fists, but also with their feet, knees, and elbows. The fighters, little men as frail looking as undernourished children, are combination boxers, acrobats, and jumping jacks.

For color and dynamism, it is an incomparable spectacle. After the initial prayers to the suitable deities (sports, like everything else in Thailand, is saturated with religion) the boxers run, dart, skip, and spin all over the ring; they leap on each other, punching, kicking, and poking each other with their elbows and knees. And the crowd roars. This is the boxing of a people who, being small and thin and lacking the muscular strength of larger-framed races, have given the body complete freedom to use all the aggressive parts and fighting resources at its disposal. A mixture of acrobatics, boxing, jiu-jitsu, and catch-as-catch-can, Thai boxing symbolizes the spirit of the Thai—agile, dynamic, nonaggressive, but willing to defend themselves to the best of their ability.

"But our favorite sport," Pen Phmim continues, "is kite flying."

And there I see them, in Bangkok's darkening blue skies, flying at dizzying heights above the heads of the crowd, all eyes turned toward their favorite kites—an entire nation flirting with torticollis.

The kites are in all shapes and colors. Green fishes, scarlet dragons, gold birds, blue flying ships, purple pagodas, silver warriors. They fly at great speed, some climbing, others descending, steered by the invisible threads that hold them and by the even more invisible fingers of the wind. Others, as swift and free as eagles, ride high in the startled sky.

In this celestial festival the sky becomes starred, as in some romantic legend, with all the things that are the romantic essence of man's dreams: flying dragons, turreted castles, sailboats, rainbowed birds, winged horses, and moons of gold: a fairy celebration in which men on earth let their most sublime inner yearnings climb to heaven astride their kites, conquering the celestial heights with their paper cutouts, over which the dying sun is but another kite.

Kite contests are held from March to June. In the most important match the field is divided in half with a cord. On one side is the *chula,* or masculine kite, a five-pointed star six feet high; on the other side is the rhomboidal female *pakpao,* with its loop and spruce white tail. Both the *chula* and the *pakpao* are made of paper on a frame of bamboo strips. The *chula,* by means of barbs attached to its cord, tries to cut the cord of the little *pakpao* and bring them down in its territory; the female kites skip, cavort, and dance all around the big *chula,* like butterflies around a hawk, and try to attach themselves to it by means of their loops and, by destroying its balance, force it down in their territory. Each kite is manipulated by a team of men who work in perfect coordination.

That afternoon I witnessed a rare event. The little *pakpao* succeeded in forcing down the big *chula,* which like an airplane hit in its vital parts, crashed with a resounding noise on the ground.

Kite contests, which have been held in Thailand for seven centuries, were once a sport of kings, who used to sponsor them and were expert kite fliers themselves, often vying with their own subjects.

An unforgettable event for the Thai was the contest held in 1906, when, to the accompaniment of the royal orchestra, twenty teams congregated on the esplanade and competed throughout the day for the King of Thailand's gold cup.

Until recently, kites were used in Southeast Asia for transporting goods from one place to another, for dropping explosives inserted in jars on enemy towns, a practice three centuries old, for transporting spies from one island to another, as the Japanese and the Thai did during World War II, and for reconnoitering enemy territories. Jets have put an end to this aspect of kite flying.

Today, fortunately, their use is limited to matches such as the one I have just seen on Pramane Esplanade. When we leave, the moon, a great silver kite, has risen in the skies and forced its painted paper rivals to descend to earth.

Sawat di, Bangkok!

I shall forever be dreaming of you, magic city of temples that glitter like jewels of silver and gold; of processions of people clad in robes tinted like a painter's palette; of young girls draped in gorgeous silks bearing silver urns in their golden arms; of women unfolding their polychromatic, flowered parasols; of bustling canals where frolicsome children swim like fish in the sunshine; of water buffaloes with hulking slate-gray bodies, antediluvian heads, tiny legs, and mighty horns, plodding through brilliant-green rice fields, each steered by a child perched on its back, who from afar looks like a bird; of children flying their colored kites in the sky; of monks with shaven heads and saffron-colored robes; of pagodas with multicolored tiles housing gold and emerald Buddhas; of snake farms where the dangerous krait and the huge cobra secrete their venom for missions of mercy; of dancers beside whom even China dolls look like strapping women, dancers with hands like stars and feet like lilies.

Sawat di, Bangkok!

My heart remains flying in your skies like one more scarlet kite.

ANGKOR

A MONKEY ON THE IMPERIAL
HEAD

WE LOOK AT EACH OTHER
with startled eyes and suddenly become immobilized,
I in my walk, and he in the restless manipulation of
his hands.

Despite the fact that I have already seen many others
like him in the neighborhood, for this is his native
habitat, I am pleasantly surprised. For I have not expected to see him comfortably seated on one of the huge
ancient stone heads of Angkor Wat here in the Cam-

bodian jungle, supremely indifferent to the steady drizzle and the suffocating jungle heat. Small faced, with
bright little eyes that twinkle with mischief, he looks
like some tiny idol abandoned here many centuries ago
by the builders of the Angkor temple.

A few moments later he has returned to the task of
defleaing himself and I to my exploration of the temple's ruins.

Thus one Sunday morning in April, during my visit
to Angkor Wat, that most legendary of all temples, a
monkey perched atop the stone head of a beautiful
statue chose to pick his fleas rather than strike up a
friendship with me.

Organizing this excursion had been a difficult and
exhausting affair. The evening before in Bangkok, I
had secured passage almost miraculously on a Royal
Air Cambodge plane. Royal Air Cambodge, Thai Air-
ways, and Air Vietnam are three of the lines that make
flights to Siem Reap (pronounced Sem Rayop), from
which one can go to see Angkor. All flights were
booked for weeks to come, but that scourge of the
traveler, dysentery, had come to my aid with a last-
minute cancellation. I was then told that I needed a
visa from Cambodia, within whose territory, bordering
Thailand, lie the Angkor ruins, and, since the consul
had already left his office for the day, I had to send
to his home for the visa. Furthermore, although the excursion lasts only a day, I had to answer an endless
series of questions written both in Cambodian and

French on an even more endless series of printed forms, to provide photographs of myself in triplicate and declare the money I was carrying.

All this finally done, I had gone to bed late, tired and ill humored.

At 5 A.M. I was awakened almost simultaneously by the triple precaution I have adopted when planning to arise very early in the Orient: the odious ring of the alarm clock, that mechanism that cans time; the telephone, a mechanism that converts the visual world around us into darkness with words; and the entrance of the smiling Thai waiter, who punctually every morning brought me my breakfast of tropical fruit, ham and eggs, and the most delicious Thai coffee.

The air conditioning was most ineffectual against the infernal heat outside, and the room felt warm—until I stepped into the adjoining bathroom. Here the heat, intensified by the maddening noise of the air-conditioning motor, was suffocating. But even worse was the heat in the foyer at the other end of my room, where the other section of the cooling apparatus was installed. Every time I crossed this foyer, a veritable furnace, I emerged drenched in perspiration.

A grayish light stole in through the bathroom window. The clouded sky threatened rain. Opposite the hotel, the Menam River, steely and quiescent as the blade of a sword at rest, reflected the black shadows of the flat-hulled fishing boats, in which diminutive Thai women gracefully stood, piercing the sky with the long poles they use as oars.

It was drizzling when I arrived at Don Muang airport, just in time to board the plane. By the time I crossed the stretch between the airport building and the plane, the rain was coming down in torrents and I was thoroughly drenched. The motionless craft at the airport looked like clumsy gray birds forced to the ground by rain-clogged wings. Royal Air Cambodge, despite its imposing name, employs planes for its flights to Cambodia that appear almost toy-sized and look alarmingly fragile. The uncomfortable seats were already filled with some twenty-odd passengers, all crammed together like little tin soldiers in a box too small for them.

We took off amid a sputtering din. Soon we were flying through dense, leaden clouds, enveloped in thick curtains of rain. The two-hour flight across the four hundred and twenty miles between Bangkok and Siem Reap we spent in vainly trying to dry our sopping clothes with our handkerchiefs and in filling out questionnaires issued by the Cambodian immigration authorities.

The Thai of Bangkok are not fond of Cambodians, and continually remind one that, whereas today Thailand is a great democracy, Cambodia on the other hand is infiltrated and headed toward complete communization. The Vietnamese of Saigon, who likewise bear the Cambodians no love, speak of them with contempt. They are fond of saying that Cambodians "not only know nothing about anything, but they do not even *suspect* anything!"

Nevertheless, Cambodia has a great natural potential for becoming a country of economic importance. It is a large plain almost completely bordered by heavily wooden highlands, and in the southeast it is bathed by the Gulf of Siam. Irrigated by the great lake Tonle-Sap and by the Mekong River and its affluents, Cambodia is mainly an agricultural country, producing rice, corn, beans, kapok, pepper, and palm sugar, and also rubber and fish.

We approach Siem Reap, whose airport is improvised in the middle of the jungle. Some distance from the airport is Phnom Penh, the capital of Cambodia, in which five hundred thousand of the country's nearly six million inhabitants live. The Cambodians are very proud of their capital, established on the bank of the Mekong River about a hundred years ago, and of their royal palace with its gilded spires.

According to legend (legends abound in Asia), once upon a time a beautiful lady by the name of Penh saw a tree drifting down the waters of the Mekong during one of the frequent floods. With the assistance of her neighbors, she pulled it out of the river. To her great astonishment she found that its hollow interior held four statues representing Buddha, whereupon she had a hill erected for these relics of Buddha. This hill, or *phnom,* and the name of the pious woman, Penh, are the poetic origin of the name of Cambodia's capital.

The city now has new hotels and even night clubs, such as the *Cambodge,* where the customers dance to American music. The country is a monarchy in conjunction with an assembly and a chief of state. But the main attraction for visitors to Cambodia is the fabulous Angkor ruins, over which our plane was now reeling like a bird lashed by a storm.

Almost in a dive, we descended upon Siem Reap, a barren field hemmed in by the jungle. Through the steady torrent of water pouring from the bleak sky we could discern nothing around us except another plane half-covered with canvas, a metal bird that seemed mortally wounded by the storm, and a small shed. Ankle-deep in water, we hastily scrambled across the muddy ground toward the shed. The rain was warm and the air asphyxiating. April is a bad month to visit Cambodia. The hot season lasts from April to August, and the rainy season, of which we were getting a generous sampling at the moment, from August to November.

Inside the shed it was even hotter, and our discomfort was further increased by the exasperating series of bureaucratic formalities we were subjected to by soldiers in shabby gray uniforms. Almost all of them spoke French, as a result of ninety years of French control over Cambodia, which lasted until 1953. Cambodia entered the stage of history in the same century that marked the beginning of the Christian era, with the establishment of Founan, a Hindu mercantile and maritime kingdom. Six centuries later it was replaced by the state of Tchen-La, part of which came under Javanese rule. In the ninth century, Jayavarman II emerged as the true founder of the Khmer kingdom, from which came present-day Cambodia.

The faces of the soldiers, who were so indifferently making us waste precious hours, revealed their mixed origin. The present-day Cambodians or Khmers represent a fusion of indigenous Southeast Asian peoples, Malayans, Hindus, and Chinese. This mixture is reflected in the folds of their eyelids, in the shape of their mouths, in the structure of their cheekbones, and in their distant gaze, so characteristic of the Hindu. Among themselves, the soldiers spoke Khmer, a language that sounds like Thai, and when we handed them the printed forms they made notations on them in an Indian-Cambodian script. Finally the signal to leave was given. We set forth in a rickety bus over a mud road flanked on both sides by an armada of lush green trees.

An amusing detail illustrated the persistent force of French influence. No sooner did the bus get started than the conductor's Cambodian assistant set a board upon a pair of wooden boxes near the steering wheel to make a counter. Then, while the bus jerked and jolted and almost did somersaults down the road beneath the downpour of rain, he pulled out bottles of Remy-Martin cognac, wine, whisky, and beer from the boxes and placed them upon the improvised bar. *Vive la France!*

Because of the heat, few people ventured to order anything. Only two Americans, with the image of businessmen stamped on their clothes and faces, made a stab at the whisky. After a few sips they turned cherry red and had to remove even their shirts. The alcohol had opened the very last faucets of their bodies and these men were now exuding more water than was pouring from the sky outside our windows.

The rain let up a little. Beyond the windows we could now see many huts made of wood and straw. Half-naked children, their dark faces lit up by warm innocent smiles, were playing in the mud or splashing alongside their fathers in the water of the rice paddies. One of them, standing alone in the middle of a stream, his torso gleaming with rain, was playing a shrill bamboo piccolo. Rather than a child, he looked like a little jungle faun.

We came to a stop in a clearing in the jungle and descended into a world heavy with lustrous vegetation and dripping with rain, which was now falling softly and monotonously, like the whimpering of a tired child. We had reached Angkor Thom, the magic city which about one thousand years ago reared its glittering gilded towers in the middle of a fertile, irrigated region, a city then more beautiful than any other city in the world, more beautiful than Paris and London are today, a city that at its apogee almost suddenly and mysteriously vanished from history: Angkor Thom, or the "Great City."

Angkor Thom was rebuilt in the early thirteenth century by King Jayavarman VII, just a few decades after Suryavarman II had built that legendary wonder, Angkor Wat, or the temple of Angkor. These warrior kings erected a walled city of five and a half square miles, with towers two hundred and fifty feet high, a city that was a temple and a temple that was a city, where between wars they carved a tapestry in stone, all splendor and royal pomp.

Drifting away from my traveling companions, I entered the maze of stone corridors beneath the drizzling rain. The remains of Angkor Thom are completely built of stone carved by the hands of mystical artists. Rows of stone giants hold seven-headed cobras. There are interminable passageways, their walls miraculously preserved, though before their restoration they waged a losing battle each day against the encroaching jungle. I can easily imagine the emotion that Henri Mouhot, the French naturalist, must have felt when, more than a century ago (in the year before the United States Civil War began) during a jungle expedition in search of rare botanical specimens, he suddenly came upon the lofty structures of Angkor Wat, the legacy in stone abandoned by the Khmer in the middle of the jungle and today regarded by the natives as having been built by the gods.

Climbing over rocks made dangerously slippery by the rain, trudging across pavements that seemed to bear the tracks of royal carriages, jumping over fallen columns, struggling up the carved faces of stone statues, clutching desperately at every protuberance while scaling the towers, losing my way amid droves of bats in a labyrinth of galleries whose walls are richly carved with thousands of figures more beautiful than the carvings I had seen some years ago in the tombs of the Egyptian pyramids, fighting with the jungle, which constantly tried to trap me in the sharp claws of its thorns, in the pointed fangs of its branches, in the slimy fingers of its reptilian leaves, in the serpentine arms of its lianas, I allowed myself to wander off gloriously amid the ruins of fantasy.

One thousand years ago Angkor Thom was a capital with one million inhabitants, the king's residence, a walled city encircled by a water-filled moat. In its center stood the temple of Bayon, a colossal mass of stone with soaring towers.

Most fascinating of all are the thousands of carvings of gods, kings, priests, warriors, dancing girls, ladies, peasants, children, animals, trees, swords, harps, boats, lances, plows, forges and workshops, temples and palaces that cover the walls of Angkor. Here, written in stone, the whole history of the Khmer empire can be deciphered. From time to time—and the first time it is startling!—a live Buddhist monk in a saffron-yellow robe deeply absorbed in prayer in a corner insensible to the rain and the heat, suddenly appears to the eye. Perhaps these monks are one thousand years old, left here by Buddha to pray to him and for the glory of the lost empire.

It was in the ninth century that Yaçovarman I (*varman* means protector), god-king (like the Egyptian pharaohs) of the Khmer empire, established Angkor Thom as the capital and royal seat.

In the twelfth century, when Angkor was at the zenith of its greatness, the Khmers, whose ancestors had come from India about the time of the Christian era, superimposed Buddhism upon the existing Hinduism (which had been imported from India), and Buddhism subsequently prevailed as it did in Japan. As a result, Angkor Wat, originally constructed, as its carvings reveal, as a Hindu temple, was converted into a Buddhist temple, as the later images of Buddha indicate.

The Khmer kings, especially Jayavarman VII, the greatest builder of the Khmer rulers, depleted their people in their frenzy of building temples, a frenzy comparable only to that of the Egyptian pharaohs. Thus was created one of the unparalleled wonders of the world, Angkor Wat, which combines the charm of Chartres Cathedral with the grandeur of the Egyptian pyramids.

I kept on walking along the corridors of Angkor Thom, suffocated by the heat, dripping with rain and sweat, exhausted from climbing stone staircases that soar to the sky, but reliving in my imagination what

Angkor Thom must have been like during its epoch of splendor.

The corridors must have resounded to the march of kings clothed in gold and silver robes overlaid with magnificent jewels, to the music of cymbals, flutes, drums, and horns, to the footsteps of Buddhist bonzes clad in brilliant orange robes, their shaven skulls shining as brightly in the sunshine as the gilded towers. At the foot of the main stone staircase stood many elephants, their tusks sheathed in gold, their palanquins draped with gorgeous silks and bejeweled with precious stones. The swords of the guards glistened in the sun. The air was perfumed with the incense and myrrh burning in little copper braziers. The wind shook the big bronze lanterns. And every lady in the royal court was an enchanted figure plucked from a tapestry of dreams.

Parades, always accompanied by a majestic procession of elephants—the symbol of imperial power—and gorgeous chariots, celebrated the great religious festivals in Angkor. Life for these people was a combination of exhausting toil, in building palaces and temples for lavish festivals, and of periodic armed incursions into neighboring lands in search of rich booty with which to embellish the magic city.

The guide's staccato whistle impatiently summoned me back through the rain to my travel companions. Beneath another downpour, as if the sky, like a cranky child, had merely been resting before resuming its celestial weeping, we returned to Siem Reap, where, in the Grand Hotel, a decrepit French provincial hotel that provides its guests with two elephant rides a day, we were served lunch by French-speaking waiters.

The menu: *Bar à la Portugaise, endives dorées au beurre, entrecôte Castillane, pommes croquettes, salade Pascale, moka, and corbeille de fruits.* There was *beurre frais,* which I was careful not to touch, and I did not drink the water even though it is supposed to be filtered and boiled. Typhoid and dysentery are prevalent here. Having disposed of my lunch, I exchanged my Bangkok ticals for riels, so that I might pay my bill. This small financial transaction and other riels similarly obtained in order to buy post cards and souvenirs subsequently caused me a small but annoying mishap.

At the burning siesta hour, always under the rain, without an umbrella or a raincoat, with my clothes turned into one more part of my body, a layer of skin so hot and damp it felt almost organic, I again headed through the jungle with my fellow travelers, this time toward Angkor Wat.

Beneath the rain, one more of Cambodia's defenses against foreigners, we reached the stone entrance of the temple. Two giant Nagas stand guard over the causeway leading to the temple entrance. It is not a temple in the Western sense of the word, but rather in the Oriental or Egyptian sense. Like the Egyptian pyramids, within whose vast precincts are temples, tombs, and quarters for both mummies and priests, the living and the dead, here the temple spreads out over a square mile of land half covered with buildings. Time has failed to raze the beautiful ruins—astonishingly well preserved in this horrendous climate where nothing can possibly endure, including man's work, and where the jungle inflexibly continues its emerald invasion. The gray stone was gradually succumbing to the engulfing embrace of the wild fig. One thousand years ago, Angkor Wat was the spiritual capital of the Khmer empire. Later, King Suryavarman III, in flight from Siamese incursions, abandoned it and moved his capital to the other end of Tonle-Sap, the "Great Lake."

The jungle at the height of the empire was the same as the one now spread before my eyes, but it had been pushed back for miles. There were rice fields, pagodas with golden roofs, monks in saffron-colored robes, and children playing in the mud banks under palm trees, not far from the sacred presence of the elephants. But where once throbbed a great pagan religious life, today there are only silent desolate stones on which the rain gently sheds hot tropical tears.

The religion, then as now, was Hinayana Buddhism, and its sacred language was Pali. Religious festivals in Angkor Wat surpassed medieval Europe's special masses to the Virgin Mary in the cathedral of Chartres in pomp and pageantry. On the walls in the nearly thousand-year-old carvings of girls dancing episodes from the Ramayana, I saw the same faces that I had seen on girls seated at the doorways of their huts grinding corn or cooking rice, on our way to Angkor Wat. But the jungle has clothed everything in vines, roots, and trees, and the moat, one mile long on each side, along which Buddhist monks once walked, is now muddy and rotting, harboring only snakes and other crawling creatures.

In those ancient temples there were no great halls for meditation and prayer; instead they had numerous terraces decorated with bas-reliefs, interminable colonnaded galleries around courtyards, and a number of shrines, all of which are now overrun by the jungle. Their buildings, like those of the Incan ruins in Macchu Picchu and the Egyptian pyramids in Giza and Sakkara, were constructed of blocks of stone with no cement in between. The carvings depict the religious and military life of a dauntless people who, challenging nature, despoiled the elephant and the tiger of their lands and built a great civilization by pushing the jungle back.

The great mystery of Angkor is that a civilization could vanish within two centuries of reaching the apex of its power. The wonderful city of Angkor Thom, created in the ninth century, was already beginning to disintegrate by the end of the thirteenth century. A supreme mystery of history, this prodigious civilization emerged from the jungle, reached the highest peak of glory, and suddenly vanished as if by magic, its people marching off, its temples abandoned, its relics subsequently disappearing, spirited away by greedy Siamese hands. In about two centuries the Khmer civilization, that wonder of history, reached its apogee and, in one leap into nothingness, vanished amid clouds of mystery.

What happened in Angkor?

The carved stones have never told the secret. Suggested explanations are that the Khmer people, drained and depleted by warfare and the building mania of their rulers, finally succumbed to their enemies, that a wave of malaria exterminated the population, that the beasts and the jungle took possession of the temples. Nothing is known with certainty. But here are the magnificent ruins, the splendid traces of an unrivaled historical and artistic feat, buried today in the middle of the jungle: a golden stage without actors, an empty stone city, a music box without music, a fabulous continent void and empty, one of the great wonders of the world now lying in utter nostalgia beneath the unremitting rain, which may be a source of nourishment for the jungle, but which for the stone of the temples is the germ of death.

We leave the temple, after having scaled, with great peril to our bones, the central sanctuary, a lofty tower whose steps, laid in the rock, are smooth and slippery from the rain and from hundreds of years of being trod upon. The descent from this sanctuary was a nightmare. Frantically we all clung to the rocks, never looking down for fear of becoming dizzy, the rain pouring in streams down our bodies. On top of all this, I assist a woman, as obese as she was old, who in a mad moment of audacity had decided to climb the tower. Under the dome of this tower, which tops the sanctuary, a millenary Buddha, as tall as the sanctuary itself, bestowed upon us a smile of stone.

Back at the airport I run into trouble. The customs officer, examining my passport and money-exchange declaration, comments that I have no record of any exchange of money. I explain that I had changed Bangkok ticals for Cambodian riels. This, he tells me, is forbidden. In any case, it should have been officially stamped on the exchange form. The Cambodians, it seems, prefer American dollars to the ticals of their Thai neighbors, who are friendly enemies.

Visibly annoyed, the guard summons a superior official who speaks a little French and who interrogates me with great difficulty. The other passengers have already made a dash through the rain to take their places in the plane. I am alone in the shed with the Cambodian soldiers. The rain turns the shed into a beating drum. The official insists that the currency exchange was unauthorized and that he cannot allow me to leave. The amount involved is a few dollars, six, perhaps seven, but the official seems determined to make a scene. Two hundred yards away, the plane is already roaring like an angry beast.

The chief official is called in. A desperate idea quickly flashes across my mind. I suddenly do not know any French. In two seconds I become a tourist who speaks only English, who has not the slightest notion of what is going on, and who is about to lose his temper because he is going to miss his plane. The new official, after making an attempt to address me in French, to which I reply with angry words in English, shrugs his shoulders, turns around, and leaves. And so do I. I dash across the muddy field toward the heaving plane and climb aboard. Twenty pairs of eyes stare at me angrily. The door is shut behind me. The plane takes off like a rocket into the Cambodian sky.

On my seat I find an airline envelope with Cambodian picture post cards inside. There is one of the coronation of the present Cambodian sovereigns. In their pointed gold crowns and gem-studded gold robes, surrounded by gilded carriages and brilliantly clad royal guards, they are a nostalgic remembrance of their fabulous ancestors.

Beneath us we can see Angkor Thom and Angkor Wat, two incredible epics of man's struggle against nature. If the Egyptian pyramids are the human epic of the desert, Angkor Wat is the human epic of the jungle.

But the great epic of Cambodia, Angkor, lies buried in the millenary sleep of its mystery, shrouded in rain, enchained by the mighty grip of the jungle, which it now seems will not release it until the green has finally swallowed the gray, the lianas, the columns, the leaves, the carved reliefs, the mud, the pavements.

I suddenly recall the monkey perched atop the stone head. Of course! That monkey was the answer to the history of Angkor. Man in his pride carved an epic in stone that was meant to endure forever. The monkey, defleaing himself beneath the rain, was concerned only with himself. And it is he who is the master of Angkor, for he knows that, when he leaves, there will always be another monkey to replace him.

LEBANON

MUEZZINS AND BLUE JEANS: THE TWO LEBANONS

Beirut and Byblos, along with Damascus in Syria, are among the oldest continually inhabited cities in the world; they are also separated by only twenty miles of space, but about two thousand years in atmosphere.

It has been very pleasant to explore for a few days the small but important cultural emporium of Beirut: its museums; its great twelfth-century mosque, al-Jami' al-'Umari, a former Crusader's church built in Byzan-

373

tine style on the site of a Phoenician temple; the Nou-
fara Mosque, which in the course of time, for some
strange reason, has incorporated into its typical sixteenth-century style some columns from a Roman temple; and the impressive American University, which I
have just finished visiting. The largest American university in the world outside of the United States, it has
a library of almost a hundred thousand volumes and
gorgeous flower gardens. I see students of every race
sprawled on the grass, studying thick tomes in the
shade of Mt. Sannin, facing the Mediterranean, which
can be seen in the distance playing its liquid blue symphony.

Tired and dusty, declining whispered offers of gold,
opium, and hashish on the street, I return to the main
part of the city on foot, for Beirut's taxis and traffic are
probably the most dangerous, and the city itself is the
noisest, in the world. I had decided to rest a while on
the terrace of the St. George's Hotel which is situated
on the spot where, according to the Lebanese, St.
George killed the dragon. The terrace overhangs the
deep aquamarine waters of St. George's Bay.

It is pleasant sitting here, sipping a French vermouth
that sparkles in the sun like liquid topaz, reading the
Paris newspapers and magazines. Everyone around me
speaks French, which makes me feel as if I were once
again in the City of Light.

A moment later I raise my eyes from my newspaper
and I am plunged back into the Arabian world. The

green gracefulness of the palm trees is emphasized by
the bright blue sky. My table is now surrounded by
Levantine businessmen clad in flowing white robes.
Their eyes are fierce, suspicious; their skin is a flaming
brown. With white or striped turbans framing their
faces, they look as if they have stepped out of an illustration for the *Thousand and One Nights*. Cloaked in
their voluminous garments, utterly indifferent to the
heat, revealing no sign of its effect except a thin, permanent veil of perspiration on their faces, they sip a
coffee so highly concentrated that it is the very fragrant
soul of the coffee bean. There is music in the background, monotonous and melancholy, an Arab song as
interminable as a night of love in a harem. Suddenly,
from the top of a minaret, the voice of a muezzin summons the faithful to pray to Allah.

A moment later everything has changed again. From
Paris I had suddenly shifted to Arabia, and now I am
surrounded by a noisy group of American girls from
the American University, some of them in blue jeans.
Waving their Pepsi-Colas, they wildly hail a shapely
girl friend, a Valkyrie of almost Amazonian proportions, who swiftly crosses the water at our feet in water
skis, enveloped in a nacreous sea spray. I am in a
French-speaking, soft-beverage drinking, Arab world.

My chauffeur and guide is a native Lebanese from
Beirut who has spent half of his sixty years driving
visitors around his country. He is very proud of his
country. Its beauty and its climate fire him with admira-

tion. He displays every ruin with the hauteur with which a society matron might display her celebrated jewels at a ball. He is the type of Levantine who has been softened by French influence and therefore is less suspicious than most of his people. His face, as round as a full moon over the desert, constantly lights up with a smile as gay as that of a happy child.

My trip has brought me in contact with three great Oriental races—the Japanese, the Chinese, and the Hindu, with their Thai, Korean, Annamese, and other variants, and of all of them I understand and like best the Japanese and the Thai.

With few exceptions, the Hindus I have encountered in my journey have been aloof and distrustful toward Westerners, which makes communication with them very difficult.

The old Chinese appear to be bewildered and disconcerted by the new China, which has despoiled them of their ancient tradition, the only thing they had left in life. The new tradition they neither like nor understand. The young Chinese are no longer so much Chinese, as Communists. They no longer think in terms of their country's culture and history. They hunger for a future. They want to replace the past as quickly as possible with a future that will provide them with the economic well-being that the past never gave them. The centuries-old situation of great luxury for the few and utter misery for the multitude must be exchanged for a future in which, even at the cost of a uniform, monotonous, collective existence, the individual's right to life is salvaged. Their fanatic attitude in this respect makes it difficult for Westerners to understand them. They themselves shut off all comprehension.

The Arabs, whose emotional inflammability I know well—I can even feel it—seem to give play to their emotions in a world to which only they have access.

In contrast, there are two peoples who have preserved their past, with all its beautiful traditions and culture, and at the same time have harmonized it with a striking advance toward the future. These are the Japanese and, on a different scale, the Thai. In Japan I encountered a people who are imbued with poetry, art, and culture, yet who have also shown great technical ingenuity, which they have placed at the service of the future of their nation. In Thailand I found a dynamic, optimistic people, unprejudiced toward foreigners, deferential toward their cultural heritage, genuinely religious but without the Hindu's fanaticism, a people who have successfully made the transition from the white elephant to the jet without sacrificing the beauty and grace of their tradition.

But now I am in the Levant, and the Levant, as exemplified by Lebanon and the Lebanese is, like all Arabian nations, a land in ferment. The Lebanese nation is divided into a number of different religious groups. Also, European influence—specifically, French —has been too long felt and too penetrating for the Lebanese ever to feel that they are pure Arabs like the

Syrians or the Egyptians. The Lebanese Arab from Beirut is as proud of speaking French as the Egyptian Arab is of speaking Arabic. The Lebanese Christian Arab enjoys his Bordeaux wines with a vehemence equal to that which the Moslem Arab from Damascus displays in shunning alcohol. Beirut, with its mixed population of Europeans, Hindus, Kurds, Bedouins, Arabs, and Christians, aspires to be the great cosmopolitan port of the Middle East, even as Damascus and Cairo desert cities, wish to be (as Peking is for the Chinese in Asia) "prohibited" cities for all except Arabs. Lebanon's aspirations to belong to the modern world point toward Europe; Syria and Egypt's toward the Arab world. The Christian Lebanese wants peace and prosperity; the Moslem Lebanese, power and political strength. Consequently, one might say that the Lebanese suffer from a politico-religious schizophrenia— exemplified by their habitually having a Christian president and a Moslem premier, or vice versa—which they cannot, do not know how to, or perhaps do not wish to cure. Instead they ignore it, living immersed in their happy Arcadia, beneath the broad celestial vault, overlooking the blue, legend-rippling sea.

MEZZE, KIBBI, AND ARRACK

FOLLOWING THE COUNSEL OF MY
Lebanese guide, I had stopped on the outskirts of Beirut
to have lunch Arab style. The modern hotels of Beirut
shun Arabian food. Instead they prefer the anonymous
type of international hotel food—the menu is written
in French, still the official language of gastronomy—
which tastes exactly the same as at the Waldorf-Astoria
in New York, the Ritz in London, the Erawan in Bangkok, or the Arawak in Jamaica.

We are at an Arabian café, the Ghalaini. It is a plain, bare room except for a few posters on the walls displaying the improbable anatomy of scantily clad girls drinking Pepsi-Cola. The music from a strident radio accentuates the intense heat. At the old wooden tables Arabs, wearing turbans, fezzes, or European-style Panama hats, noisily eat, chatter, and laugh, turning the room into a maddened cage of birds with their clamor. The smell of coffee drifts through the air.

From a small water-filled tank sparkling in the sun, I select a fish scaled in iridescent red to be sautéed for me. The meal begins with *mezze,* an endless assortment of hors d'oeuvres, including thin long strips of roast lamb and goat, a variety of salads with lemon and sesame oil dressing, and salted almonds and walnuts. Served with the hors d'oeuvres is the national drink, *arrack,* a colorless liquid with a strong aroma and the taste of anisette.

After the hors d'oeuvres we are given *kibbi,* a national dish made with pounded meat, ground wheat, onions, and pine nuts, which can be eaten either raw, like a "cannibal steak," or cooked; *tabbouli,* boiled ground wheat with chopped parsley, mint, onions and tomatoes mixed with olive oil and lemon juice; and *hummos bi tehini,* boiled chick-peas mashed into a paste and mixed with sesame.

I decline the next dish, *kefta,* ground lamb with chopped parsley grilled over charcoal, since I am already familiar with a similar dish, *kebab,* having con-

380

sumed it in Istanbul and Cairo. At other tables people are eating stuffed vegetables, eggplant marinated in lemon, and *mehshe,* or grape leaves, stuffed with lamb and rice, very similar to the *dolmades* I once ate in Athens.

With the fried fish a sort of pancake is served, which torn into pieces is used as a spoon and moistened in different sauces. With the *hummos* mentioned before, strips of thin toast cooked in olive oil are also used as a spoon. I also pass up the *moghrabiyeh,* a semolina dish, and the traditional *yoghurt* and Arabian pastries and sweets. Instead, I have fresh fruit, the best the Arabian world has to offer—oranges, peaches, apricots, melons, grapes, all piled up into a porcelain-like architectonic pyramid in a basket lined with fresh grape leaves dotted with glittering drops of water.

Soon after, the smoke from our cigarettes merges with the vapor exhaled by the motor of our car as we race toward Byblos along roads ablaze with sunlight.

CEDARS AND VIRGINS

Beirut's landscape is famil-
iar to everyone even without their having been in Lebanon. It is the landscape of the Bible.

On one side stand bald hills of rock and earth tinted
in bright colors: red, purple, ocher, sulfur, and lemon.
There is no vegetation and the land is dry and hard,
for the sky rarely sheds its tears upon it. On the other
side, the sea stretches far into the distance, almost white
beneath the haze of the heat on the horizon, but all

382

blue and silver sparks as it joyously breaks upon the platinum sands of the beach.

The traffic is light, almost all of it old, dusty, European cars; goats, lots of goats, led by women whose heads, deep in the folds of their shawls, appear to be enveloped in a cloud; shepherd boys; young girls washing clothes in the streams; little donkeys panting in the sun under the weight of great loads of kindling; squat houses, blocks of stone with hardly a window to stave off the blazing heat, mere sentry boxes where poor peasants dwell with their wives, children, goats, and donkeys.

Dust, sweat, heat, all are starkly accented by the vast horizon, and there is nothing, neither clouds in the sky nor trees on the earth, to provide man with a little shade. Water more precious than jewels is carried in jugs, which exude moisture as if they were weeping, aloft on the heads of flaming-eyed, full-lipped girls dressed as if for a masquerade with brightly colored rags wound tight round their young bodies. We pass salt flats in which the mining is done by the wind and the sun. The villages are poor: humble little shops, ancient cars and even more ancient donkeys standing everywhere, one or two little restaurants that are more dives than restaurants—and everywhere radios strident with Arab café music or American dance music.

But the entire way is paved with history. We stop at a few places where within barely one hundred paces more than two thousand years of history are contained (at the Dog River, for example). On one side of the hill, I see stone carvings dating to Ramses II in the thirteenth century B.C.; Roman inscriptions overrun with the creeping roots of a neighboring vineyard; a time-eroded bust of unmistakable Byzantine origin carved in the mountain; the remains of a fortress constructed by the Crusaders; the ruins of an eighteenth-century mansion; a plaque in French commemorating the name of the regiment that entered Damascus victoriously; and one in Arabic commemorating the final evacuation of French mandate troops in 1946—in all, nineteen inscriptions.

A similar accumulation of centuries of history is to be found all along this route. It is as if man, unable to move, blocked on one side by the quivering blue wall of sea and on the other by naked rocks and burning mountain wasteland, had devoted himself to expanding in time the small area allotted to him in space.

There is a statue of Our Lady of Lebanon, as dazzling a white as an apparition in a religious legend, standing on top of a mountain. Tall and beautiful upon a high pedestal inside a lofty tower shaped like a lighthouse, the Virgin dominates the scene with her pure whiteness.

From the Virgin's pedestal can be seen a vast expanse of parched earth sparsely dotted with trees and vineyards, the chain of mountains the color of copper oxide, the desert stretching toward Tripoli, and, always, the blue vastness of the sea of romance.

A small, bearded monk, who looks like a storybook

pirate, with a huge crucifix hanging from his waist like a six-shooter, sells me a little plastic statue of the Virgin marked "Made in USA."

A grove of cedars surround Our Lady of Lebanon. Nearby a goat, dark brown and shaggy as the husk of a dried coconut, gently nuzzles a cat as white and glossy as the meat of the coconut. Invisible nuns are singing a litany in French. The fresh air carries the fragrance of the pine and the sweetness of the date palm. The sun vibrates on the white Virgin, standing strong and dauntless in the solitude of her altitude, like a magnificent invitation to heroism.

The cedars that surround her are beautiful, sturdy, solemn. Soon I shall be seeing many of these cedars about forty miles from Beirut, in one of history's most symbolic sites: the grove of the Cedars of Lebanon.

This was in Bsharre, the ancient B'sharra, which is one of the last forests still existing from Biblical times in Lebanon. I stand in awe beneath the shade of that legendary band of giants, which, immobilized in time and space, are imbued with poetry and history. Their trunks are huge, one hundred feet high and forty-five feet in circumference. Their branches, like a giantess' fan, unfurl in a regular fashion, as if they had been deliberately carved and arranged by a skilled craftsman. The wood is a soft reddish color, smooth, shiny, hard, and has a bitter taste that protects it against insects. Clustered together upon a hill, as if for protection, like an army of defeated but never conquered heroic Crusaders, these trees are an alert sentinel of history. There are about four hundred of them, the youngest is two hundred years old, the oldest, close to two thousand years. In their shade, poets and writers from all epochs have sat, and lyric poems of all varieties infused with an almost sensuous love have been dedicated to them.

When I visited the cedars the Maronite monks call *Arz el Rab,* or the Cedars of God, I saw a group of these monks enveloped as much in the aura of their hushed saintliness as in their dark habits. They were making their annual visit to their precious cedars, which are today under the protection of the Patriarchs of Lebanon, who in 1845 had a small chapel built there and have for centuries tried to prevent the trees from being cut or profaned. In August of each year, the devout celebrate the festival of the cedars in the shade of the trees, while the Patriarch caressingly strokes them. I saw a monk caress a tree with an almost voluptuous gesture, as if it were a woman's body.

What thrilled me most, however, was the recollection that these cedars were utilized by Tyre and Sidon to carve their statues and construct their houses and the masts of their ships, and above all by the wise Solomon to build the temple of Jerusalem and to fashion jewel boxes that he later presented with passionate hands to that woman with the beauty of an untamed panther, the Queen of Sheba.

CASTLES AND CRUSADES

A FEW HOURS AFTER VISIT-ing Our Lady of Lebanon, I am hopping through the ruins of Byblos, the Gebal of the Bible, the Gubla of antiquity.

The entire historical panorama of Lebanon is re-flected in Byblos. Byblos' great antiquity is recorded in cuneiform writing in the tablets dating from the four-teenth and fifteenth centuries B.C., unearthed in Tell el-Amarna, the Egyptian capital of Akhenaton and

387

Nefertiti. What is now Lebanon was conquered by the Romans under Pompey the Great, after whose time the territory was called Colonia Julia Augusta Berytus, after the daughter of the Emperor Augustus. In A.D. 3 the Pax Romana made possible the founding of Beirut's great and famous law school, which forged learned men with minds finer than its famous silks. Later, much of Lebanon was dominated by the Arabs; it was then conquered and ruled by the Crusaders, fell into the hands first of the Arabs again, then the Egyptian Mamelukes and Ottomans, was a French mandate between the two World Wars, and finally attained its independence in 1943. But the antiquity of Byblos itself makes Beirut seem like the youngest child of a mother who is almost as old as the Egyptian pyramids.

Here is Byblos, where in the shadow of past glories more than six thousand inhabitants dwell, dedicated in the present day to small handicrafts, the sale of tourist souvenirs, the cultivation of small fruit orchards, or the weaving of cloth. There once dwelled the god el, subsequently identified by the Greeks with Cronus.

This was the city of the Gublites, a Hebrew people, and the cradle of Phoenician activity, influenced by Mesopotamians, Egyptians, and Myceans. In the fourth millennium B.C., Byblos was the great commercial and religious center of the Syrian coast, eclipsing even Tyre and Sidon. Thirty-two hundred years before Christ it already had the famous temple of Balaat. Later it harbored the cult of Isis, and its kings became vassals of the Egyptian pharaohs.

In the seventeenth century B.C., the Hyksos, the warring shepherd kings, swept through Byblos as they had before through Phoenicia, and in the fifteenth century B.C., the Egyptians overthrew the Hyksos, thereby freeing Byblos. Later Byblos was conquered by the Assyrian kings and subsequently incorporated into Cyrus' empire. In Byblos, in the grotto of Afquah, was born the Ishtar and Adonis myth. (I saw the stream of Adonis there, today a mere thread of cloudy water.) The natives still go to light oil lamps in honor of the phantom lady who, according to legend, appears there. Moslems, Christians, and Druses still venerate trees, a remnant of ancient Canaanite phallic rites in Lebanon. In 1103 Raymond de Saint-Gilles, Count of Toulouse, with his valiant Genoese Crusaders, wrested Byblos from the Arabs, and occupied the castle of Byblos. In 1187, during the Third Crusade, the town was again lost to the Sultan Saladin, who sacked the castle.

It is precisely before that castle of the Crusaders, here in Byblos, that I now stand, near the mosque of al-Jami' al-'Umari. Some say that Byblos is the source of the name of the Bible, that the name is derived not from the Greek word *biblion,* a scroll of papyrus, but from the fact that the papyrus on which the Bible was first written came from Byblos.

The ruins of the castle are in rather good condition.

Its towers and turrets are still standing, and so are part of the moat around the castle, the ramps leading to the top, and the windows, which no longer gaze out at the enemy but at the fields of history. Here are the ruins of the Crusaders, and not too far away there are Roman ruins, and a little farther, Phoenician ruins, and in the cemeteries, in earthern urns containing skeletons, the remains go back to neolithic times.

Standing in the tower of the fort, in the same spot where once many a Crusader must have stood looking at the Mediterranean and dreaming of recovering Christ's sepulcher and of returning to Venice, Valencia, Genoa, or Paris covered with laurels, I too gaze out at the *mare nostrum* and try to visualize the Crusaders emerging from the horizon in their vessels, their impatient swords gleaming like silver needles in the sun, while the sirocco inflating their sails pushes them swiftly to the holy shores. I then turn and look in the other direction, at the scorched, barren plains and, beyond them, at the mountains, which, fierce and naked, lie like a burning curse beneath the pallid sky.

But then, not far from the ruins, I see a Lebanese family passing by, their plain white robes drenched in blazing sunlight. The mother, riding a little plum-colored mule that placidly chews sun-burnished straw, is holding an infant in her arms. The father is carrying a small basket of figs and dates and a jug of milk. This living Biblical scene reminds me that through the ages, even mightier than the swords of the Crusaders, whose only remains are the ruins of their castles, has been the example of love left by that other family who, nearly two thousand years ago, at the slow pace of a mule, like the family I am now watching, passed through these honey-colored Biblical lands.

EPILOGUE IN THE CITY OF THE GLITTERING TOWERS

M Y JOURNEY AROUND THE
world completed, I reached New York at the amethyst
hour of twilight.

From my window high above the city, I look out
at the Neo-Gothic city, whose towers are staircased like
Mesopotamian ziggurats and pointed like Gothic spires.
In the Middle Ages, man through his Gothic architecture ascended vertically into space in quest of God
and of his own soul; in the Renaissance, he expanded

horizontally, craving to explore the mystery beyond the horizon and that of the human body. In our Neo-Gothic era of vertical cities, like New York, a rebirth is taking place, fomented by our desire to explore both cosmic space with satellites and man's inner realms via the microscope and depth psychology.

Standing at my window high above the city, I realize that my travels around the world have revealed much to me about other people and other places, but more about myself, about the geography and history of my soul.

In my journeys I learned a great deal about the peoples I visited and about their preoccupation with two eternities: their millenary past, with its rich philosophic and religious legacy; and their future, their history in the making, which is being forged through the dynamic aspirations of their new generations. Between these two eternities lies the present, which to them represents a mere twinkling of an eye.

I learned that in the face of the horizontal vastness of our planet, man's aspiration to create vertical cities like New York, bristling with stalagmite-shaped skyscrapers, is trivial and pathetic, and that, irrespective of the difference in their human geography—race and anthropology—and in their history—religion and culture—the family of man is one and the same the world over. When one probes deep enough into the spirit of man, one reaches a land filled with millennial memories, eternal hopes, and human ideals, which overshadow the difference between peoples and provide the basis for the unity of the family of man.

Slowly night descends upon Manhattan. The towers glitter against a sky ablaze with their reflection. Far below, the traffic lights bedeck the avenues with emeralds and rubies.

The traveler, now returned from his trip, meditates, dreams, waits. Soon, he knows, he must continue his barely begun, ever-unfinished journey around himself.

INDEX

395

INDEX

404